Best

MW01039398

World Class Runners and Races

by Kenny Moore

Cedarwinds Publishing Company
Tallahassee, Florida

Published by Cedarwinds Publishing Company.
P.O. Box 13618
Tallahassee, Florida 32317
Telephone: 904/224-9261
Fax: 904/561-0747
Telex: 650-303-5591

Library of Congress Cataloging in Publication Data

Moore, Kenny, 1943-   Best Efforts

  1. Runners (Sports)—Addresses, essays, letures. I. Title
GV1061.14.M66   796.4'26 [B]   AACR2

ISBN 0-915297-10-8
Library of Congress Number 80-2057
Copyright © 1982 by Kenny Moore

CONTENTS

For Gilbert Rogin, literally.

The Long Blue Line:
Munich Olympics, 1972

The Olympic marathoners of 1972, sixty-nine skittish, prancing men, were called into the tunnel that led from the practice track to the stadium. I said good-by to my wife and the coaches. Stan Wright, our sprint coach, sat with his back against a post watching his 400-meter relay team warm up. It was Wright who had accepted the blame for two of our 400-meter men having failed to get to the stadium in time for their heats.

"One more day," he said, "and it's all over." Flippantly I said, "No it's not. Life goes on."

He looked straight at me. "That's what I'm living for. Life has to go on."

In the tunnel I saw Ron Hill, the renowned English marathoner. His drooping mustache was gone, as was most of his hair, and he was conspicuously tanned from training close to the sun in the Swiss Alps. Ron is a textile chemist and occasionally seems possessed by the scientific method. Here in Munich he had dressed to reflect as much heat as possible. His shoes and shorts were coated with silver. His shirt was made of glittering mesh. The Union Jack on his chest seemed to be done in sequins.

An official assigned us lanes and rows. Hill and I were in the front, flanking Derek Clayton of Australia, who has run the world's fastest marathon. Clayton stared out at an angle somewhat above the rim of the stadium. As if savoring every aspect of the moment, he drew in deep breaths through his prominent nose, closing his eyes as he exhaled. "It's finally here," he whispered. "It's all come to this."

Hill seemed vexed, complaining about the warm weather, the course, the time it took to place us on our marks.

"Hey, take it easy," I said.

He snapped at me. "Certainly, when we've had two death threats from the IRA."

The starter's gun went off and conversation ceased. We circled the track twice at a moderate pace. I drifted toward the center of the pack, picking out the experienced marathoners I had met before. Jack Foster and Dave McKenzie stood out in the all black of New Zealand. Fragile Mamo Wolde, the defending champion, wore the Ethiopian green, Seppo Nikkari the pale blue of Finland. Akio Usami of Japan, who had calmly removed all his clothes in the warm-up area, was in white from shoes to headband.

When Jim Ryun fell in his 1,500-meter heat, people said to me, "For God's sake, be careful in the marathon." I explained that marathoners are gentlemen compared to milers. The race sorts us out perfectly well. We don't have to hit each other.

Save for the two walks the marathon is the only race in the Olympics for which no qualifying time is required. Every country has the right to enter three men. If an eccentric Argentine or Ceylonese is determined to be an Olympian and can persuade his national Olympic Committee to enter him, and can pay his own way, he can run. Or, to put it more accurately, he can start.

So as we swept through the marathon gate and headed out on the roads the pack included stumpy little men struggling even then to hold their positions. They jockeyed incessantly. They bunched too tightly toward the inside on curves. They ran like milers, and a few hundred yards after leaving the stadium I was caught in a jam on a corner and tripped. I curled into a ball on the warm asphalt until an opening appeared in the slapping feet and was up quickly, with a stinging elbow and knee, a sore calf, and a 30-yard deficit. As we flooded over the cobblestones of the Press Village and set out on wide, unshaded thoroughfares between cement factories and apartment houses, I told myself to relax, to harbor the surge of aggressiveness I was feeling. An electric bus with a revolving red light led us between rows of applauding spectators. I let the leaders draw 50 yards ahead and tried to take myself to a more natural, peaceful setting.

*   *   *

U.S. distance runners prepared for Munich in bucolic near-isolation. We were a week on a piney, stony peninsula near Brunswick, Maine, and spent twenty days exploring the blueberry-strewn forest above Oslo, Norway. That city maintains miles of trails for cross-country skiing in winter and hiking in summer. We ran upon them daily, peering into the trees after moose, marveling at rushing cataracts and the way Norwegian families push baby carriages on fourteen-mile hikes.

We were equally struck by the garrulity of our own Doug Brown, a steeplechaser who had just completed his sophomore year at Tennessee. Brown must have been a hyperkinetic child, for he is now a hyperkinetic postadolescent. As we ran, his stream of consciousness mingled with the waterfalls: "*Thunderball*, that's what we're seeing tonight. Love James Bond. All those gimmicks. I'm not grown up yet. Fat? I'm not fat. One hundred fifty-two pounds. Of course, I eat a lot of dinner. I never make it to breakfast. That's my schedule. I go out a lot at night. I figure eight or nine hours sleep is eight or nine hours worth, no matter when you get it. So I sleep from two to eleven. Never go to morning classes. Sure rains a lot here. Like Oregon. This is supposed to be *summer*. What's everybody acting so tired for? This is Sunday. The first day of the week. You're supposed to be chipper. . . ."

One afternoon, jogging back from the stadium, Brown and Jeff Galloway, a 10,000-meter runner, noticed a yard containing a stately cherry tree burdened with fruit. Later, under cover of darkness, they returned.

Brown gave this account: "It was a big house, two cars, nice furniture, so let's face it, it wasn't like we were taking cherries from the mouths of starving babies. Besides, we decided to concentrate on just one branch. Or at least I did, because Galloway said I should go into the yard and pick while he kept a lookout on the sidewalk. So, great steeplechaser that I am, I jumped over the fence and fell down. I finally got under the tree, whipped out my sack, and went to work. Every so often Jeff would whisper someone was coming and I'd hit the ground. I was ready to run every time, I tell you. Finally I had enough for a snack, about four pounds, so I quit, cleared the fence and we started ambling home.

"Pretty soon this *politi* car comes rolling along slow and they call us over. They were great, spoke good English. We got to talking, told 'em we were on the U. S.

Olympic team. To be friendly I offered 'em some cherries. They looked at the sack and back at the yard where I'd been, and then they started talking Norwegian to each other. Finally they said, 'Get in.' I was on the verge of taking off when I felt Jeff's hand on my back. I got the idea he didn't want me to run, so we got in. They took us to the front of the house and I—Galloway made it very clear who had been doing the picking—had to go up to the door.

"A nice man came out when I knocked and I told him how I was on the U. S. Olympic team and that I admired Norway and Oslo and particularly his cherries so much that I'd picked some without permission and I was sorry. He said that was all right, it happened all the time, and if I would come to the house after this and ask, I could pick all the cherries I wanted. I mean, let's face it, he was really nice. So the *politi* were happy and Jeff and I got home with our cherries and you know what, these Norwegian cherries, my Lord, are they sour!"

*   *   *

Six miles from the start we entered Nymphenburg. The marathon course was conceived by Willi Daume, head of the Olympic Organizing Committee, with an eye to scenery. The painted blue line marking the route wound past most of the notable Munich landmarks and through the city's two large parks, Nymphenburg and the English Garden. When a number of countries protested the eight miles of loose gravel or dirt in these stretches (IAAF-International Amateur Athletic Federation-rules require marathons to be run on pavement), the committee said the paths would be swept and covered with a "special plastic." The yellow dust that now rose behind the bus was testimony to that promise broken. Our eyes filled with grit. There also was profanity in the air, much of it Frank Shorter's, and eventually the bus turned aside.

We came to the first refreshment station. On a hot day it is essential to replace as much lost liquid as possible. Once you have sweated away more than ten or twelve pounds, your blood becomes too viscous to be pumped easily and you court heatstroke. Frank and I had spent half an hour in the morning shaking the carbonation out of Cokes and pouring the flat liquid into plastic squeeze bottles marked with our numbers. These now were arranged on card tables beside the path. An Ethiopian, Lengissa Bedane, took Frank's. Frank took mine. I took nothing. Frank couldn't return my bottle to me because it is against the rules to aid fellow competitors. We discussed the situation through the remainder of the park. "Sorry," Frank said.

The route to Munich was cluttered with airports. Including Portland, Maine, there were, at least five—LaGuardia, JFK, Oslo, and Copenhagen. Most of my teammates also went to pre-olympic meets in Italy or Sweden. Sauntering through these terminals in our double-knit suits with red-white-and-blue-striped belts and two-tone patent-leather loafers, we sparked some curiosity in our fellow travelers. People often seemed surprised when they learned what we were. We in turn wondered what they had guessed. A tour of super-patriotic circus performers? *Reader's Digest* editors? George Wallace supporters? (No, there were too many blacks among us for that one.)

Americans, especially in Europe, often treated us possessively, which was understandable but sometimes got on our nerves. Once when we were seated for a meal, a lady who had learned to speak in the vicinity of Brooklyn, perhaps near a boiler works, materialized behind marathoner Jack Bacheler.

"Are you Ryun?" she shouted in his ear.

Jack said he wasn't. Jim was training back in Kansas.

"Oh, then we're disappointed," she said, and glanced around the table, meeting Frank Shorter's icy stare. "Well, not really disappointed. . . ." She began to make her withdrawal.

"Yes, you are," said Frank. "Admit it."

In the passenger lounge at JFK, an AP reporter presented himself to Head Coach Bill Bowerman.

"I have to file a story on the team's departure," he said. "So what's the big news?"

"So far as I know, there is none. We're all here. We leave from Gate 29."

The man's brow knitted. "Well, let me ask you about some of the big names. Randy Matson. Al Oerter. Hayes Jones. How is Hayes Jones doing?"

"Hayes Jones is no longer with us."

"You mean he died?"

(Jones competed last in the 1964 Games, Oerter retired in 1969, and Matson had not qualified for the team.)

Pole vaulter Jan Johnson and runner Steve Prefontaine, inseparable companions, softened the tedium with nips from a flask wrapped in a brown paper bag. Later Johnson reflected on the journey.

"The Olympics have always been a shining dream for me, unreal and mystical, where everything takes on deep meaning. So at JFK, when we got on that funny container bus that took us out to the aircraft, Steve and I were giddy, saying, 'This is the slowest plane I've ever been on,' but I was thinking, 'Here's where the fantasy begins.' Then I looked around and it was nothing special, just a bunch of guys I knew. Coming in to Oslo, I got ready for the magic to hit me. But it was only rain."

Johnson provided his own magic, as at breakfast, mixing the contents of two bowls. "Ah, oatmeal and applesauce. Gives you the strength of a thousand butterflies."

*   *   *

Before we emerged from Nymphenburg, Clayton and the iridescent Hill, who had pushed the early pace, dropped behind. Usami and Foster took the lead. Once out on pavement again, Frank cruised through the front group, now down to eight, observing runners closely. With seventeen miles to go, as we ran beneath maples lining a murky canal, he surged ahead.

Nobody went with him. It was hot, and it seemed he had spurted too sharply. He would pay for his extravagance later. So as he moved away we each sought our most economic rhythm, and the pack split up. I ran for a mile with Gaston Roelants of Belgium, whose shoes were bound to his feet with yards of tape to prevent friction and blisters. He slowed with a side ache.

I caught Jack Foster and tried to cajole him into running the slightest increment faster. He looked at me stonily. Then a rejuvenated Clayton pounded by and I took up with him. Along a smooth stretch of road our shadows preceded us. Clayton's was full of movement, his arms clawing high across his chest, his head bobbing. I looked over. His tongue rolled in and out of his mouth.

We came up to the men closest to Frank: Usami, Wolde, Karel Lismont of Belgium, and Bacheler. When Clayton and I ran past, Wolde joined us. But Clayton lingered too long at the 25-kilometer refreshment station, and Wolde and I were alone.

*   *   *

On the warm afternoon of August 26 the Games were opened. In white coats and vermilion pants we trudged to the grassy assembly area at one o'clock, there to mill and grow stiff until four-thirty when we could begin the march to the stadium half a mile away.

Distance runner George Young, a four-time Olympian, examined the five United States Olympic Committee (USOC) officers who would lead us. "I just realized," he said, "that the last time I saw any of those distinguished gentlemen was when we were marching in Mexico."

Traditionally, neither coaches nor managers parade with the athletes. But the USOC appeared to have given its seats to friends and relatives, so many coaches had to enter our ranks to see the opening ceremonies. The head track and field manager, George Wilson, who is the deputy chief of the U. S. Army sports program and who until then had shown a determination to stick to every nit-picking rule, came too. This is my first protest march, he said.

Jon Anderson, a 10,000-meter runner, moved through the crowd patting strange bulges under his coat and conferring with others similarly misshapen. Every U.S. athlete had been given an Instamatic by Kodak, which had paid the USOC handsomely for the privilege, yet a notice had been posted that morning that read: "One's sense of national pride ought to prevent the carrying of cameras in the opening parade." And if somehow that were not sufficient, they would be confiscated at the gate.

"I'm afraid my personal pride and my national pride are in conflict," said Anderson.

"Pride, my foot," said Shorter. "The Germans just want a monopoly on pictures of the opening. And the USOC wanted Kodak's largesse. And Kodak wanted the Olympic shield on its ads."

Said Anderson, with mock astonishment, "You mean if you follow a gift or a rule to its source, you don't find appreciation for the athletes or concern for our best interests?"

"Only money," said Frank. "Only money."

Once under way to the stadium, our mood continued to be one of sarcastic festivity. Ticketless people lined our route and hung from overpasses. Steeplechaser Mike Manley instructed them in cheering: "Let's have it louder there on the bridge. You, sir, with the flag, wave it like you meant it. Wottle, do you think it would be possible for you to assume an upright position?" As we approached the gate and darkened tunnel, someone shouted, "O.K., everybody, get out your I.D.!"

Then we emerged into the light at the bottom of that great bowl of humanity, and there were no more wisecracks.

During the long wait those of us who had been in Mexico had said to the cranky new Olympians, "It will be worth it," and in those first moments in the stadium we all experienced a surge of happiness over having come together again. But it was not Mexico.

In 1968 the International Olympic Committee (IOC) members presented a sharp contrast to the singing, celebrating Mexicans around them. They sat quietly in their special box with an air of detached pride, basking in the glow of what they had wrought.

In Munich the crowd and the IOC were indistinguishable. The stadium was filled with politely clapping people of means, as intent on being seen as on welcoming the world's athletes. The pageantry, which was nearly identical to that in Mexico, was enhanced by an international escort of Ryun, Kip Keino, Kenji Kimihara, and Clayton for the young German torchbearer. There were no hitches. But Mexico's fire was not rekindled. We stood and squatted on the infield as the speeches rolled over us, and gradually sore backs and pinching shoes took on greater importance than the Olympic oath. When the time came to leave, we were glad to go.

*   *   *

Mamo Wolde runs, soundless of foot and breath, with his head tipped slightly forward. I sensed his presence only from that distinguished widow's peak floating above my left shoulder. We ran along boulevards, around statues, fountains, arches.

Downtown Munich exudes prosperity. Furs, and jewelry are displayed behind plate glass. Marble buildings seem more substantial, portly, in the soft afternoon haze. But we were beyond noticing. Our universe was asphalt, tram tracks, and a faint blue line.

Mamo is knock-kneed and points his toes slightly out. I am grossly knock-kneed and also toe out, both conditions being accentuated by fatigue. Since we ran so close together, once in a while our shoes brushed. "I'm sorry, I'm sorry," Wolde said each time, displaying the manners of a true marathoner.

*   *   *

The mayor of the Olympic Village, Walther Troger, made us to understand that all officials' and athletes' wives or husbands who had come to Munich would receive plastic-coated, color-coded passes with photographs of the holders that were required to get into the Village. Each delegation was told to submit a list of names to be so accredited. The mayor, shocked at the number, reneged. This list was shortened by lopping off athletes' and coaches' wives. Only spouses of high officials were given passes.

My wife Bobbie was upset at the injustice of the ruling. Others had a more urgent need. Connie Manley and Peg Savage, our steeplechasers' wives, had been thrown out of their Munich room (found for them by the USOC, which had also accepted full payment) and had nowhere else to go but the Village. "I guess they oversold," said Connie. "Peg and I slept in a double bed, and last night the Frau who runs the operation was sleeping on the kitchen floor. Five minutes after we got to bed, two more people came with a blue card from the city. Out we went."

Emboldened by necessity, Connie and Bobbie investigated the pass-making machinery in the administration building, an assembly line of typists, Polaroid photographers, and laminating machines. Picking a moment when the room was packed with impatient Poles and chattering Colombians and the clerks were busiest, Connie and Bobbie strolled behind the counter, lifted what they hoped were the proper forms, and casually but officiously typed their names on them.

Mike Manley and I sat by the door. I couldn't look. He described the scene to me: "They're sure smiling a lot. . . . By God they've got their pictures. . . . I don't think each station in the line knows what any of the others is doing. . . . Wait. There's a guy at the end who seems to be inspecting the cards before they're given to the athletes. If anything's wrong . . . The room is a lot emptier than ten minutes ago. The thieves look so obvious out there. . . . Oh, they're so close. So close . . . Bobbie's through. Connie's got it. Connie's got it!"

Within days, everyone knew six ways to produce bogus credentials. "The Village drugstore is doing a land-office business in laminating kits," reported walker Bill Weigle. "Isn't it just like the Germans to bring in a thousand more laminating kits?"

Not once, even during the security crackdown that was to come, were any of the wives' passes questioned.

* * *

With nine miles to go we plunged into the greenery of the English Garden. People shouted that Shorter was one minute ahead. Wolde and I looked behind us. Clayton was gone. There was only a pale little man in white, 150 yards back. The day had cooled. The next five miles through the park would be in shade. And Frank had said, "I've never tied up, you know. I've never really died after getting a lead." I believed him now. He could hold his minute. Wolde and I were running for silver.

We dipped and rolled and sometimes stumbled on the dusty, rutted path. The applause of the city streets fell away. On some wooded stretches, we were alone with our struggle. I drew on the competitive responses I had restrained earlier, imagining how I would bolt away from Wolde with a mile to go, recalling his 57-second last lap in the Mexico City 10,000, where he had been a close second, and reminding myself of the other side of the coin, his thirty-nine years.

In a clearing the trail widened. A cluster of spectators pushed to see. Trotting straight at us was a long-haired dachshund. I went left. So did he. I cut back. So did he. To the amusement of the crowd, I had to hurdle him. A few yards farther on stood three policemen whose duty it was to keep the path clear. They were taking pictures of us.

* * *

I had been torpid, just out of bed, ready to jog on a humid, glaring day. The Olympic Village gate was locked. A guard, dressed in silly turquoise, said, "There have been shootings in the night. You cannot leave."

I started back to my room. On the way I met my teammate, hammer thrower George Frenn, whose parents were born in Lebanon. He told me Arab terrorists had broken into the Israeli quarters, shot two people and taken others hostage. George was seething. "I hate lunatics," he said.

I lived in an apartment on the fifth floor of the U.S. building with Shorter, Steve Savage, Jon Anderson, and Dave Wottle, all middle or long-distance runners. Frank was on our terrace, staring at police lines, ambulances, and newsmen assembled under cover near the Israeli dorm 150 yards away.

"I haven't felt this way since Kennedy was killed," he said. "Imagine those poor guys over there. Every five minutes a psycho with a machine gun says, 'Let's kill 'em now,' and someone else says, 'No, let's wait awhile.' How long could you stand that?"

We took turns on the terrace, plucking seeds from a fennel plant there and grinding them in our palms. Below, people played chess or Ping Pong. The trading of Olympic pins continued. Athletes sunbathed by the reflecting pool. It seemed inappropriate, but what was one supposed to do? The scratchy, singsong notes of European police sirens sounded incessantly. Rumors leaped and died. There were twenty-six hostages. There were seven. The terrorists were killing a man every two hours. They were on the verge of surrender.

At 3:30 P.M. I phoned a friend in the Press Village.

"Have you heard?" he asked. "The Games are stopped."

"Stopped? You mean postponed or canceled?"

"Postponed for now. But they say it may be impossible to start them again."

I went back to the room, where Bobbie was waiting, and I wept. I experienced level after level of grief: for the marathon, those years of preparation now useless; for the dead and doomed Israelis; and for the violated sanctuary of the Games.

In Mexico and here the Village had been a refuge, admittedly imperfect, from a larger, seedier world in which individuals and governments refused to adhere to any humane code. For two weeks every four years we direct our kind of fanaticism into the essentially absurd activities of running and swimming and being beautiful on a balance beam. Yet even in the rage of competition we keep from hurting each other, and thereby demonstrate the meaning of civilization. I shook and cried as that illusion, the strongest of my life, was shattered.

In the evening Bobbie and I walked around. We met Ron Hill, the British marathoner. Ron was agitated. "Why should this stop the Games? It's all political, isn't it? Let the police seal the thing off. The rest of the town isn't affected. I want that marathon to stay on Saturday."

"They're talking about a one-day postponement," I said. "Surely one day shouldn't matter."

"It does to me," he said.

Tom Dooley, one of our walkers, responded, "All political? Those people are just politically dead?"

Hailu Ebba, the Ethiopian 1,500-meter runner, said, "I have led a calm life. I can't believe those people are in that building and could get killed. They could shut this whole place down. Running is not that important."

At 10 P.M. Bobbie and I decided to spend the night away from the Village. On our way to the front gate, the only one where exit or entry was permitted, we met John Carlos. John, often strident, now was muted, thoughtful. He shook his head. "People were upset over what I did in 1968," he said, "but I just expressed my feelings. I didn't hurt anybody. Now what are they going to say? Can they tell the difference?"

At the gate, the guards were now admitting no one, nor permitting anyone to leave. Hoover Wright, one of our assistant coaches, and his wife were also trying to get out. We looked at each other in confusion. Someone who knew him shouted from the crowd, "Hoover, there's going to be shooting! There's going to be shooting!"

We turned to check other exits and met Lee Evans, who said it was impossible. We went back, through the rising furor, to the room.

After a few minutes Dave Wottle came in from, to our amazement, a run. "I went out the back gate," he said. He had covered a three-mile loop and returned to the rear of the Village, where he found his way barred by ropes. He jumped the ropes and then the fence. "I heard some guards yelling 'halt' but I just waved without looking. After fifty yards I came to another group of guards. One recognized me. He said, 'It's Wottle,' and they laughed." When Dave looked back, he saw five guards returning guns to their holsters. "If I had known they were so jumpy, I'd have walked around out there all night."

Then it seemed over. Anderson and Savage, who had been kept outside the main gate for an hour, came in and told how helicopters had taken terrorists and hostages to an airport. The late news said the Israelis had been rescued. We went to bed, shaken by the prolonged anxiety but relieved.

We awoke to the final horror. The first newspapers said, *Sixteen Dead.*

I walked to the memorial service. Russian soccer players were practicing on a field beside the stadium. Concession stands were open, smelling of sauerkraut. The program was long-winded in four languages. The crowd applauded when IOC President Avery Brundage said the Games would go on.

"The Games *should* go on," said Tom Dooley, "and they will. But for the wrong reasons. The Germans don't want any hitches in their organization. There are the financial considerations. Those people who applauded just want to see who will win the 5,000 meters and the hell with the rest."

"What are the right reasons?" I asked.

"Just one. To stay together. Who wins or loses now is ridiculously unimportant, considered against these men's deaths. But we have to stay together."

"Can we go to future Olympics, knowing this might happen again?"

He was quiet for a moment. "I don't know. Maybe Olympians will have to be like the early Christians now. We'll have to conduct our events in catacombs, in quiet forests."

* * *

With five miles to go, a cramp shot up my right hamstring. Wolde passed immediately and looked around. He watched me hobble, clutching the back of my thigh for a couple of steps. Then he turned and ran on.

As I slowed the cramp eased. I couldn't risk a second attack. I had accelerate carefully, if possible, to just below my previous pace. Wolde quickly had 100 yards. Then Lismont, the European champion, the man in white we had seen behind us entering the park, stormed past, running with his head down and a powerful arm action. I had visions of myself in the coming miles, a crawling, agonized figure, being passed at the end by wealthy Argentines. But then, mercifully, the park ended and I got back on level streets. I found a rhythm and began to move again. There was no reason to look back. The last medal was disappearing ahead of me.

* * *

For a period of two days before the Games, every American athlete faced the decision of whether or not to compete. On August nineteenth black U.S. trackmen withdrew from a meet at Kempten, sixty miles from Munich, rather than go on the field with the Rhodesian team. Late that night and again the next morning the entire team held meetings, in which it was established that the blacks were united in their decision and that many whites, out of conscience or brotherhood, would back them. Coach Bowerman said, "By admitting Rhodesia to the Games under the flag of Great Britian, when Rhodesia has severed all ties with Britain over the issue of white supremacy, the IOC has committed a political subterfuge. If any of our athletes feel they cannot in good conscience compete against Rhodesians, I'll support them all the way."

A statement urging the IOC to expel Rhodesia was given USOC President Clifford Buck to deliver. It was by no means sure Buck would even be heard. "I know the temper of these aristocrats," said Tokyo Olympic Coach Bob Giegengack. "They will lock the door if they think they are going to be pressured."

We cast about for other ways to avoid a boycott. "Can't we just ask the Rhodesians to leave?" said Walk Coach Bruce MacDonald. "If enough countries told them they weren't welcome, wouldn't they go?"

"If they were that rational," said Frank Shorter, "they wouldn't have apartheid."

Buck was allowed to present our appeal. While the IOC deliberated, athletes mulled over their personal courses of action in the event Rhodesia participated.

"I don't have any question about which is the more important, my jumping in sand or the inhuman treatment suffered by more than 90 percent of Rhodesians population that is nonwhite," said triple jumper Art Walker. "If that team stays, I'll have to go."

Shot-putter George Woods: "I didn't have to pass a political test to come here. I put the shot seventy feet. That's what I'm here to do, regardless of my sympathy for oppressed people. There are so many issues we could boycott over—the Russians' treatment of the Jews, the Nigerians' treatment of the Biafrans, the Pakistanis' treatment of the Bengalis. . . . We're vulnerable ourselves over our Vietnam bombing. None of our governments are pure, so let's leave them out of it. When all those people who can't be athletes first have gone home, I'll be here putting my shot."

Our anxiety was to no purpose. The IOC ousted Rhodesia. But the debate, once ignited, did not die. Instead, it widened into a discussion of the true ends and essences of the Olympics.

"Before I made the team," said intermediate hurdler Jim Seymour, "I thought of all the things I'd do, like I'd just wear a plain white uniform because competing for a country is political. Then I swung the other way and figured I'd wear a McGovern button. Now I know that's wrong. The Games' only value is their universality. Even though I'm against bombing, any bombing for any reason, I couldn't wear one of the OLYMPIC PROJECT FOR PEACE buttons unless I could take the 'Olympic' off it. I can't stand the Games being used."

Others decried the imperfections of the Games themselves. The "representation" of countries by competitors not only introduces nationalism but, because teams are limited to two or three people per event, some fine athletes are prevented from taking part. Three quarter-milers capable of winning medals stayed home in the United States, for example, and at least two of the finest steeplechasers in the world were not entered because they were Kenyans.

As Mark Spitz began stacking up his seven golds, one of our oarsmen spoke of the inequity of opportunity between sports. He said, "Swimmers and sprinters can double or triple without any trouble, and then get together on relay teams, so they're always the heroes of the Games. An oarsman in the eights, by comparison, can only take credit for one ninth of his medal. And that kind of unfairness aside, I find it hard to call people in yachting, equestrian, and maybe shooting real Olympians. In my mind an Olympian is an individual who approaches the limits of human performance. That entails enduring a kind of pain that you don't get riding in a sailboat." As he spoke, he scrutinized me very carefully. "Marathon," he said. "Yeah, I guess you're legitimate."

*   *   *

The final four miles were through a chasm of yelling, clapping people. Where in the beginning this noise was a distraction and an irritant, it now kept sense in our suffering.

If it is run right, a marathon inflicts considerable physical damage. The cell walls of muscles rupture. Tendons become in inflamed. Joints, crunching together fifteen thousand times, wear away at cartilage. I ran it right, with the crowd's approval roaring in my head, on a cushion of blood blisters. I tempted my twinging thigh, forcing the pace, frantically trying to get back up to third, but as I approached the stadium Lismont was out of sight and Wolde still had me by 200 yards.

In the tunnel I felt the other hamstring going. On the track I just tried to hold together, to hide my weakness. Around the last curve, when the crowd buoys you and you sometimes experience a perverse desire that the race not end, I felt only a great weight.

I finished fourth. Frank was waiting beyond the line to catch me; he was the first American to have won the Olympic marathon in sixty-four years. We walked on the grass outside the track, leaning on each other. Photographers screamed incomprehensibly from their moat. Bobbie was there, holding me, and I came apart, pain and frustration forcing out tears. "I tried so hard," I said. She just held me. In a few seconds I knew it was all right. She was more important than any medal and it was over and it didn't matter if I cried. I was amazed at having the moisture.

I walked and jogged a lap, letting the feeling come. I was an Olympian again, bruised, bloody, half-delirious. Legitimate.

*   *   *

A most congenial adventurer, William Norris, twenty-eight, of Beverly, Massachusetts, three-time IC4A steeplechase champion, has hitchhiked across Africa, cornered the Manhattan market in Christmas trees, and traveled a hundred thousand miles while in the U. S. Army without ever taking a day's leave or lifting a rifle in anger.

Bill Norris came to Munich from Eugene, Oregon, where he was employed as a carpenter, having learned the trade in a week by watching other carpenters. Within days he was working for ABC, UPI, and Time. It was Norris who noticed sprinters Eddie Hart and Rey Robinson in the ABC-TV building when their second-round heats were being run. He got them to the stadium, but too late.

Early on the afternoon of Tuesday, September 5, when the Village was coming to the realization that it was under siege by murderers, Bill Norris burst, panting, into my room. He carried a camera with a monstrous telephoto lens and a Hungarian Airlines bag that emitted growls and spitting noises.

"Have you got a glass of water?" he said. "I haven't had anything to drink for two days."

He collapsed onto a bed while I brought him a quart bottle of Coke. He drank it right down, his eyes filling with tears from the sting of the carbonation. "At last," he sighed. "What a morning."

"What in hell have you been doing?"

"Taking pictures of terrorists. The Hungarian and New Zealand buildings are across from the Israelis."

"I thought they were sealed off."

"They are, kind of. The airlines bag got me in. I crawled around on the terraces. Once I was sitting up on a cement divider, clicking away at the negotiations, and a guerrilla aimed his machine gun at me. I never felt so naked in my life. I went inside and an official came through and said absolutely no one could leave until the thing is settled. I said, 'Sure' and got up . . ." Snarls erupted from the flight bag. Bill fished out a walkie-talkie. The press center was calling. "Yeah," he said. "I got a few pictures."

"Are they any good?" asked an irritated metallic voice.

"I guess so. Remember, I haven't had much experience with this sort of thing."

Growing exasperation. "Look, on a scale of one to ten, what would they be?"

"Well . . . ten."

"Get them over here, Norris."

The following day I saw Norris sitting on a bench near the U.S. building, fiddling with his camera. "I'm learning," he said. "I'm to where I know what maybe half these buttons do."

"Were your pictures any good?"

"Yeah. UPI moved four of them on the wire."

"My God, you've found your calling."

"I doubt it." Bill was clearly drained, his eyes bloodshot, his hands unsteady. He leaned back against the wall and put down the camera. "During the heat of the moment it seemed like something worth doing. It was exciting, scrambling around with the snipers, being in on something I knew would be history. I didn't see any bodies or blood, just some nuts parading around with weapons. The feeling of death never reached me. But, this morning, when I heard all the hostages had been killed . . . That was no game yesterday. I'm a little ashamed of myself."

Bill donated the payment for his pictures to the fund for the victims' families. "I couldn't take advantage of someone's death," he said.

* * *

A trainer disinfected the abrasions from my early fall and took me to the doping test. I submitted a urine specimen to one of a row of cubicles. The female attendant was asking if she couldn't work in another room.

"It makes me sad to be always with the fourth-placers," she said. Thunderheads were building. My mood was worsening from fatigue and the pressing, curious crowd. A boy begged for my number and I let him pull it from my sweat suit. He yanked so hard I staggered back, instantly detesting him for an absurd sense of values. What possible good was my number to him? When he got it off he shoved it in my face to be signed.

"Hey, no," I said. "You can't know how tired . . ."

"You must!" he demanded.

"I will not!" I raged, shoving him away. I was incredibly close to swinging at him, a twelve-year-old. Bobbie soothed me and we kept on, she waving away the autograph hunters, me limping and whining when the cobblestones found my blisters.

Inside the Village we met a boxer who stopped to observe my crablike attempts at climbing the stairs. He had a mouse under one eye, tape above an ear. He said "Why would anyone want to be a marathon runner?"

* * *

Frank and I sat in our room the next morning. It had been an effort of will to jog three miles around the soccer fields. The weather had turned in the night and a wintry wind had cut through our sweat suits. We were caught in the melancholy that follows a well-run race, deepened now by the griefs of these Games. Neither of us said much, but the feeling persisted that something ought to be said.

"How do you think the medal will change things?" I asked.

Frank shook his head. "I'm no different. No delusions of grandeur. Hell, I couldn't run five miles this morning. If my life changes it will be because other people change the way they behave toward me."

We moved slowly around the apartment, rearranging dirty towels and boxes of once-worn white boots, thinking about packing. Frank talked for a while about taking up cross-country skiing.

"You know," I said, "all this time I thought the Olympic champion was somebody incredibly special."

Frank gave me a consoling look, as though he would have liked to protect me from this final disillusionment. "And then you found out," he said, "that it was only me."

—April 1973

The Observer

The balance of this book is simply findings about other splendid runners, made in the years following Munich. And while there has been no restoration of my illusions about the Olympic Games, the fine, hard, sometimes whimsical characters of these men and women continue to be affecting.

Most of the pieces were written in the third person, to avoid a relentless "I" being interposed between subject and reader, to lull the latter into an unwarranted sense of objectivity. Thus the recurring "visitor" or "friend" or "observer" who views the action in so much of what follows.

It is a device that can become tedious, especially when the watching euphemism is known to be always me, but I'm going to leave it in, because in the case of this observer, it is perfectly apt. I am conscious of myself as an outsider, shy, peculiarly suited to peering for a while into lives and worlds then withdrawing to muse over what seems interesting. In this I found myself similar to a few of my subjects, different from far more.

So here I write something of my own early career and wanderings, to tell about the runner who is telling you about all these other runners. The snippets that follow, of imperfect truth and little beauty, still are all you need to know.

I am in class in the third grade, Howard Elementary School, Eugene, Oregon, in a reading circle. We come across the word "Navaho."

"Wrong," I say. "Navajo is spelled with a 'j'."

My next sensations are of being seized and shaken, feet off the ground, the teacher's nails driving into the narrow flesh of my arms. Her words do not come across the years, but they are hissed, the low voice of fearful hatred, and I am crying back in angry, righteous wails that it *was* wrong.

There the scene ends. Surely it was resolved in favor of Mrs. Anderson and equally acceptable spellings. She was not an old woman, even as I judged at age nine, probably less than thirty. But what arrogance of mine had gone before to build such a reaction?

In grade school I was a strange, imperfectly socialized thing. Photographs show a stick figure, pale and knock-kneed, with hair more closely resembling fur. I had had two operations to correct amblyopia, or lazy eye, and I wore glasses until I was twelve. With or without them the child's eyes are wedged back in hollows, his look the hunted one of ineradicable self-consciousness.

We had moved to Eugene from Portland when I was four. My father had come to start the Moore Steel Service Company, a warehouse operation, with backing from a Portland industrial family. He was successful. I remember a cavernous building of corrugated metal, booming echoes out of the dark, a whining overhead crane from which dangled chains and hooks. Men in oil-blackened coveralls cut through dusty plate with acetylene torches, sparks flying, dribbles of steel dropping white upon the plate below, congealing red, then gray.

Prime customers were the sawmills and logging equipment manufacturers. The dirt and noise and force of these places repelled me as a child. Later, in college, I would work weekends and summers in the plywood mills north of Eugene, and though I developed a perverse pride in being able to do the filthiest jobs without complaint, I still detested that world.

Yet there were compensations. To his two sons crawling upon red leather and brass-riveted armchairs in his office, Melvin Moore was an observably capable and respected man. We belonged to the country club, its pool a refuge on hot summer days, a place to lie on the fir-shaded grass and watch my father walk, intent on his final pitch shot, up the emerald light of the last fairway.

He had written sentimental poetry on shipboard during the war. He was a determined gardener, working the good, deep river soil of our yard. I remember him tanned, with short, sunbleached hair, hard in the stomach, sweating behind a Rototiller or setting posts and stringing wire to support boysenberries. Summer flowers were his pride—zinnias, asters, and snapdragons standing against drifts of shasta daisies. A four-hundred-year-old white oak grew between house and garage, and in the fall it was drudgery to rake and haul the tons of wet, acrid leaves it shed, but upon that compost my father grew pumpkins so large my brother at six could squeeze inside and the lid be put on.

We had a console phonograph beside the dining room table and every evening my father chose our "dinner music." I recall the "Saber Dance," though I've forgotten what sort of meal it might have complemented. He had the company sponsor a weekly hour of classical music on a local radio station.

From the example of his father in Pittsburgh, who gathered mushrooms and wild greens to eat with raw oysters, he had learned courage in dining. He brought home finnan haddie, butter clams in the shell, pickled pigs feet. And always in the freezer were joints of deer and elk, wrapped in white paper. It is a requirement of business people in Oregon to at least pay lip service to hunting and fishing. Among the steel fabricators and scrap iron dealers of those days there were few who did not drop an antelope quarter or salmon on my father's desk once or twice a year, usually because their wives had forbidden them to bring any more home.

My father was an instrument, as a member of the building committee, in the foundation of Trinity Methodist Church. I wonder at this now, for he never enjoyed the actual going to church, and his efforts seem more than what was necessary to placate my mother, whose lash got us there each Sunday. This memory is practically palpable:

The sermon rolls on. My brother Bob and I flank my father, pressing in on him, close to odors of nicotine and heavy suit cloth, intent upon the church bulletin in his lap. Slowly, with great consideration, he draws a picture with his mechanical pencil, a vague and confusing sketch, a line suspended in air here, a shadow off to one side, a connecting curve . . . The object of the game is to be first to identify what is taking shape, a railroad track or toilet bowl or piece of farm machinery. Care has to be taken to avoid disturbing my mother, who is devotedly attending the preacher, so my father's kidneys are subject to sharp digs from children's elbows as the picture comes clear. When I had to take the Army induction tests that ask you to find a given diagram within the network of another, or to identify a complicated shape as seen from a different angle, I thought of those hours in a hard pew, my father drawing in the margins of the litany, a faint rumble of contentment in his chest.

We traveled then. From the age of eight I can watch myself grow ever skinnier and more strange looking—in the home movies my father took of our summers. To Yellowstone Park for bears and moose and a snowstorm in August; to the long, windswept, driftwood-piled Oregon beaches; to Vancouver Island on the ferry, to walk in the old quarry that the Bucharts turned into a sunken garden near Victoria, British Columbia, always on the watch for unusual trees, from which cuttings might be stolen and nurtured.

Fishing. Deep sea fishing for salmon or halibut, relishing rough water because there was always the chance everyone but my father and I would get seasick, and we would get to catch everyone's limit. Or crabbing in Coos Bay, he dumping nets full of scrabbling, hard, pointy, mechanical crabs in the bottom of the boat for amazed, timid boys to sort. Or, to do important fishing, to the McKenzie River and the high lakes in the Cascades for trout. We would rent cabins or pitch tents. There was little pretense of these expeditions being for the kids or to get away for some time to think or a return to nature. The object was to kill trout, the heaviest possible.

Usually another couple or set of relatives would be along. The men would venture out in the boat or along the stream at first light, and the women and kids would be left to amuse themselves until things had been settled with the fish. I recall catching huge, soft frogs at Elk Lake, watching three-pound trout gliding through the reeds next to shore. My father, returning with one-pounders from trolling the deeps, refused to believe this. Three Creeks Lake had a cliff above one end, with snow in the shadowy overhangs. Clear Lake, the headwaters of the McKenzie, was formed when ancient lava flows dammed the outlet of the creek, submerging a forest. The water is a constant thirty-seven degrees, so cold that it forestalls bacterial action, allowing the trees at the bottom to remain unrotted for centuries. Great trout, fifty feet down, look like minnows among the snags.

The McKenzie's woods are so silent, the dogwood and vine maple so luxuriant under fir and cedar canopies, its water so clear over stones so colorful that it seems the Platonic ideal of a woodland stream.

I recall a day. My father is off drifting the river with customers and I am poking around the bank near our rented cabin. I have a little steel pole with a length of leader and a tiny gold hook and a few salmon eggs. I let the line down into a hole, a place overhung with mossy logs. A bending alder trails in the current and the water flashes with the stone and sky colors, shadows and gleams through the depths, impossible to tell fish from swirl. I have bite after bite, the sharp tug sending me into wild recoil, the hook flying up, shorn of egg. The excitement grows unbearable. I would throw gill nets across the river, use dynamite, to have a fish to show my father when he came back. And finally I do, and squeeze it all out of shape awaiting his return.

He makes me clean it, explaining what each of the entrails is, and coming to the stomach we find that its recent diet has consisted of salmon eggs.

We went, annually it seems, to Ten Mile Lake, near the ocean, staying in a white cottage set upon stiff dry grass. One walked down hot, chirping beach sand to a silverwood dock. Pilings receded into dark, brackish lake water, thick with underwater plants, sunken rowboats, catfish.

One afternoon, the family lying on the beach, I walked into the water up to my chest and started jumping up and down. Each jump carried me a few inches down the slope to deeper water, until suddenly I had to jump just to get my face up for a breath. I saw streams of yellow bubbles in the black water, the shining surface shattering as I jumped, dimming as I fell back, shouting underwater, surges of bubbles, not having enough time to get a breath and shout while above the surface, sinking back, yellow bubbles. Then my father lifting me out, unworried, soothing, dropping me on the hot sand. My mother got a towel around me while I choked and shivered. There were tears in her eyes and she made it plain that she felt my father had waited too long to retrieve me.

He visited my room that evening and said he knew it would be hard but if I were not to be marked by my fright I ought to go back in the water and really learn how to swim. I shook my head, mute, abject. For days be kept after me, wearing me down, just to wade, just to have the water around me. Later we went up the McKenzie to Belknap Hot Springs, which fed a swimming pool. There are home movies of the first time I swam across it.

*   *   *

From eight to twelve I had a dog, a collie touched lightly with St. Bernard, for he was more muscular than a true collie, and more imaginative. He came, when he chose, to Chipper, a name given in puppyhood which later suited him not at all. He could run forty miles an hour, kill all the cats in the neighborhood on a single day, swim two miles to be near me in the center of a lake, and bring home the goods. He brought: fifteen doormats, which he piled in a kind of friendship offering on our front steps (and which my brother and I returned to bemused neighbors, pulling them from house to house on a little red wagon), those dead and torn cats (buried in haste), and once a casserole of steaming macaroni and cheese. My mother told him to take it back where he got it this instant. Chip took it into the backyard and ate it. My mother still uses the dish.   •

He was wild, with a madness of loyalty. He once jumped from a third story window when he thought I was leaving him. When he caught some sort of disease which afflicted male dogs, and became listless, eventually having to be fed dextrose and orange juice from a squeeze bottle, pathetic in his submission to this ignominy, it was my first prolonged anxiety. Then one morning he was gone. I was hopeful. His energy had returned, he was off on a neighborhood romp. Soon we would get the gratifying news that he had bitten a paper boy somewhere. But the day passed—and others.

There was no grace in my grief. I cried bitterly and long. My father left me alone. There was no mention of another dog. My brother looked at my rages wonderingly. And I hated everyone for their stupid acceptance.

I looked for him. I ran through the slough that wandered near the house, picking my way through brush and roots whitened by the dried slime of winter's high water.

I hunted the miles of filbert and walnut orchards that stretched off to the north, away from settlement.

My father told me, years later, that a neighbor had come to the house and said he had found Chipper where he had gone to die, under some alder trees, hidden by deep summer grass. My father couldn't bring himself to tell me, so I was left to accept the loss in increments, to give in to my mother's and brother's patient remarks about how life went on. And I respect now how very long it took, because part of him has stayed within me since, that willful child, blind against the odds.

In the sixth grade I was selected to attend a special class, across town at Dunn School. This was for "gifted" students—a word which made my father smirk—to challenge them beyond what was possible in regular, undifferentiated classrooms, so to prevent the habits of laziness. It was too late. I did no more under Mrs. Moomaw's expectant gaze than I had earlier, just enough to get by.

I was unhappy during my first weeks in this class, from a combination of intimidation, homesickness, and the uncomfortable burden of great expectations. Most of the other kids were children of professors or other professionals. Many came from the same neighborhood, the hilly, maple-shaded area of South Eugene near the University of Oregon.

A five-minute walk from school uphill through a stand of pine brought one to the farm of Senator Wayne Morse. I came from the flatland north of town, near the railroad yards and lumber mills, where less than 10 percent of the residents have college degrees. These indices are too easy to set down. At the time, I only knew there were differences, that other kids had read more, had developed more interests, which they pursued in a more adult manner than I had imagined possible for twelve-year-olds. Perhaps they were gifted. As for me, it often seemed that a terrible mistake had been made. I demanded that my parents have me returned to comfortable Howard School. My mother, thrilled by the social implications of my rise, would not hear of it.

After school I had to walk a mile to South Eugene High, where I'd take the bus home. On the way I often stopped to moon over the clownfish in an aquarium shop on Willamette Street. There were blind cave fish, clouds of sparkling, iridescent neon tetras. Had I been given a choice then of growing on or staying in that shop, dim and warm and humming with the pumps and heaters, I'd have gladly stayed.

These trials were mitigated by finding a friend. Don Porter was the son of a congressman and cherished the same resistance to hard work as I. We giggled through math and music, put cherry bombs under Mrs. Moomaw's chair, laced our conversation with the innocuous Yiddish expletives of *Mad Magazine* ("I will not eat my fursh-lugginer peas."), and ran around the playground at recess. If we ran far enough, it seemed, nearly everyone else got tired before we did.

When I was eleven, my father bought a cottage on the wooded shore of Dexter Reservoir, a new lake then filling on the Willamette River, twenty miles southeast of Eugene. His father, an elemental man of huge strength and energy, came from Portland to rid the land of its mounds of blackberry and poison oak. My grandfather's name was Fred but the family knew him only as Grandad, with its connotations of whisky and vigor. He had worked for nearly fifty years in the steel mills of Pittsburgh.

When I was thirteen, I hunted with my grandfather. I walked through the Oregon uplands ahead of him, carrying a 16-gauge shotgun loaded with No. 6 shot, for pheasants and squirrels. My instructions on seeing a deer were to lie down flat in a hurry because Grandad brandished a double-barreled 12-gauge loaded with solid lead slugs. We never saw a deer, which saved me, as I surely would have stood transfixed before the muzzle of that elephant gun, and Grandad, inflamed with buck fever at eighty, just as surely would have let loose.

Because my father had told me of his hunting with Grandad, these times seemed to have a certain resonance, the echo of generations. "Dad hunted rabbits around Pittsburgh," my father had said, "and we ate rabbit often. We took walks, hunting mushrooms, collecting May apples and poke and dandelion greens, and one of us always carried the old single-shot .22. Once, walking, Dad took my shoulder and said 'Look, there's a rabbit.' I peered into the thicket he was pointing at, but I couldn't see any rabbit. He carefully described the limb I was to follow, the twig, the leaf that was just above the rabbit's ear, and told me to aim just below there. I fired twice, and nothing moved.

"'You missed,' he said.

"'Of course I missed because there's no rabbit there.'

"'Shoot again.'

"'Can't. No more shells.' I started into the thicket to show him he was just looking at a lump of sod, but he held me and took a quarter out of his pocket.

"'Run down to McKees Rocks and get some more.' So he sat down and chewed tobacco and watched while I ran the two miles to McKees Rocks and got the cartridges and ran the two miles back. And when I shot again, a rabbit came kicking out of there and died at our feet.

"'Don't tell me about rabbits,' he said."

Grandad was an instinctively combative man. As he told it, his fighting had started around home. "My Dad wouldn't let us work on the farm (in Columbia, Pennsylvania) in the heat of the day, so he taught us boys how to box under the chestnut tree. Then later when I was weaving silk in Paterson, New Jersey, I took boxing and wrestling lessons with a professor at the YMCA. I'm a left-handed man, and a left-handed man has it easier in fights." This left-handed man had a lot of fights. "I boxed in smokers in Paterson and Pittsburgh and all the little towns. I wrestled at carnivals, challenging the carnival man, and mostly I won. I was quick and agile and I liked to surprise people." I could vouch for that. When I brought two pairs of boxing gloves up to the lake when I was fourteen and he eighty-one, he jubilantly bloodied my nose with his first sneaky right-hand lead.

My father had swum and dived for the Langley High School team in Pittsburgh, and ran cross-country as well, finishing eighth in the 1932 City Championships. The first time Grandad saw his daughter Wilma swim, she won the Pittsburgh city championship in the 100-yard freestyle. In 1932, Wilma finished second behind Lenore Kight in the Pennsylvania qualifying for the Olympic Trials, but couldn't afford to travel to New York City to try out for the team.

"He encouraged us in sport," said my father, "but not with pressure or what you would call intense interest." Not the way he would have if the sports had been those of combat.

His bad teeth had kept him out of the Spanish-American War, but in 1917, at age forty, he tried to join up for World War I. "I think it took some nerve to try to enlist with five children," my Aunt Vivian—one of those children—told him once.

"Well, I said I only had two," Grandad explained, and added with a disgust carried across sixty years, "They wrote me a letter saying to 'hold myself in readiness.'"

Aunt Vivian, as curious as the rest of the family about the roots of his disposition to engage an enemy, any enemy, asked why he was so eager to serve in that war.

"Why, I wanted the experience of a soldier," Grandad replied. "Everybody wanted to wear a uniform them days."

Grandad worked in the Pittsburgh mills until 1947, when he was seventy. Then, on the urging of his children, most of whom had come west, he moved to Portland and took a job in a boiler works as a night watchman. At seventy-five he broke his back in two places by falling twenty-two feet out of a plum tree. He was told to wear his cast for a year and a half. But he kept a penknife beside his bed and in the evenings whittled away a bit of plaster here and there "to get at the itches." In six months he had only a little vest remaining, and the doctors gnashed their teeth and fitted him for a brace.

There was something of the medieval concept of scourge in Grandad's view of disease or affliction. The invader must be driven out. So when he endured a siege of arthritis, be heated his room to one hundred degrees. Grim and sweating, he worked his hands up the wall as far as he could reach, first to his shoulders, then his head, clawing a little higher each day. For hours he squeezed rubber balls in his gnarled hands. Gradually, at great cost, the arthritis eased, astonishing the doctors. Grandad then uttered the phrase that would become the traditional pronouncement of a cure: "I beat that rap."

There was a catalog of other injuries, other illnesses beaten back. Grandad's primary legacy, the example he set a young athlete, was that drive to keep his body his own.

But my town has long provided examples of athletic excellence. In the spring of 1956 there was inordinate interest in Eugene in running. Jim Bailey, an Australian studying at the university, had run the first four-minute mile on U.S. soil, a 3:58.6 in defeating world-record holder John Landy in Los Angeles. A year later, my father took me to see the Pacific Coast Conference championships at Oregon's Hayward Field. Bailey was in the half-mile against California's Don Bowden. For some reason we only went the first day, so all I saw were the heats. Both Bailey and Bowden won their qualifying races, but their superiority was not so impressive as the simple sensations of the event. I gripped the low wire fence on the north end of the track. The middle-distance runners pounded by thirty feet away, their spikes making a wonderfully loud gnashing sound on the moist cinders. Their faces were controlled, distant in their concentration. How could human beings run like that? I left with the sense of an unbridgeable separation. All this elegant and austere power, so close, only accentuated the weakness and awkwardness of the wondering observer.

About that time my father left his company because of differences with the owners. I remember angry telephone calls, silent dinners, forced good spirits. There was a recession; the owners needed money so the company was not to grow any larger; its profits were to be siphoned off. Over this decision my father quit. We never spoke of it, but dreams were involved. By then a church builder, a member of the Chamber of Commerce, he seemed to connect the company's growth with responsibility to the community. He began again, and left a second firm for similar reasons. Money was lost in a company which made boat trailers, more in an insufficiently capitalized steel warehouse. Real estate was sold to finance ventures, second mortgages taken.

He was able to keep the urgency of these setbacks from me, but some of the physical aspects of our life changed. We traveled less, except for one summer of touring the western states with an empty boat trailer, visiting distributors. We lapsed at the country club. Such marginally reduced circumstances didn't worry me at all, but they must have torn at my father. He seemed to age, to become distracted. Determined to shield his family, there was no one to whom he might transfer the shocks. He drank more heavily. Even in good times and good jobs he had to work around the rawness of construction. That may have been a stimulus to sailboats and flowers. Now he stuck, duty-bound, to industry, to selling and importing steel pipe, getting by on his knowledge of the market but never making headway, and growing yearly less exuberant, more potbellied, deaf and repetitious, blending in with all those deadly people in offices beside whom he once seemed so alive.

*   *   *

In the seventh grade I rejoined the mainstream of my classmates at Colin Kelly Junior High. In many ways it was a return to old paths, with the exception that social functions—dances in the gym even at noon in some libertine departure from disciplined education—now were sanctioned by school officials. It happened that no matter what presence of mind I might show in classwork, when plunged into social affairs I went haywire. I seem to have operated on an earlier code, a fourteenth century sort of romantic commitment, disguised with an uneven nonchalance, as in the eighth grade, when I fastened upon chubby Duretta Roderick, an alert Mormon girl who lived behind our church. I attended from afar, so far that when I betrayed myself she was appalled. A Christmas dance: Shavings and crepe paper and sticky punch on the gym floor. Paul Anka sobbing. I pressed a small package of perfume into her hand. She resisted. "I can't take this," she said.

"Why not? You haven't even opened it. It might be a joke."

"It's not a joke and I can't take it." And she didn't.

I sailed it into the slough while stumbling home, castigating myself for expecting anyone else my age to act in a rational manner, asking why I was the eternal outsider. So, against cold rejection, or the chance of it, I sublimated.

*   *   *

I played no school sports until the ninth grade, but seem to have labored for years in solitary contentment in our backyard. My parents endured hours of vibrating phone wires as I attempted through several autumns to kick a football over them. One summer I pole-vaulted, using a fir pole the diameter of a mop handle, until one day, at the apogee of a leap, it split and I fell heavily onto sun-hardened earth, where I writhed, my breath knocked out of me, until I rolled against the lower half of the pole, now a spike rearing up from the ground, where it had been ready to run me through.

I don't know how I came to think of myself as one who, once sworn to a task, would never give up. My past record spoke otherwise. I quit at homework if it seemed too hard, at mowing the yard rather than refilling the gas tank, at bean picking once I'd earned enough for a water ski.

My mother ranted whenever I abandoned a job or project that continuing would instill discipline. Instead, exposure to the world of farm labor, and later that of the plywood mills, only spurred a determination that I would find some way to get by in the world without having to work.

In the ninth grade I turned out for cross-country running, moved by the apparent promise of freedom to go one's own way, and by memories of my endurance on earlier playgrounds. I found I wasn't very good after all, because most of the team had been running in an organized sort of way for two seasons, but I quickly claimed a parity, not in races but in the length of workouts. Every day the team was asked to do several laps around a half-mile course. It was then up to the individual whether he wanted to do anything more. Even faint and nauseous, I would decide to run around the old gravel pits, filled with scummy water and bluegills, which lay beyond plowed fields near the Southern Pacific tracks. The run was done very slowly, with great appreciation for startled ring-necked pheasants rising out of the fence rows; more in the manner of a leisurely recovery jog than any real work, but it increased the total of my workout miles, sometimes to as much as four.

This diligence was unctuously supported by the coach, a man named Morgan, who was not perfectly versed in running theory but who substituted the song of all coaches everywhere: the more you put in, the more you get out. The simple pleasure of surpassing most of the rest of the team in mileage formed the basic pattern of my running for the next eight years: train on the track with the others, then add the long solitary run.

Occasionally that autumn a teammate would accompany me, especially if I were heading out on Park Avenue, which joined River Road in a stand of fir trees which had been topped in their youth and so grew stunted and branching, like great shaggy menorahs. On the side streets of that region lived most of the acceptable girls in our class. My companion would suggest that we stop at one or another of these residences for a lemonade or to check a homework answer. I did this a few times, coming sheepish and dripping into carpeted living rooms, sinking down beside floral silk divans, the point of a piano leg in my back, finding I had nothing interesting to say. I had not the nerve to stop at the houses of girls I liked, or thought I would like if I ever had the nerve to stop. So I began running alone all the time and not stopping at all. And when winter came—Oregon's chill, soggy dreariness of five months away from the sun—cross-country races ended and I was the only one who kept on, in tennis shoes and dark green sweat suit, through the rain with a rash in my armpits. And I was not at all unhappy.

I only remember a few competitions from junior high cross-country. On a race day my nerves made me feel sleepy to the point of trance. "That will all be over the instant the gun goes off," Coach Morgan said, watching me yawn and yawn and slowly slide to a squat in the locker room corner. But it wasn't. The gun would be perceptible through my fog of apprehension, and I would start to run, but with huge effort. Sometimes more than half of the 1.4-mile race would pass before I seemed to come to myself, recognize that I had performed this activity before, and strike a rhythm that let me pass a few people. By then the leaders would be far out of range.

I remember experiments in which I would go slowly at first, in hopes of preserving energy for a last blazing 440, but I went so slowly that even if I could have sprinted the last mile I couldn't have caught up. Or racing with the front runners for the first 880 and staggering the remainder. Thus came clear the harsh realities of pace, the very narrow limits between going too fast to sustain a speed and too slow to remain in the race. It required a delicacy under stress, a self-knowledge that seemed impossible then, in my nervous mist.

In the spring I fell to training on the track, intending to be a miler. In my first timed mile I did 5:40. By the end of the season I got down to 5:23, in the city junior high championships. I ran third until the last lap. Crowds of kids lined the inside curb, releasing shrieked encouragement into my left ear as I faded to fifth. I finished spent, to be caught up by teammates and walked around, eyes rolled back, toes dragging, the coach pressing the breath out of my chest. Usually on the periphery of these scenes was my father, jovial but holding back, waiting for me to go to him. I seldom did.

Later, at home, he would say, "It appears that you are taking this running seriously. I just want you to know that no matter how you do, whether you never win a single race, I'll still love you exactly the same."

I would allow as that was good to know and we would sit quietly for a while. Then he would add, "But couldn't you have squeezed a little more energy out of your legs that last time around?" This with a wincing grin.

And I'd protest that he had forgotten how it felt to run for his high school cross-country team in Pittsburgh. More silence.

Then he would say that he might have forgotten most of it—he remembered the breathing near the end, the involuntary sobbing—that his remark had been made out of wanting me to do my best.

Once, coming awake, I heard my father talking to a late-night visitor, a neighbor or perhaps the preacher. "He gets awfully tired and he really doesn't do very well," he said. "Frankly, I can't understand why he hasn't quit."

*   *   *

It certainly wasn't winning which drove me on. More often escape. In those weeks of the summer when there was nothing to be picked, my mother determined that I ought to clip the laurel hedge which ran the length of one side of our yard, a formidable ordeal. I was allergic to many things, grass, pollen, dust, cat fur, feathers—all of them collected in the dry and impenetrable interior of that hedge. After hacking away at it for half an hour (perhaps one fiftieth of the job) I was swollen around the eyes, hoarse, unable to breathe through my nose and shaken by repeated, explosive sneezes. I made a mask from a handkerchief folded over a filter of Kleenex smeared with Vicks VapoRub. That let me breathe a little easier, but the rising camphor fumes made me cry. By the end of an hour I was in tantrum at the imbalance of my mother. Having a smoothly trimmed hedge simply wasn't worth a fraction of what I was going through. That decided, I was off, to a shouting match with her, or a sullen run along River Road, silently cursing what I later teamed to call middle-class values.

I will not say I felt unappreciated, but when North Eugene High Vice Principal Bob Newland, a courtly, relaxed man who was also the track and cross-country coach, sent me a note asking if I would do him the honor of running for North, my direction was sealed.

I remember my first run at North, the newness and light in the looker room, with freshly varnished birch benches bolted to red steel supports. I ran with Robin Manela, a junior whose best event was the half-mile, through the fields where lumpy, grunting football players flung themselves on the ground to a coach's whistle and out round the filbert orchard to the west.

It was September before the rains. The ground had been plowed and pulverized and then rolled with a huge smooth roller, to make it firm and level to receive the falling nuts. Our footsteps were well received, settling lightly onto the land, accompanied by little puffs of dust which crept slowly into the air behind us, motes in the sun filtering between the ragged, dark green leaves.

To finish we did 110's up and down a smooth length of grass, Newland making the challenge not effort (as we heard the football coaches demanding) but control, not allowing us to stop until we had done five in a row within half a second of 20 seconds. Eager, one first day, we all ran too fast, laughing.

*   *   *

Young, growing, and flu-ridden, I ran poorly my first year. In the state junior varsity meet in Portland the start was a stampede up a grassy bank. Someone ahead fell. He came rolling back down the hill and I had to hurdle him, seeing, as I did, a single scarlet footprint on his back. I never seemed to find much room to pass and finished in the middle of the field, shocked to find afterward that a teammate, Lynn Adkins, a football halfback who had only begun running when his season was over, had won.

My sense of justice was devastated. Any runner can explain that there are profound emotional and philosophical differences between the autumn disciplines. The qualities necessary for success in football—size, aggressiveness—are liabilities in cross-country running. (It happened that my state champion teammate was a natural runner and something of a misfit in football, but that was where the glory was.) The more confirmed practitioners of the two sports tend to grate upon each other, nowhere more abrasively than in high school, as in what follows.

With our hours of exploring the thousands of acres of nearby orchards, Robin Manela and I and Harlan Andrews, who was the best of the North runners, had come upon some remarkable trees. One was a tall, rather fragile Gravenstein apple no more than a quarter mile from school. The farmer had picked most of the lower fruit. Perhaps that had made the apples in the top branches grow so heavy, as much as a pound apiece. It took a little work to get them. Andrews, much larger than I, would pitch me up to the first crotch and I'd shinny from there, tossing down one apple per runner to observe the conclusion of a particularly satisfying workout. We would sit in the locker room after our showers and polish these voluptuous things on our damp towels, savoring them while the football players clattered in, getting mud on the floor, staring at us with animal jealousy. The apples surely looked spectacular for being held by such frail, white little boys as we were.

With some urgency the guards and tackles demanded to know where we had gotten them, and we would reply with gently elusive accounts of how much country we'd covered that day and it was hard to keep your bearings straight, but we vaguely recalled it was this side of the river. "Pumpkins, now do you need pumpkins? We could take you to eight or ten *tons* of pumpkins, or walnuts, or rotting cucumbers for sure, but apples . . . apples are so ordinary. Didn't they just sort of come to hand somewhere along the way? You ought to run with us some time, an easy six or eight miles . . . Tell you what I can do. I can let you have this core."

This ended, after some weeks, abruptly. A gang of football players beat the location of the tree out of another junior varsity runner, went there en masse, and tore down all the branches, whether in trying to get at the remaining apples or in revenge, we never discovered. They killed that tree.

Even then the incident seemed richly symbolic, representing the diverse approaches of two cultures, one close to the land, and the other defined more by the use of force.

* * *

It has been my luck never to have been coached arbitrarily. When Robin and I spoke as if we would like to understand the ideas behind our training schedules, Newland pulled open a drawer in his desk and gave us folders of raspy onionskin letters. They were filled with advice from the most famous coaches in the world— Gösta Holmer of Sweden, Percy Cerutty of Australia, Franz Stampfl of England—for at that time American runners were not competitive in international distance running. Using the principles of these men, and consulting with Bill Bowerman, who was producing many of the best U.S. runners at Oregon, Newland worked out individual training plans with each North runner based upon the boy's strengths and likes and enthusiasm. There were no uniform requirements in the sense of regular workouts or number of miles to be run. Our best quarter-miler, Ralph Rotter, had to get up at four every morning to milk cows and crush silage and spread topdressing before school. He managed to train only three times a week, forty minutes a session. Yet Newland was as happy with him as he was with Harlan Andrews' exhaustive drive to be the best miler in the state.

Once a week Newland would pile half a dozen of us into his battered old green Chrysler and drive us six or seven miles into the country, for us to run back. As we began he would cruise alongside in the car admonishing us to be comfortable, not to kill ourselves. As soon as he had driven ahead, Harlan would kill us all. We were crueler then, it seems, more blithe about running off and leaving teammates. It seems so because I was always the one left.

There was one glorious fall day, with the pops of hunters' shotguns floating through the soft rural quiet, when Bowerman brought his stable of Oregon runners, including Olympic 1,500-meter men Dyrol Burleson and Jim Grelle, to run six miles with us. We were giddy on the drive out, listening to these wondrous milers say how unfit they were, how this was going to be too far for them. Then when we started they were soon gone, disappearing ahead after the first few hundred yards.

I remember running through the little town of Santa Clara, two miles from the finish, in the greatest distress of my life—and suddenly I was catching an Oregon runner. I couldn't tell who it was yet, but here was a chance for a coup beyond price.

"Was that Burleson?" I screamed at a farmer ambling out to his car from the barbershop. Puzzled, he simply looked behind him to see who I could be addressing.

"Was that Burleson?" I cried to other people. "Don't you know what's going *on*, you idiots!"

Robin caught up to me and said it looked like George Larson, not an Olympian but an excellent runner. We cut the corner of Silver Lane through the filbert orchard and came out onto the road 10 yards behind Larson with 300 to run. When we passed him, he blinked and smiled. We sprinted our hearts out, collapsing in the furious pleasure of finishing ahead of him with Bob Newland looking on.

* * *

On the Oregon coast, sixty miles west of Eugene, there are regions of sand dunes, miles of blowing, soft emptiness, broken only by a few clumps of twisted hemlock. One summer Robin and Harlan and I gathered up a tent and camping gear, and spent a week running across the strength-sapping sand. Far out across the dunes were shallow depressions which filled with water during storms, then crusted over with blowing sand. As we approached one of these places, the sand grew damp and firm, and we would lift and begin to sprint, three abreast, running lightly, bursting with anticipation, for suddenly the surface would heave and give way, and we would be sucked into quicksand, slamming into the cold mess up to our thighs or waists. I remember going from a wild sprint to stunned half-burial while Robin and Harlan strode blissfully by on either side, howling.

Once, heading back, struggling through the loose, hot sand near the woods and campground, Robin and I crested a dune and saw before us on the opposite slope, nestled beneath an overhang of dune grass, a couple, clothing cast aside, rapt in each other's arms. Robin and I scurried back over the ridge, only to have Harlan, mystified, roar from behind, "What's going *on*?" Myopic Harlan, running without his glasses, plunging madly down the sliding sand, while the lovers disengaged and covered.

Once past, we growled at him. He was silent, unbending, for awhile, and then said, "How would you like to be spied on?"

"One must get in the situation first," said Robin, his tone so wistfully mild as to be bereft of hope.

In the spring of his senior year, Harlan won the state meet mile in 4:16 and the 880 in 1:55. I had done 4:49 and 2:05, times which did not qualify me for the subdistrict meet, so I watched from the stands, sitting next to a girl whose looks and good sense I had been taken with in chemistry class. She bruised my shoulder, hitting it for Harlan as he blew around the pack on the final curve of the 880.

"You know him?" she said when he had won. She was flushed, unguarded. "You *really* know him?"

* * *

A week before my senior year began it appeared that I had finally eked my way into a position to win a varsity race. Andrews' graduation was the prime factor, but through the summer I had run consistently and was feeling a new ease, both with myself and the sensations of running. Enter David Deubner, a six-foot-two, 165-pound arrival from Orinda, California. He would be the best high school middle-distance runner in the country that year, with times of 4:11.2 and 1:53.6, and would win the Golden West Invitational mile. His greater gift was to be able to do this, as well as making off with Eunice Wheeler, with whom I'd hoped to curry favor, while evoking friendship from me, and now, looking back, a sense of great fortune. He was to become for me, so conscious of my adolescence, a steadying influence, tipping the scales toward what I wanted do, regardless of its eccentricity.

He was a superb student, earning thirty hours of advance placement credit at Stanford while in high school, but more than the results, he moved me with the means. He burst out in delighted guffaws while reading calculus texts. In literature, he seemed to get to know and judge and predict the behavior of the characters we came across in Shakespeare as easily as he did our classmates. I suppose I must have added something, but now remembering, it is all David.

He lived one street away from our house, and in the first weeks of school we established a routine. After a breakfast of uncooked oat-meal mixed with walnuts and filberts, bananas, raisins, honey and milk (David preferred orange juice), a meal recommended by Australia's Cerutty, who had deduced a runner's greater need for carbohydrates, we left our respective houses, turned away from the other kids waiting for the school bus, and walked the mile and a half to school. This was one of several exercises in toughening, another being to end showers with fifteen seconds of icy blast. Even in the rain we walked, mildly gazing back at the stares through the steamy windows of the passing bus, although we were known to accept a lift from Newland on the worst of days.

We ran everywhere together. David was eager to learn all of my slowly researched courses, and within a month was showing me places to run, along the railroad tracks and through the industrial district, just to see what was there.

We went longer and longer on our one exploratory trek each Sunday. The longest was a wet, slogging climb a thousand feet through pastures and woods to the top of the Coburg Hills, then along the crest to Bowerman's house above the McKenzie, then back home, eighteen miles in four hours of battling through grasping mud, barbed wire, blackberry-choked hollows, descending through undergrowth and fern in the dim light below conifers—what Kesey has called "The Druid Woods." I had never run so far before and with five miles to go was weak and will-less. David, who had never run that far either, was patient and kept to my pace, rather than floating off ahead as he might. "We just have to go along slow," he said. "We'll make it now." And we did. And we walked to school the next morning, stiff and drained, and I for one, profoundly gratified. My affection for marathoning dates from that run.

We were first and second in the district cross-country meet, and won the team title from Thurston, coached by Bill Dellinger, who would take the bronze medal in the 5,000 in the Tokyo Olympics in 1964. I outkicked a Thurston runner in the last 150 yards with a panicky sprint that surprised me because I thought I'd been running as hard as I could.

I considered all this and concluded that I'd developed more quickly physically than I had mentally. In my next race I would be ruthless with myself.

The next race was the state meet in Salem. I was brought to unprecedented eagerness by the smell of wintergreen on the breeze, the good firm turf of the course, winding through oaks and rose gardens. This was the time, not to beat David, but to show all these other runners, boys I had started behind as a sophomore in that bloody race in Portland, boys who'd had as much time and opportunity as I, that I had done better.

I sprinted hard for position in the first rush from the starting line, driving along faster than I'd ever begun, and by the time I'd made the top of the first hill, oxygen debt was working its sour change in me. David came past, then others, and I slowly, grudgingly, fell back into the pack. Just before the finish line, sick and disgusted, I saw the purple uniform of a South Eugene runner looming up, John Crowder, who hadn't beaten me all year. I used a wild elbow to keep him from passing, but it was no use. I wept at his back.

That evening over dinner, my father said he'd been astonished at my behavior at the finish, that it did not seem that my avowed concern for fairness and discipline was consistent with slugging opponents. I went away from the table in interior storm, wanting to shout, "You win any way you can!" and knowing that was absurd, that was what football players said. Everything seemed an acid turmoil, rationalization contending with the truth of what had happened. Out of it came a resolve that I would never go out of control again no matter what the goad.

I went over to David's house, where there was a cake, in celebration of his state championship. His parents, uncomfortable but brave, said that if they hadn't brought this machine to town, I would have had more victories to celebrate. They asked how I felt about that. I smiled wanly and said there was plenty of time for winning, that David had been more of a help than any number of good races. And as I said it, I knew it was true, and I felt better.

*   *   *

Ultimately, I *would* do plenty of winning. I went to Oregon, and with the physical maturity and the stern and quixotic guidance of Bowerman, I improved dramatically. In my sophomore year I beat both Harlan Andrews and Dave Deubner. I won my first national championship—AAU cross-country—in 1967, then made the 1968 and 1972 Olympic teams in the marathon, and most of the national teams in between at 10,000 meters. I met Frank Shorter on the final turn of the AAU six-mile in Miami in 1969, whereupon I outkicked him.

But such rewards carry little of the essence of the runner, who was formed long before. He is still very young, the child within that paradox of abandoned effort and firmly held civility.

The view of such a runner is therefore limited, missing a great deal, but willfully convinced that what he misses is unimportant. For once in his life, he is an insider, albeit in his own career, and as he proceeds to write about his fellows who have made great attempts, he does so with the calming knowledge that the attempts have also been his, and they are worth the effort even if you don't win.

Bowerman

The next fall I began at Oregon. I could afford nowhere else. For years my father had kept five acres of land out by the airport, leased to a wheat farmer. Whenever, in the autumn, we hunted pheasants over it, he would stamp his foot in the muddy loam and say, "This is your college education."

But I wanted to try to make it without his selling the land. As I also wanted to live in a dorm on the campus, I needed some money. Bowerman had far better prospects than me waiting in line for partial scholarships (he seldom permitted full ones), but when it reached him through Bob Newland that I was headed for Oregon, he said that I was welcome to work weekends, night shifts, in the plywood mills. He had long-standing arrangements with the owners and foremen that let him place athletes in part-time jobs.

Sunday's graveyard shift, from midnight to 8 A.M., the mill was shut down. All I did was carry a watchman's clock hourly through the still machinery and steaming lumber kilns and warehouses, alert for fires. But Saturdays the mill ran three shifts, and I had to work like any other hand. As one might expect in the case of a quiet, disapproving youth who read Plato's dialogues in the lunchroom, I was tested early.

One night I was assigned to cut core, which meant sawing eightfoot-long sections of dried fir veneer in half. These would then be used to make the middle of the three-layer, four-by-eight sandwiches that are quarter-inch plywood panels. I worked with a partner, who grabbed perhaps a seventy-pound stack of veneer from a cart and slid it onto the bed of a circular saw. Together we rammed the pile of splintery sheets into a raised steel corner to square the edges, pulled the wood through the saw, then lifted our halves of the cut veneer onto waiting carts.

My partner was a large and profane man who had come to Oregon with his parents from Arkansas during the Dust Bowl years. Later, I would think of him as representing that faction of manual workers who had surrendered themselves to prejudice. Lord knows what I represented to him. That night he cared only to work me until I broke.

For an hour we went along establishing a pace, which was his to call, because he was the one to slide down each new stack of veneer. If I were a split-second late in returning to my position after depositing a shifty thirty-five-pound load on a cart, he would shout at me that I was a lazy, goldbricking jock, and other things obscene and obscure (his accent was so thick I could only understand about half of them). For a second hour I held my own.

Gradually he began to increase the size of the loads until I was staggering to get them over the edge of the cart. For the hour and a half before the lunch break, I strained in a red fury, my back knotting, salt running in my eyes. I remember flashing an expression of appeal at the jitney driver who carried away the core and brought new stacks to be cut. He stared back impassively. The foreman strolled by once in a while, always silently.

At lunch I sat gasping in the corner of the smoky, grimy, laughter-filled room, gulping Coke after Coke. My partner was the object of some attention, in the form of backslaps and shouts. "Keep him honest," was said.

As we went back into the mill, he asked if I wanted to change ends. "Whatever you say," I said, so we did. Now I had the extra work of sliding down the eight-foot veneer, but I had control of the pace. I kept the size of the loads small enough to move easily, and in an hour felt stronger. I picked up the pace, keeping an eye on my opponent. While his raw strength had let him slowly lift large loads, his rolling belly kept him from moving quickly. I began spinning back from the cart to slide down a new pile and have it on the saw bed before he was back in position. At such moments I kept quiet, only regarding him steadily. He kept up, but was going red and sweaty, making mistakes. Men began to gather. I could see them behind the presses and glue-spreaders, the shadowy parts of the mill. Once the foreman came by just as my man spilled an armload of veneer across the floor and I knew I had him. We ended with me slowing things down, thinking this was a hell of a thing to look forward to every weekend, trying to guess whether the sopping, shaking wreck on the other end of the saw would now hate me forever.

The whistle blew and a circle of men was around us. The jitney driver and foreman conferred and announced that we had cut the third-highest volume of core on one shift in the history of the mill, and the total was spray-painted on one of the high beams. My opponent said, "Well, however else you screw up your life, you know you can work."

There was never another day I had to work like that. While my letterman jacket and odd studies kept me from being accepted, neither was I an outcast.

Yet being able to endure nights in the mill was part of measuring up to a larger set of expectations, those of Bowerman. You found that by joining the Oregon track team you entered a world that he permeated. If you had done especially well or especially poorly on an examination, Bowerman knew it. He wrote your training schedules and watched you follow them. He made you shoes. He found you jobs. He judged your associates.

These are things of some intimacy, yet Bowerman did them in a way that kept an uneasy distance around him. He never traded intimacy for intimacy. And his originality was sometimes so great that it was bewildering.

For example, simmering in the basement of the University's creaking basketball pavilion was a dim, redwood-paneled sauna. Memory of its 180-degree heat was sometimes all that gave purpose to a sodden, chilled distance runner over the last half of a winter workout. You could sit in there with your eyes closed, letting the dry heat play over you, until that disciplinarian part of your mind, which had driven you fifteen miles in the rain, curled up and went to sleep, and you could drip and stretch and simply, dumbly, relax.

You could, that is, unless William J. Bowerman entered. He was a big man, with exceptionally powerful arms and shoulders, although his legs were slender. He put his towels and heavily laden key ring on the bench and sat in silence, without acknowledging your presence. You kept a wary eye on him. The heat built rapidly in your body, but just as you were about to head for the door and a cool shower, he spoke.

"You know that the U.S. Olympic Committee refused to recognize the Track and Field Federation and actually rescinded recognition of the Wrestling Federation, giving it back to the AAU." It was not clear whether this was a question or a preface.

"Uh, no."

"Well, they did," he said indignantly. "I don't know how those old men figure to keep from stagnating if they don't let in new blood."

He paused. You began to make another move for the door. He spoke again in a more scholarly tone.

"As any institution grows into wealth and power, its practices, which are necessary to maintain or increase that power, can come to contradict the institution's original philosophy. All societies that get rich go through that, including the Olympic movement."

Again a pause while you roasted.

"I feel like Elijah," he said, "giving the kings of Israel and Samaria hell for their royal greed, for abandoning the old ways. But then Elijah could call down the fire of the Lord and behead the false prophets, and he went out on a whirlwind. I'm more likely to go out on my shield."

He stood and took up his towel. "It's understandable," he continued. "They're crotchety old men, those kings of Olympic House. They don't want to change. It hurts to change." Suddenly he snatched up his keys and slapped them on the inside of your thigh.

"Doesn't it hurt to change?" he asked in a voice of oil and sweet reason as the 180-degree brass scalded your tender flesh. You tried to squirm away, but were easily pressed to the bench by a great, burning hand.

"Sometimes it hurts more," you shouted, "just to sit and take it!"

For one important moment before he turned and shouldered through the door, his eyes crinkled; he was pleased. A lesson had been absorbed. You bore the mark for days.

* * *

William J. Bowerman was the head U.S. track and field coach in Munich.

"Bill Bowerman is absolutely frank," says Bob Giegengack, the Yale track coach who took the U.S. team to the Tokyo Olympics. "If I ask him a question, I know he'll give it to me straight, regardless of whether I'm going to like what I hear. That bluntness is rare. Almost all of us will bandy words. We'll circumlocute. We'll try to soften the blow. Not Bowerman. In fact, when I think of Bill, I'm a little ashamed of being diplomatic. I wonder if I might have compromised somewhere."

Not Bowerman. So outspoken has he been in defense of what he considers the best interests of U.S. track and field that the recognition implicit in the Olympic coaching position came years after he earned it. In 1959 Bowerman was an assistant on the U. S. Pan American Games staff, normally a prelude to greater service, but when his name was placed in nomination for the 1960 and 1964 Olympic posts, it was killed by an AAU member of the Olympic Committee who felt, quite rightly, that he was unsympathetic to the former organization. In 1968 Bowerman was again nominated, but asked that his name be withdrawn. "Hell, I wouldn't have won, anyway," he says.

Even when he did, he continued to give officialdom fits. The USOC made no provision for the expenses of track men who qualified for the 1972 trials in Eugene. Bowerman solicited a promise of $50,000 from General Motors, which would easily have covered the athletes' room and board. The USOC said no; GM will have to put the money in our general pot and we'll decide where it goes. GM withdrew the offer.

Bowerman petitioned the USOC on behalf of the athletes, asking that at least the top twelve or sixteen qualifiers be reimbursed for their expenses and that machinery be set up for such payments in future Olympic years. Four years later it was done.

"I've heard our officials make plenty of sanctimonious noises when they were looking at a guy with a rap on him (Boxer Bobby Lee Hunter) who might have made the team and wondering if his morals were up to theirs, and then they won't reimburse fine athletes, some of whom weren't getting enough to eat."

Bowerman actually considered seeking an injunction preventing his own Oregon Track Club from turning over the proceeds from the track and field trials (the gross was $300,000) to the USOC until the matter was adjudicated. Finally, and one feels, reluctantly, he decided against it. "My attorney thought it was the wrong approach. If you threaten somebody, and he doesn't give in, you put yourself in the wrong position."

Bill Bowerman came to the University of Oregon as track coach in 1948—pre-eminently the right man in the right position. His background included a boyhood in Fossil, a small central Oregon town with the remarkably stable population of 528 ("Every time a baby is born, a man leaves town," said Bowerman). At Medford High School he played in the band and edited the school paper besides lettering in football and basketball. Bowerman took his degree in business and premed from Oregon in 1934 after giving up on journalism. "I never could feel I was learning anything from those people," he has said.

He quarterbacked the Oregon football team for two seasons in the days when a quarterback was a team's most vicious blocker, and in 1931 led the Ducks to a 14-6 upset of NYU which ruined the Violets' national championship hopes.

Bowerman returned to Medford in 1935 as football and track coach. His football teams had a 64-8-3 record, won three state championships, and he was invited to apply for the head coaching job at Oregon but declined. "Track men have a higher general level of intelligence than football players and the competition in an individual sport is much keener," he said. "A lot of football players can't tolerate being all alone out there with nobody to hide behind." Bowerman emerged from World War II a major in the 10th Mountain Division ("We made the world safe for Communism"), and when Oregon offered him the job as track coach, he went. Bill and his wife Barbara, a comely, awesomely energetic woman, have three sons: John, an Alpine ski instructor; Jay, a biology teacher and member of the U.S. biathlon team in the 1968 and 1972 Winter Olympics; and Tom, an urban planner.

It is tiresome and by far the lesser story to recount the records of Bowerman's tenure at Oregon: four NCAA team championships, thirty-three individual NCAA and AAU titles, eleven U.S. Olympic team members, and ten sub-four-minute milers. "No man has contributed as much to track and field in the U.S. as Bowerman, says

Indiana (and ex-Oregon State) Coach Sam Bell. The accomplishments, however, cannot be appreciated apart from Bowerman's' character.

Few men are embodiments of a philosophy. Rather, they are constructed piecemeal—a principle here, a judgment there—and if subjected to scrutiny, the parts don't mesh. In Bowerman paradoxes seemed to abound. He often illustrated his points by quoting Scripture, but could be so earthy in conversation that Bouncy Moore, his 1971 NCAA long-jump champion, called him "that obscene man." He was devoted to winning yet branded recruiting "immoral." He despaired of the creep toward the welfare state ("You hand-feed a wild duck, pretty soon it can't fend for itself anymore"), but urged his athletes to apply for food stamps. His gruff, countrified manner ("You run like a turkey in a plowed field") belied an extensive, often arcane, knowledge of history and the classics.

Yet any assessment of Bowerman that has opposing values constantly at war is superficial and ultimately incorrect. One encompassing fact sweeps away the contradictions: Bowerman, perpetually and compulsively was, and is, a teacher. His choice of the sacred or the profane depended upon which would be more effective in prying open minds. He justified the food stamps with the worth of his pupils' efforts. "These men are holding down two jobs as it is," he said. "Studying and running."

He scorned recruiting because anyone can be taught (". . . and those who don't expect a handout most easily of all") and because young men ought to select their colleges primarily on the basis of academic offerings.

In 1962 I went with Dave Deubner to talk with Bowerman. Deubner had won a National Merit Scholarship and wanted to study geology, which he could do best at a California school, but he also wanted to train under Bowerman. He explained his dilemma, and Bowerman told him flatly, "You can't run forever. Consider your education first." Deubner went to Stanford. To Rick Rojas, a 4:11-miler for Los Alamos (New Mexico) High who had been offered a full scholarship to Harvard, Bowerman said, "You'd be crazy to come to Oregon."

Bowerman's methods were grounded in a belief that "You cannot just tell somebody what's good for him, because he won't listen. First you have to get his attention." His sharpest attention-getter was kicking people off his team. A survey of Oregon's recent Olympians reveals that a significant percentage at one time or another found their names painted out above their locker-room stalls. But the boot, being a teaching aid, was practically never permanent.

There were other means of instruction. Wade Bell, a 1968 Olympic half-miler, told a tale of horror: "I never used to shave the day of a race. Bill always made remarks, but I didn't take him seriously. The morning of the 1967 NCAA finals I woke up being carried down the hall of the dormitory by our shot-putters. They took me in the lavatory, and there was Bowerman with a fiendish grin, a cup of lather, and a rusty old straight razor. He got that blade right under my nose before I convinced him I'd do it myself." Smooth-cheeked, Bell won the 880.

Bowerman had no explicit training rules, preferring to depend upon the common sense of dedicated athletes. "People are taught more by the vicissitudes of life than by arbitrary rules," he said, but occasionally he would give the vicissitudes a shove. During a spring vacation training camp at a California air base it came to

Bowerman's attention that one of his quarter-milers was returning from nearby San Francisco at dawn. When the miscreant had had just enough time to undress and go to bed, Bowerman burst in and rolled him out for a bracing, early-morning jog, remarking, as they ran, on the beauty of Marin County. A series of errands kept the runner from sleeping after breakfast. Then during the midday workout, Bowerman put him through endless 220's while his teammates, long since finished with their training, watched in silence. Yet after dinner he caught the bus back to the city and again returned in the wee hours. Piqued, Bowerman dismissed him from the team, but upon further reflection reversed himself. "The man was simply one hell of a competitor," Bowerman said. "Trouble was, he was competing against me."

Bowerman's humor seems to flow from an overpowering desire to consternate. I once found caddis fly larvae in the steeplechase water jump. Bowerman ordered me to interrupt my workout to collect several dozen, which he surreptitiously introduced into the indoor fountain in a crony's law office. In the warm water, the larvae soon emerged as diaphanous-winged insects. Bill paid frequent calls, beaming at the spectacle of the hatch and the frantic secretaries. Too, each year when the circus visited the basketball court, Bowerman associates were apt to receive large, gift-wrapped boxes of elephant droppings.

This frightening joviality unified the often diverse personalities of his athletes, if only in self-defense. Bowerman valued a sense of common purpose, and annually took his team to a relatively isolated retreat for a week of "coming together." Dressed in baggy shorts, an aromatic T-shirt, and some touch of the outlandish—a beret, perhaps, or a pair of enormous, hexagonal women's sunglasses—he led his party aboard a chartered bus and gave wearying, pun-filled commentories on the flora fauna, history, and legend of the passing countryside.

The vigor of the man captured the loyalty of many of his athletes. The day before the 1963 NCAA cross-country race in East Lansing, Michigan, the first that Oregon runners had ever entered, Bowerman jogged the four-mile course with his team, pointing out potential dangers and likely spots at which to pass. The other coaches stood on a knoll and smoked cigars. There were no Steve Prefontaines on the Oregon team then, but it finished second. "Bill communicated a sense of confidence," recalls Clayton Steinke who, in eleventh place, was the Ducks' first finisher. "He cared enough to go out and see what it was going to be like for us. And seeing those other coaches puffing away on the hill made it more than a race. It was a contest of life-styles."

Bob Newland, who went on to direct the 1972, 1976, and 1980 Olympic Trials in Eugene, and was team manager in 1976 and 1980, played quarterback and high-jumped for Bowerman. He remembers football at Medford: "Bill always encouraged us to think and react on our own. He never called the plays from the sidelines, but there was an aura of dead certainty when we talked about game plans. He was such a student of the sport and of our opponents that we were absolutely convinced anything he suggested would go all the way. In practice most coaches act like infantry commanders: they like to see the bodies fly. Not Bill. He taught us *how* to hit, but we really did it only in the games. That way we kept all those fine athletes who like to play football but hate getting beaten up every day."

Bill Freeman, a graduate student, in 1972 found the man's sheer competitiveness his most pervasive trait. "Even his interest in jogging (Bowerman coauthored a book on the subject which has sold over a million copies), to all appearances the least competitive aspect of running, had a competitive origin," Freeman said. "Bill was touring New Zealand in 1963 with his world-record four-mile relay team when he took his first jog and found himself running with a seventy-three-year-old man. He soon learned the old man was holding back and staying with him out of kindness. 'That old man beat me,' he said. 'That's not going to happen again.' After that he ran every day, and on his return to Eugene he began his jogging experiments."

Bowerman constantly formented small competitions with his athletes. "But always under his rules," said Jim Grelle, an Olympian and former American mile record holder (3:55.4). "He badgered me to race him a two-twenty for weeks, and when I accepted, he gave me the outside lane and told me over and over again that I'd run a poor race if I looked back." Suspicious, Grelle looked back and saw Bowerman cutting across the infield.

Bowerman success has not been limited to guiding champions. He has advanced the state of his art in several technical areas, chiefly through incessant experimentation. He did the earliest—and smelliest—research in rubber-asphalt surfaces and devised elastic cloth tops for practice hurdles so runners could work closely over the barriers without bruising knees and ankles. A skilled cobbler, he has done prototype work on training and racing shoes for several large manufacturers and made lightweight shoes for his milers out of snakeskin. Beginning in 1971 he developed a special, shock-absorbent "waffle" shoe which revolutionized the industry.

These putterings seldom proceeded smoothly. Barbara's waffle iron fell victim to a batch of urethane, destined for shoe soles, which cooked too long and bonded it shut. In the early fifties Bowerman found that long underwear, like a wet suit, keeps a runner warmer in the Oregon rain than do bulkier sweat pants, so he outfitted his Ducks in long white drawers. In the following days he was swamped with calls from indignant matrons, protesting the indecency of such attire. Bill stopped the fuss by dyeing the long johns green, which in turn dyed the legs of the runners splotchy green.

One August, before the advent of Gatorade, Bowerman tried to develop a liquid that would replenish a marathoner's salt and other essentials lost in sweat. He sent one slender guinea pig—me—six miles under a beating sun and prepared a mixture of lemonade, salt, honey, and tea which, when fed to the panting runner, was promptly spewed across the track.

"What do you think this is, the Cordon Bleu?" Bowerman said. "If it makes you run faster, that should be enough." Later, he sampled it himself. "It does taste like sheep's piss," he admitted.

The single-mindedness of Bowerman was at once asset and liability. "Over the years Bill has offended people," says Sam Bell. "He's been so preoccupied with what he's doing that he's ignored them. I think you'll find quite a few men with genius are that way." Bowerman's candor extended to himself. "I have feet of clay," he once said. "I have prejudices against certain types of personality. But if I have an athlete who rubs me the wrong way, I'll try to see that he works under a different coach."

Although he has had national champions in fourteen of the twenty individual Olympic events, excluding the walks, Bowerman's most striking success has been with middle-distance runners, especially milers. Again, experimentation seems to be responsible. "Every kid is different," he said. "Unless you understand that, you can't coach." Eschewing team workouts ("The best man loafs, the worst tears himself down, maybe only one guy in the middle gets the optimum work"), Bowerman wrote an individual program for each runner, scheduling two or three weeks of workouts, in advance. He tested each man's responses to widely differing types of running, and it was not uncommon for two Oregon milers of equal ability to go an entire season without running the same workout on the same day. In addition he conducted yearly goal-setting sessions to make sure runner and coach had the same ends in mind. He expected runners to understand the principles at work in their training so that they could carry on to physical maturity. Bowerman's last seven Olympic distance men all ran their best times after graduation.

He was most stern in his injunctions against overwork. Runners are permitted only easy jogging and weight lifting or a swim on days following hard runs. "The idea that the harder you work, the better you're going to be is just garbage," he said. "The greatest improvement is made by the man who works most intelligently." Runners who were frequently sick or injured were suspected of secret workouts or intemperate living, and "intemperate" covered a range of behavior. Bowerman once kicked 1967 AAWU steeplechase champion Bob Williams off the team for sweeping out his church. "If he'd just sat there and prayed, I would have encouraged him," Bowerman said, "but be was doing too many extracurricular things." When Wade Bell failed to make the finals of the 1966 Pac-10 half-mile, Bowerman boiled out of the stands. "Bell, have you been romancing on me again?" he growled.

Bowerman long regarded women as subversive. In one of his early seasons at Oregon a pulchritudinous jogger appeared daily at the track, bent on distraction. Bowerman effected her departure with a barrage from a pellet gun. In the sixties he appeared to mellow, often bantering with coeds who came to watch the sprinters practice starts. Occasionally, however, Bowerman would turn to the infield with a beatific smile as the girls, with burning faces, rose and dispersed and the sprinters giggled and slapped hands over his newest obscenity.

In the seventies he came to the view that women could run as seriously and as hard as any man. "I enjoy working with them more than with men," he said in 1980. "They have fewer bad habits to unlearn."

Bowerman lives in a comfortable split-level home he built himself on a cliff overlooking the McKenzie River. Projects such as new patios, bathrooms, and vineyards are constantly undertaken, giving the place an air of incompleteness. Barbara is accomplished in bonsai, the Japanese art of cultivating miniature trees. Stately pines and gnarled firs eighteen inches tall grace the terraces, and the yard is a showplace for native shrubs.

When an Oregon runner visits to discuss his training he may be given a shovel and told where to haul a pile of sand. There is always a pile of sand. Once a truck driver, bringing more sand, knocked down a prized holly. Expressionless, Bowerman grabbed the six-foot bush and wrenched it from the ground.

"I'm awfully sorry," said the truck driver.

"It was an accident," said Bill, "but my wife won't want to see her tree like this. Why don't you take it with you?" He rammed the needle-tined bush through the window of the cab. The driver yelped for some time before driving off.

Bowerman has kept much of his sixty acres in its natural state and has considered willing the property to the county to be kept as a park. He knows all of the great variety of birds which nest in the area, and on summer evenings raccoons can be seen receiving bread and milk on his front deck. Lane County's largest recorded rattlesnake was killed by Bowerman—with a clipboard—on the road to his house.

One Bowerman project was a large fishpond which he built by damming a spring-fed creek several hundred yards from the house. One evening in the spring of 1972 Bill and Barbara and a frenetic Llewellin setter called Gilgamesh (the Bowerman cat, which floated down the river on the high flood of 1964, was named Ashurbanipal) accompanied Frank Shorter and me to the pond, walking through fields of sheep, stands of ubiquitous Douglas firs, and a tangled undergrowth of wild roses, watercress, and poison oak.

"I have a total disinterest in making money," he said. "Two or three years from now, when I get thrown out of the university, I may change my tune, but now, so long as we're eating well, I can't get worked up about it. We have the fish. There are plenty of acorns around here. Ravens fed Elijah when he was hiding in the wilderness from King Ahab."

In Bowerman's case, the ravens weren't necessary. His interest in the Nike shoe company would make his retirement comfortable.

A pileated woodpecker called raucously from the forest. Bowerman addressed himself to the question of where the Olympics are going. "The role of all sport," he said, "is to help people learn competitive responses. Beyond that, the big international games and tours serve to increase understanding between cultures. They keep people from being isolated and provincial. Now, you always strive for excellence. But in the emphasis on winning, some of these goals can be obscured. For example, we always dominate the Pan-American Games. I have proposed, and been hooted down, that we continue to send our national champions to the Pan-Ams, but that the second entrant in each event must be able to speak one of the other languages of the hemisphere, Spanish or Portuguese. I have no illusions that many officials agree with me. The USOC generally seems preoccupied with running up the score.

"Winning is nice," he said as he cleaned the trout with a pair of Barbara's scissors, "but you savor that victory for an evening and you wake up the next morning and it's gone. I believe we compete for every breath we draw, but competing well is just not to be equated with winning." Bowerman glanced up at his patiently listening wife. "Barbara doesn't buy all this," he said. "She says I have to win."

"Never believe he doesn't," she said. "He'll die when he stops. It was an effort, but I've come to see that there just isn't any other way people could do these great things like four-minute miles without the drive to win."

Bowerman stopped eviscerating the fish and turned to look at her. His eyes crinkled. He was pleased.

—July 1972

But Only on Sunday: Ron Clarke

In 1970, Frank Shorter and I ran in an international 10,000-meter in Oslo. Frank won. I was fifth, and a gentleman named Ron Clarke was sixth, the pair of us laboring silently together for the last mile.

At the award ceremony we pushed the bone-tired Clarke onto the top level. The crowd stood in tearful ovation as the Norwegian officials presented him with a pair of cross-country skis to symbolically ensure his return. This had been Ron Clarke's last race.

Later, I visited him in Australia, to review a career as important for its philosophical integrity as for its world records.

Sunday mornings Ron Clarke drives out from Melbourne past Puffing Billy and up Ferntree Gully into the Dandenong Hills. He parks near a roadside general store and waits. Other automobiles arrive filled with men wearing running shoes and shorts, T-shirts bear the names of nations, universities, beers. When their number reaches two dozen the men set off, trotting comfortably along the road's grass verges. Suddenly a runner veers into the bush and sprints away madly. The rest, Clarke among them, give howling chase. The trail, rich with loose rocks and tree roots, is overhung with brittle eucalyptus and huge wet ferns that Clarke, taller than his hurtling companions, catches squarely in the face. In half a mile the leaders regain the road and jog, listening to the stragglers, the thump of bodies against the trees. The pack re-forms, gathers its strength, and begins another wrenching charge through the forest. "I've been doing this since 1961," pants Clarke. "I don't care if I never set foot on a track again but I can't leave this."

The run is seventeen miles. The road, with Australian bluntness, goes right at its hills, two- and three-mile stretches of rough gravel without a curve or dip or chance to rest. On the summits everyone wheezes and looks vaguely ill. "This is the best," says Clarke at the base of a mile of thirty-degree pitch. "You know Dave Power, the bronze medal in Rome? He had to walk here." When Clarke has willed himself up and some color has returned, his voice is touched with reverence: "Such a hill. A brutal, magnificent hill."

Between 1963 and his retirement in 1970, Ron Clarke took part in 313 races over distances of half a mile to a marathon and won 202 of them. Along the way he broke 17 world records. Yet Ron Clarke did not win an Olympic, or British Commonwealth Games gold medal and upon that omission he has been sternly judged.

Derek Clayton, once the world's best marathoner, trained with him. "I know Clarkey better than he does himself. No emotions. The man couldn't lift himself in the important competitions. A machine. The Olympics or a club race, it was all the same to him."

"He was gifted physically, his records prove that," said Coach Percy Cerutty, who attempted to advise Clarke early in his career, "but he had no real mental drive. When he came up against men with spirit, he let them beat him."

In Australia, Clarke has in fact become a symbol of promises unfulfilled, of excellence somehow gone to waste. "Ron Clarke?" asks the cabbie or the girl who brings your bitter. "Isn't he the bloke who never won anything?"

* * *

The kids are in bed. Ron and Helen Clarke, the latter a composed, capable woman with a soothing, mellifluous voice, invite friends over for an evening swim. After a few laps in the frigid little pool, Ron climbs onto one of the rocky ledges that make up the backyard. His Afghan hound, Shendi, attacks him with love. Since his retirement from racing Clarke has reversed the aging process. The graying crew cut has given way to thick, black curls that frame a face less drawn, less lined than the one that agonized through all those miles.

"I apologize for the mess this place is in," he says. Barbells and pulleys and sit-up boards that once had dominated the family room are being moved outside, displaced by a billiard table and a bar. "I've been too busy to see to things properly." He is general manager for Australia's largest sport-shoe company, has three corporations (to receive royalties from endorsements and development of health and fitness products), a position on Australia's Film Censorship Board of Review, and a newspaper column.

Despite the assertions of his countrymen that his racing character was flawed, Clarke, relaxing in the warm December night wind, is clearly not freighted with remorse. "That's over," he says. "The races blur. My God, most of the time it seems as if the competitive runner was another person." Reminded of the 10,000 meters he won in the 1969 U.S.-U.S.S.R.-British Commonwealth meet in Los Angeles, Clarke had to consult a log of his travels to satisfy himself that he had run in the Coliseum at all that year.

"I did not win the Olympic gold medal," he says, "and that has given rise to the idiotic idea that I was no good in *real* competition. My only contention, and I'm leaning over backward to be fair, is that because of the altitude at Mexico City I had no chance against the Africans, and therefore the critics' point that I was incapable of winning remains unproved. Personally, I have no doubt at all that I was the best 10,000-meter runner in the world in 1968. At sea level I would have won easily." With some finality he dives back into the pool.

Clarke seems justified. In Europe before the Mexico Games he defeated 10,000-meter champion Naftali Temu of Kenya and 5,000-meter gold and silver medalists Mohamed Gammoudi of Tunisia and Kip Keino of Kenya by margins that were comparable to those by which they beat him in the Games.

But there were other chances for gold. In the 1964 Olympic 10,000, Clarke led for most of the race and was outkicked by Billy Mills of the United States and Gammoudi. In the 1966 Commonwealth six-mile in Kingston, Jamaica, Clarke led most of the race and was beaten by Temu. At the 1970 Commonwealth Games in Edinburgh, Clarke was still in front down the last backstretch, but was outkicked by Scotland's Lachie Stewart. These races gave him his reputation for crumbling under pressure. And even though they came following injuries or in tropical heat or during Clarke's decline toward retirement, in each he was probably the equal of any other entrant. Except for the peculiar nature of his running, he might have won them all.

Ron Clarke defied the one edict that, in contests among equals, approaches law: *The pacesetter never wins.* Front running has an element about it of keeping one's nerve, familiar to those who move in high, unprotected places. The leader competes against footsteps, specters. He struggles to escape the clinging pack at the same time he fights to down his own cowardice. "There is fear," says Clarke. "I usually didn't think I'd be able to finish until I got into the last lap."

The follower has only to match the leader's pace. He enjoys a comparative calm in which he can relax and conserve his emotional energy for a final, unanswerable assault. Given these realities, few men running at the head of a pack can avoid a feeling of sacrifice. Steve Prefontaine explaining the savagery of his bursts to break contact with his followers, said, "I hate to have people back there sucking on me."

Ron Clarke was a front runner, yet not in the classic mold of an athlete who has no finishing kick and therefore must set a hard pace out of desperation. On those rare occasions when Clarke followed instead of led, he outsprinted such fast finishers as Keino and West Germany's Harald Norpoth. Shunning expediency, Ron Clarke was a front runner out of principle. He accepted each of his races as a complete test, an obligation to run himself blind.

Over a late dinner of salad, a lean steak, and five glasses of chartreuse Vigorade, he makes his case.

"The single most horrible thing that can happen to a runner is to be beaten in the stretch when he's still fresh. No matter who I was racing or what the circumstances, I tried to force myself to the limit over the whole distance. It makes me sick to see a superior runner wait behind the field until 200 meters to go and then sprint away. That is immoral. It's both an insult to the other runners and a denigrations of his own ability."

So Clarke took the lead in Tokyo and Kingston and even in Mexico with the understanding that doing so was likely his ruin. "If you're the world-record holder, as I was, and nobody else will set the pace and make a real race of it, and it's your style to have a demanding pace, then you have to do it yourself. If that is going to diminish your chances of winning, well, you still have to do it. I was very conscious of that pressure. Perhaps one should resist it. I couldn't."

Although he calls it his "style" or "impatience," Clarke's flaw was a driving moral imperative to go flat out, to impose an order on each race, to make sure the winner was the fastest, toughest competitor. "I loved testing myself more than I feared being beaten," he says, "and front running is the ultimate test. You need a total, irrevocable commitment to see the race through to the end or it cannot justify your effort."

Clarke takes a text from his bookcase. "Any athlete who thinks he suffers ought to read this." The book is Heinrich Haerer's *The White Spider,* an account of the climbing of the north face of the Eiger in Switzerland, of the men who died attempting it, and of those who finally succeeded. In it, one finds a passage Clarke has underlined: "There is nothing new to be said about the behavior of man in exceptional circumstances of danger or crisis. . . . I would not find better words than those used by the Athenian, Menander: 'A man's nature and way of life are his fate, and that which he calls his fate is but his disposition.'"

Ron Clarke's fatal disposition took shape early. His older brother Jack was long an outstanding professional Australian Rules football player. "My only consolation," says Ron, "the only one I could have, since he beat me at everything, was the satisfaction of trying my hardest."

When he began running competitively Clarke was moved by the examples of two men, Emil Zatopek and John Landy, both inexhaustible trainers, front runners, and gentlemen. Zatopek, the only man ever to win the 5,000, 10,000, and marathon in one Olympics, was the more distant idol. The Czech ran as if tortured by internal demons. He seemed a sign, a proof that if athletes chose to force themselves through the pain and doubt, there could be no limit to human performance.

Landy, the second four-minute miler, helped plan Clarke's early training. His races, as did Clarke's later, often demonstrated a kind of noble perversity. Though he recognized that his best chance to win the 1954 Mile of the Century against Roger Bannister lay in upsetting the Briton's wait-and-kick strategy by sitting back himself, Landy led from the gun. The race had been the object of so much attention he felt obliged to ensure a fast time, "otherwise the sport might have suffered." Bannister outkicked him.

In the 1956 Australian National Championship mile, Clarke, then nineteen, fell during the third lap. Landy bounded over him and, thinking he had spiked him in the head, stopped, came back, and helped him up. Once assured of Clarke's safety, Landy went after the field, now 60 yards ahead. He drove into the lead with 110 yards to go and won in 4:04.2.

In that same year Clarke set a world junior mile record Of 4:06:8. Thereafter, because of a chronic sinus infection and the demands of business and family, he fell away from running. In 1961 through the urging of a neighbor, former Olympian Les Perry, he began again. This five-year hiatus, which has no parallel in the career of any other world-class runner, seems a key to Clarke's determination to run on his own terms. "It was a hobby when I came back to it, and although I was totally involved in each of my races, my whole life did not hang on the results. I could afford to take a few chances." Clarke had then and has today strong views on the relative importance of amateur sport and earning a living. "I just read something of Jim Ryun's financial sacrifices for his running. Jim was wrong. If you have that conflict there is only one way to resolve it. You shouldn't run."

Clarke's confirmation in his ethic came when he began to break records. "I've never felt more depressed or disappointed than in the days following my first world record. I was down, completely adrift. I realized that the excitement had been in the challenge of the training and in the race itself. The competition was what drew me on, the actual testing, not the hope of good results, because the best of all possible results, a world record, made me miserable."

He understands the strangeness of this remark and turns to Helen, across whose lap he is sprawled, for corroboration. "Do you remember how bad it was?"

"Yes," she says softly. "And everyone else so happy."

For years Clarke scoured the world for tough races. "I had a need, almost like a gambler's compulsion, to test myself against the best." It didn't matter that he had raced hard the day before or that the local champion was lying in wait or that the distance was not his best. In 1965, to have a 10,000 put on the program, Clarke had to promise an Oslo meet promoter not only that he would break the world record in the event but would come back the next day in a featured 3,000 against fresh Olympic champion Mills. He set his world record, one that stood for seven years, and won the short race as well, but neither was in the Olympics.

Clarke changed his basic tactic in the last years of his career. He devised one that added to his suffering: a full-bore sprint away from he field with a mile or more to run. "It increased the challenge. But in a way it was refreshing. I knew I could make it through. So instead of dreading those footsteps behind I wanted them to stay there because whoever was making them was killing himself." If the footsteps were not there and Clarke had broken contact in this way, he was never beaten. He tried to sprint away in Mexico during the 10,000-meter race with a kilometer to go, but he could not escape the altitude natives who swarmed past on the last lap. Clarke finished sixth. Three steps past the line, for the only time in his career, he lost consciousness. When he awoke a few minutes later, an oxygen mask was pressed over his face. The Australian physician attending him was cursing the IOC for having permitted the Games at that altitude. "Oh, God," he railed. "Look what the bastards have done."

"I wanted to tell him it was all right," recalls Clarke, "but I couldn't. My tongue was so swollen it filled my mouth. I couldn't speak for two hours."

The Melbourne newspapers shouted CLARKE FAILS AGAIN.

*   *   *

Ron and Helen Clarke are dining at a friend's Melbourne beef house. The friend is not much in evidence but a hostess keeps fluttering by, demanding to be told how she can serve.

"Well, I want a very simple salad," says Clarke. "Just lettuce and tomatoes, no dressing, no croutons, no frills."

Derek Clayton has been invited. "He claimed he had another engagement," says Clarke. "Then I told him I was paying. But it was too late."

The salad is placed before him, with parsley and sculptured radishes. Clarke sighs and picks out the offending vegetables. Only very gently does he try to make the nature of his running understood to the others with him, perhaps reasoning that a world that cannot hold the parsley is not ripe for a philosophy of sport any more complicated than winner take all.

"It's been upsetting that people have seen my attitude not as recklessness but weakness," he says. "The Australian behavior toward losers is far from healthy. If youngsters are taught that losing is a disgrace, and they're not sure they can win, they will be reluctant to even try. And not trying is the real disgrace."

*   *   *

The chorus, whenever Ron Clarke is consigned to insignificance, is "Who ever remembers second place?" But that is the gulf between spectators, who seem to believe that runners are drawn to compete only in order to make themselves immortal, and amateur athletes, who are private men doing what they do for myriad private reasons. Among distance runners, who understand something of what Clarke attempted, will be found his most thoughtful judges.

In 1966 Clarke sent a week in Prague with Zatopek, who at the time was not yet cast into official disgrace for having supported the liberal Dubcek government. Clarke retains the whole of that visit in softly gilded memory. He speaks of his boyhood hero's grace, his standing in the eyes of his countrymen, his unabated fitness and energy. As Clarke departed, Zatopek accompanied him through customs and, in violation of regulations, onto the plane itself.

"He stood by me and then slipped a little box into my pocket. He seemed embarrassed and clearly didn't want anyone to see what he'd done. For a moment I wondered what I was smuggling out for him. Later, when the plane was in the air, I unwrapped it."

The memento that dropped into his palm, inscribed "To Ron Clarke, July 19, 1966," was Zatopek's Olympic gold medal from the 10,000 meters in Helsinki.

"Not out of friendship," Zatopek had whispered to Clarke as he turned to go, "but because you deserve it."

—February 1973

A Play of Light and Shadow:
John Akii-Bua

The gold. If Clarke is representative of Olympian achievement unrewarded, a man named John Akii-Bua illustrates the power of one decisively won medal.

E ven before he ran a step in the 1972 Olympics, Akii-Bua was amazing. As the other finalists in the 400-meter hurdles stared blankly down at Munich's dried-blood-red track, grimly adjusting their blocks and minds for the coming ordeal, Akii danced in his lane, waving and grinning at friends in the crowd. Then, when it was over, after he had won the race in world-record time and kept on going past the finish, barely slowing while his victims slumped and dry-heaved on the infield, right then an attendant came over to take him to the doping test. The organizing committee had not allowed time for victory laps but the crowd was on its feet, calling, and Akii heard. He eluded his officious pursuer by bounding over a hurdle and then he floated down the backstretch, clearing each hurdle again, a crimson and black impala leaping joyfully over imaginary barriers where there were no real ones, creating one of the few moments of exultation in the Olympics. And after the Games had ended, on notes of violence and regret and disgust, it seemed that Akii-Bua most symbolized what they might have been. He seemed a man eminently worth knowing.

But John Akii-Bua lived in Uganda, which was even more beset with troubles than the Olympics. In an attempt to unify a country ripped by tribal factions and economic crises, the xenophobic president, General Idi (Big Daddy) Amin, conjured up a mixed bag of scapegoats. Forty thousand Asian residents, branded "economic saboteurs," were expelled. Invasions from neighboring countries were periodically announced.

The Ugandan chief justice disappeared. Two weeks before I arrived in October 1972, foreign journalists were accused of espionage, rounded up, and pitched into a Black Hole of Calcutta jail. In rapid succession General Amin praised Hitler's treatment of the Jews, said Tanzania had invaded, and had four roadblocks erected on the twenty-one-mile stretch of road between the capital, Kampala, and the airport at Entebbe. His army, which had a reputation for loose discipline and drunkenness, was given license to shoot anyone who did not identify himself at once, and to conduct vigorous searches for firearms entering and Ugandan currency leaving the country. If all this weren't sobering enough, I could always consider Uganda's crocodiles, black mambas, and malaria. As my plane banked in over the swampy expanse of Lake Victoria, the pilot came on the intercom: "To the left is a phenomena which might be of interest to some passengers. That cloud of reddish-brown smoke above the water there is not smoke at all, but billions of flies, hatching out of the lake."

Stepping from the plane I was seized by a smiling animated Akii-Bua. Dressed in gray slacks and a Commonwealth Games T-shirt, he gave an impression of greater bulk than when seen running. His features are fine, almost delicate, and his complexion very smooth. His eyes are small, allowing his face to be dominated by perfect white teeth. He swept me through customs with a single telling phrase—"This man is with me"—and we got in a National Council of Sports car and started up the worrisome road to Kampala. Akii chuckled at my fears.

"This is a land of rumor," he said with a loose gesture that seemed to include all of East Africa. "I don't know why. We get enough news. But the rumors still fly. Last week everybody ran out of Kampala because rumormongers said there was fighting at Entebbe. There was none. I think you will find Uganda a peaceful country. Just maybe a little nervous."

The road, which ran through thick tropical foliage, was lined with black, yellow, and red bunting and freshly set banana plants. The next day was the tenth anniversary of Uganda's independence. Dignitaries were arriving. The roadblocks had been cut to two, manned by soldiers bristling with automatic weapons. When we pulled up at the first, the sight of Akii transformed the dour men of war. They became schoolboys who flocked around the car to shake his hand, saying, "You did very marvelous in the Games. Thank you."

"Thank you," said Akii, and we were on our way. "It's easy," he said, "see?" I also saw a carload of Asians looking on forlornly as soldiers tore through their belongings. Akii read my thoughts.

"The army is worse in the countryside and near the frontier. There they speak no English, not even Swahili, only tribal dialects. You can't compromise with them. They kill you like that."

There had been a crush at the airport, and we encountered more busloads of Asians coming out from Kampala. "Do you agree with making them leave?" I asked.

"Asians are not good people to me," he said. "I am not educated. I do not know much about economics. But Asians stay off to themselves. They don't want to mix with black people. Once in a busy restaurant the only place for me was at a table with three Asians. When I sat, they all went away from there without eating. I don't like that. So, I don't care much if they leave the country."

We climbed through rich, red soil. "That hill there," said Akii, pointing out a slope covered with bamboo paw-paw, and tall serene trees he called *kalitusi*, "reminds me of home in the north. Look, do you know cassava?" We slowed by a roadside stand and he showed me the staples of Uganda: millet, sweet potatoes, beans, maize, bananas, and dry, white sticks of cassava root.

"I don't eat a lot of meat," he said. "Maybe once, a week. Usually just beans, cassava bread, or porridge and a plate of greens. I like greens. There is one in the northern regions which is very sour. Especially pregnant women like it. You don't feel lazy after you eat that one. And another is bitter. It's nice, too. You can't eat it if you're not used to it." He laughed at the thought of my tasting it, imitating the pinched face I would certainly make. "It's a good land," he said. "A big garden, a cow, and you can live."

Women along the way were wrapped in flowing print dresses. "They are called *busuuti,"* said Akii. "Since the law forbidding mini-skirts, they have come back. It takes seven meters of cloth for one."

A barber had placed his table, mirror, and chair in the deep shade beneath a mango tree. He approached his customer with shears while other men waited, sprawled on the grass.

"Spiffing up for tomorrow," said Akii. Near the edge of the city was the other roadblock. Akii was not immediately recognized and we had to show identification. His did not produce the hoped-for sensation.

"And where are you going in this official car?" was the question.

"This man is an official guest of the National Council of Sports," said Akii, "and I am responsible for him." After much riffling of my passport we were cleared to go. During a moment's wait while a truck in front of us got in gear, I picked up my notebook from the seat. Instantly a soldier's head leaned in over my shoulder. His machine gun cracked against the door. "What are you writing? What are you writing?"

"About cassava. About bitter greens."

There was further discussion with Akii-Bua in Swahili. Finally we were allowed off, and drove into town.

Kampala then was a city Of 330,000. Alabaster mosques topped its hills, and glass and stainless-steel hotels, banks, and government buildings stood in tiers amid jacaranda and bougainvillea.

We drew up at my hotel and Akii joined me for lunch. He carefully read the entire menu while the waiter shifted from one foot to the other. Finally, perplexed, Akii tossed it on the table. "I am best in cafeteria," he said. "I shine when I can see and point." He closed his eyes to visualize the ideal luncheon. "Soup and chicken and beer," he said, and that is what be got.

English is Akii-Bua's third language after Swahili and his Lango dialect. Occasionally he would pause in our conversations, faced with concepts for which his English was inadequate. The Swahili he spoke in my presence was, by contrast, a torrent. I have no doubt that his is a swift, innovative mind.

I said he struck me as a man having close ties with the land. He nodded and told me about his early life. "My father was a county chief of the Lango district in the north. He died in 1965 when I was sixteen. At that time he had five wives, but he had divorced three others. We all lived together and moved with my father from county to county. There was Moroto, where I was born, Dakolo, Kwania, Oyam. I have forgotten some of them. Now my family lives in a small village, Abako, on three square miles of land. At one time I had forty-three brothers and sisters. Now, I don't know." (Milton Obote, the deposed president, was a Lango tribesman. When Amin took over in January 1971, he purged the army of Langi. Those who escaped fled to Tanzania. Akii-Bua had eight brothers in the army at the time of the coup. He said only, "We have not heard from them."

"I remember my father bringing home sweets. There weren't enough for everyone. He set up competitions, races over different distances. We ran in groups the same age. I don't think I ever won. I had to beg sweets from my brothers.

"I left school in 1964 and stayed home to look after the cattle. We had a hundred and twenty. I milked them, I plowed with them, everything. In 1956, when I was very young, lions took sheep and goats from our farm, even cattle. But none came when I tended them. I did have a close look at some very big pythons. And we have wild monkeys. They can tease you and throw things. They make you run away.

"Then I was picked by a brother to be a cashier in his bar. I did that until I joined the police in 1966. I passed my training in 1967." Akii-Bua is now an assistant inspector, the equivalent of lieutenant.

"Uganda's first athlete was Lawrence Ogwang, a triple jumper who went to the Commonwealth Games in Vancouver in 1954 and to Cardiff in 1958. And I knew athletes like Patrick Etolu, high jumper, and Tito Opaka, a high hurdler, but I never ran until I joined the police. We had to go to physical training at five-thirty A.M. We did three miles cross-country and exercises. Because I could do good stretching I was selected for the high hurdles. Jorem Ochana was black African record holder in the 440 hurdles and he coached me hard. He put a high-jump bar a couple of feet above the hurdle so I would learn to keep my head and body low. Can you see this scar on my forehead? Ochana was a superior officer. He made me listen. I used to bleed a lot in our exercises, knocking the hurdles with my knees and ankles, keeping my head down."

In the police championships of 1967 Akii-Bua won four events and ran on the winning mile-relay team. Thereafter he was put under Malcolm Arnold, a British coach. The qualifying standard in the highs for the Mexico City Olympics was 14.1; Akii's best was 14.3. A few months before the 1970 Commonwealth Games in Edinburgh, finding Akii unable to improve over the shorter distance, Arnold had him concentrate on the 400 intermediates, in which he ran 52.3 and qualified. In Edinburgh Akii was eighth into the final turn, finished fourth in 51.1, and entered the hospital for a hernia operation. Six months later he did 49.7 on a lumpy grass track in Kampala and was invited to compete in the Pan-Africa-U.S.A. International Track Meet in Durham, North Carolina. "The Kenyan officials didn't like me to go," said Akii. "They wanted their men William Koskei and Kip Kemboi. They said my 49.7 was timed with an alarm clock." Amply motivated, Akii-Bua whipped Koskei and the Americans in 49.0. "I waved to the crowd before the tape. Maybe without that playing I could have run 48.7, 48.8." As he recalled that finish he was refilled with its happiness. "I'd wave again," he said.

In early 1972, Akii-Bua embarked upon six months of training unprecedented in ferocity. "I started with lots of cross-country. I ran twice a day. Then I set up five hurdles, high hurdles, every lap and put on my twenty-five-pound coat (a weight vest) and did four times fifteen hundred meters over the hurdles. That was it every day, building stamina. The police gave me a hundred and fifty dollars to go Kabale in the west where the hills are very steep."

"The hills are steep here in Kampala."

"Not like Kabale. It is high and cold. Twice a day I ran six times a six-hundred-meter hill, always with my heavy coat. I had two coaches at that time, Arnold and George Odeke. They gave me a program, but I did more than they asked. I don't think it was natural do as much as I did, but I grew strong." John Velzian of Kenya, who has coached Koskei, has one word for Akii-Bua's pre-Munich regimen: "Madness."

"What possessed you?" I asked.

Akii put aside the remains of his chicken and cleaned his large hands in a finger bowl. "We don't have good facilities. Only a grass track. It takes months to get spiked shoes sent from Europe. For three or four years no one in Uganda was good enough to represent us overseas. I wanted to change that, to show that Uganda could also produce good athletes like the Kenyans. I wanted to show that if we had the facilities the Ugandan people would be as good as any other." He was silent for a while, sipping his beer. When he spoke again it was in a less ringing, more offhand tone.

"There are always many reasons why someone does something well. Of course, I wanted to run in the Olympics because of my future, but you have to understand about being from a small country. I had a chance to be the first champion from Uganda. I worked hard." Akii went to Europe over a month before the Games and polished his speed over the hurdles. "I think it is better to always combine sprinting and hurdling in training if you want them to go together in the race. So for a week I sprinted over two-hundreds with five hurdles. Then three-hundreds with seven. Then two weeks over all ten. Six days before the competition I did a time trial: 48.6. I was relaxed. I didn't think of beating any individual when I trained. I just thought of the gold. Oh, I watched the others in the heats. They seemed tense and tired-looking. I thought Ralph Mann's hurdling technique was cuckoo."

The feeling might have been mutual. Mann of the U.S. and most other world-class quarter-mile hurdlers lead with their left legs. This allows them to run on the inside of the lane. Akii-Bua often leads with his right. To avoid violating the airspace of the man to his left he must run at least two feet out from the line, and landing on his right foot tends to throw him even farther from the inside of the lane. His disadvantage around two turns can be as much as four yards.

There were other reasons why the odds seemed against Akii. A week before the Games he had a tooth extracted and it still was bothering him the morning of the final. He hit the first hurdle in his semifinal, giving himself a tender, swollen knee. "I didn't report anything to my coaches. I was afraid they would say I was fearing."

The world record of David Hemery of Great Britain (48.1), set in a flawless race in Mexico, was thought to be unapproachable in the thicker air of Munich, yet Akii, with all his aches, predicted 47.5 for himself. Then he was presented with the lane assignments for the final.

"When I saw I was in lane one, I was very disappointed," he said. The more sharply curved inside lane is detested by all one-lap runners. "I went through emotional stages," said Akii. "I went behind the stadium on the day of the race and listened to music on American Armed Forces Radio. I became determined, not sad. After that I just tried to be calm. I ran over hurdles outside the stadium and got very warm so I could relax before the start."

Akii hit the sixth hurdle in the final, but his calm resolve carried him past Hemery just before the eighth. He beat Mann by a good five yards in 47.8.

Velzian was deeply moved. "That is not just a world record," he said. "It is an incredible world record. Out of the worst lane, running twelve feet farther than anyone else, hitting that hurdle hard . . . The man's strength is simply awesome."

"At the other end I didn't feel tired," said Akii. "At first I thought it wasn't the final. I had energy for another race."

He sat back from the table and folded his hands over a pushed-out stomach. "Now I am resting," he said. "Enjoying."

We strolled around downtown Kampala. Perhaps two of every five people we passed raised a thumb or eyebrow at Akii, usually with a deferential greeting. Ugandans don't seem to care about autographs. Akii's adulation is therefore far less oppressive than it might be.

"It is good you came when you did," he said. "In two days I am going to Addis Ababa, and then to Paris."

"I thought you were resting."

"Oh, I have no races. I am just going . . ." he laughed and got his arms, elbows, wrists and fingers tangled together in a child's gesture of shyness. "I am just going to be famous."

"How much has your life changed since the Olympics?"

"Oh, very much. The changes have been coming since 1970 when I first represented Uganda. My promotion was based in part on running. In the last two years I have been able to support my family. . . ."

"Wait a minute. I forgot to ask. Are you married?"

"I have a fiance," he said. "And a baby, one year. But when I say family I mean my mother and brothers. I have eight brothers in school. American colleges offer me scholarships, but I can't afford to go because my brothers need me."

I asked what part the tribe played in his life. "It is important. Since I am a Lango, I don't think I'd like to go and live in the West Nile District. I will always have the feeling that it is better to stay with my parents, to live where I was born."

We walked downhill from the gardens and high-rises of central Kampala into the business district. Independence Day banners swathed shops and light poles. Plastered in rows across all vacant surfaces were portraits of General Amin, his collar pushing up his jowls, furrows of worry around his eyes.

"I didn't expect the reception I got when I came home," said Akii. "There were two thousand people at the airport. I met ministers, there was a VIP luncheon. The president came. It was the second, time he had spoken to me. Last year he said he hoped I'd do my best in the Olympics. It was good to know I had.

"Everything has come my way since Munich. You know, since my father died we have been poor. I had not much schooling. I was not a middle-class man. But now I have so many friends, so many invitations. Every night I have to break promises."

Farther down the slope we came onto a dusty street which led past shuttered and barred wholesale-furniture houses and ended in a great mass of haggling people.

"That is a market," said Akii, "and this . . ." He turned and extended his arms, both ways along the road. "This is my street."

"Your street?"

"I don't know for sure yet. The government has said they will name a street after me. This one has no real name yet. People just call it South Street. It's a good street, don't you think? Busy, with solid buildings."

"Yes, it's a fine street." I stood still, affected. That his name was to be given to an enduring public landmark seemed suddenly to elevate Akii out of the world of games, or records inevitably broken, feats eventually surpassed.

"Remember," said Akii, with a sly look, "there has never been anyone from Uganda like me." Then he laughed, an open, intelligent guffaw at the silliness of it all.

Not far from Akii's street we came to a soccer stadium. Knots of frantic Ugandans, worked to a frenzy by the cheers exploding from within, pounded on every gate. People stood on rooftops. Akii led me around to a small iron door. He knocked and a plate snapped back, revealing a single brown eye. Then the door flew inward and we stumbled into darkness. Men embraced Akii amid waves of Swahili and ushered us down a passageway into the rear of the officials' box. A game between Uganda and Kenya had just begun. The box was packed, so we went to the end of the field where rows of state limousines were parked. Between cars stood sober policemen. Chains led from their wrists to the collars of nervous attack dogs. Whenever the crowd responded to a play the dogs snarled and strained against their chains. The policemen stepped on them, driving the animals to the ground.

"Don't get too close," said Akii, "and don't wander too far away from me." He showed me where a track, now overgrown, had once circled the ground. "They moved our track to a small stadium four miles from here. We protested, but they said this stadium was to be only for football. There is so little interest here in athletics. When we finish running in a race we go to the stands, so the others will have someone watching. I helped as many young athletes as I can. I give them my training programs. But the standards are not high. We have six athletes on the police club. We fight the other clubs like the army, the prisons, and we win with just our six. I do both hurdles, relays, four hundred, javelin. I want to try the decathlon, but my coach is not encouraging me."

"What are your goals now?"

"I want to stay well for 1976, to try to defend. I'll only be twenty-seven then, still able to run. Next year I'd like to better the record. All I would need is some more good training on a Tartan track. We have the hills here. I have my heavy coat. But you need to sprint on that Tartan.

"After I finish with sports, I want to concentrate on police work. I haven't any other good career than that." He demonstrated his aptitude later in the day. When we stopped for gas, Akii leaped out and caught the station attendant in some hanky-panky behind the pump. "They hold the hose high so it fills with petrol you have paid for," he said. "Then when you have gone, they pour it out and sell it again." This time there wasn't quite enough gas in the hose to press charges. The man got off with a blistering warning.

At dusk we stopped by a gathering at a local tavern. Singing, shoving matches and the swigging of millet beer seemed well under way, but Akii assured me the party hadn't started. He spoke into the ear of the proprietor, whose face fell, and we left. "I was to come later and crown Miss New Kampala. But I am a policeman. I cannot do those things without permission from my superior officers. Besides I am tired. Tomorrow I have to lead the Olympic athletes in the Independence Day parade. And we must get you to Entebbe early."

Early, because the departing Asians jamming the airport made it necessary to reach Entebbe two hours before my 9 A.M. flight. I bravely considered taking a cab and letting Akii sleep, but he wouldn't hear of it. "It will be better that I go," he said.

At 6 A.M. on Independence Day it was night in Kampala. At six-fifteen the sky was purple velvet brushed with pink and filled with birds. Crows, kites, canaries, and eagles dipped and wheeled and darted above the greening silhouettes of *kalitusi* trees. The driver for whom Akii-had arranged did not appear, so he ran a mile and a half from his police academy quarters to the nearest cab stand, and called for me in the only vehicle he could find, a groaning Peugeot driven by a sixteen-year-old. Before leaving town we had to stop at a service station to fill the radiator. The first roadblock was peopled by a handful of nodding, chilled sentries who waved us through. Vultures prowled beside the checkpoint. One flapped clumsily into the air and our driver had to swerve to avoid taking it in the windshield.

On the open road he whipped the car up to an car-splitting 120 kilometers per hour. After fifteen miles the radiator blew, spattering the windshield with steam and rusty water. The driver calmly turned on his wipers. When the vehicle started banging and missing, he pulled into a clearing beside the road and shut off the engine. Huts enclosed a bare-earth yard. We sat in the suddenly bright morning, listening to the car hiss and drip. Akii said something sharp in Swahili and the driver got out and went behind the huts. A mass of yellow weaverbirds shrilled from a small, denuded tree. I counted fifty-four swinging, woven grass nests. An old bicycle leaned against an oil drum. Akii and I looked at it, and at each other.

There was a scraping noise and the driver and another man appeared, dragging a twenty-gallon tin of water. We filled the radiator and paid a shilling (fifteen cents). The driver wanted change, but Akii popped him on the shoulder and told him to start the car. The starter ground away for two minutes. We got out and pushed, swearing at the boy, who kept engaging the clutch before we had the car moving more than half a mile an hour. Finally the engine caught and raced, and we were covered with red dust stirred up by the exhaust. We jumped in and were off. We had to push again at the second roadblock, under the baleful stares of unamused soldiers, and as we rolled into Entebbe the radiator burst. Akii wouldn't let me pay the driver so the boy lurked, vulturine, on the edges of our vision as we entered the terminal.

The check-in line for my flight to Nairobi stretched across the room, a caravan of disconsolate Asians sitting on chests and crates. I took my place at the rear. Akii looked at his watch, borrowed my ticket, and strolled toward the harried clerk. The man glanced up, did a double take and beamed at him. In thirty seconds Akii handed me my boarding pass.

"You're shameless," I said.

"You have to remember . . ."

"I know. Uganda has never had anyone like you before."

He made sure I would pass customs and then left me. I watched him go, moving through the throng of waiting Asians, followed by a few worshipful eyes and a teenage cab driver, into the warm, humid Uganda day. As in Munich, an example, a counterpoint, a glimmer of happiness over a landscape of rejection and sorrow.

—November 1972

Postscript:

In the years following Munich, as conditions in Uganda deteriorated under Amin, Akii-Bua's position as a national hero was all that saved his life. He was prohibited from leaving the country for competition for long periods. He did make it to Montreal in 1976, but was quickly recalled by Amin in enforcing the black African boycott of those Games.

When Ugandan exiles, aided by Tanzanian troops, overthrew Amin in early 1979, Akii-Bua and his wife and child fled over the border into Kenya. It was a harrowing experience, as Kenyan police had no immediate way of telling who, in the flood of people from the west, were genuine refugees and who were Amin's retreating butchers. Akii-Bua was jailed for a month and scheduled for return to Uganda before he was recognized and freed. He now lives in West Germany, where he is employed by the Puma shoe company. He raced several times in the 1980 season. "Not well," he said. "But for joy."

Four Minutes and Twenty Years:
Roger Bannister

All fine runners, through success, have to deal with the question of acclaim. Some are given a little recognition and allowed to get back to normal. Some, whose achievements take on a symbolic resonance, find their lives absorbed in the public imagination, none more inextricability than the world's first four-minute miler, Roger Bannister.

I t is an impertinence," declares the Secretary for Science and Education, in opening the 1974 British Medical Association Seminar on Sport and Sport Injuries, "to offer an introduction to our first speaker, who the other day made us feel so very old by celebrating the twentieth anniversary of his running the four-minute mile–Roger Bannister."

Bannister, still an angular, though slightly stooped figure, faces a stuffy gathering of perhaps eighty physicians, nearly all male and middle-aged, putting aside their morning papers. Few appear physically fit and some display beneath their tweeds and pinstripes sizable convexity. They seem the sort of staid British doctors who, in the phrase of Dr. Hugh Burry, regard sports injuries as "self-inflicted."

Bannister's talk is graceful and conciliatory to those in his audience unconvinced of the causal connection been exercise and disease prevention. "The relationship of health and sport is a tangly web," he says, "but I believe sport is a natural, wholesome, enjoyable form of human expression comparable to the arts, which deserves support for its own sake. Whatever improvement in health that may come through participation ought to be viewed as a bonus." He outlines the advice doctors might give to patients champing to take up sporting pursuits, warning against sudden unaccustomed exertions and the "unfortunate fizzling out of fitness schemes like physical jerks (calisthenics), which often seem too sterile to truly engage many participants."

He describes his hopes as chairman of Britain's Sport Council, which this year will channel $16 million in government funds into sport. Its theme, "Sport for All," is based upon the assumption that in England's highly urban society all that is needed to promote sporting activity is to provide facilities. Hence the council has encouraged the construction of indoor sports centers in major population areas, of which two hundred of a projected eight hundred are in operation. "Sports facilities–squash courts, recreation rooms, swimming pools," Bannister predicts, "will become a mandatory part of every new hotel, factory, flat or office building, as usual and necessary as modern plumbing."

He remarks on the boredom, and vague unease which send one third of all patients to general practitioners. "Sport is not a panacea or religion, but I think we have yet to find how many of these troubled people might be helped by recreation and physical activity. As doctors, we seem cast in the bleak role of saying 'no' to so many things—eating, smoking, drinking, drugs and now even to too many babies. Our cumulative advice is deadening, giving people a negative view of health. Instead, could we not say a massive 'yes' to recreational pursuits, thus giving a buoyant, positive view of health?" His audience murmurs approval.

Bannister first began giving this speech in 1972, had it printed in the *British Medical Journal* late that year, and squeezed most of it into an article written for *The New York Times* this spring on the anniversary of the four-minute mile, yet his delivery gives no hint of the age of his material, and his listeners are rapt. He is a bubbly man, informed with energy, given to quick leaps. Often he speaks from a crouched, praying mantis position, straightening suddenly and throwing out his hands at the arrival of a crucial point. It becomes clear in a brief question and answer session that he has aroused a rather naive fervor. One excited doctor propounds an impromptu plan "to turn Hyde Park into a country club for the working people." Another asserts that the health of the nation surely would be advanced by showing a film of Dr. Bannister jogging on the common in his neighborhood. A third proposes a revolutionary physiological course: rather than exercise so vigorously that the heart rate rises and respiration increases, he urges moving so slowly that none of this happens. "More beneficial by far," he says, "to exercise so gradually that every muscle fiber must for a moment bear the weight of the entire limb." The man seems to have arrived independently, though thousands of years late, at the oriental discipline of t'ai chi ch'uan.

Bannister is equal to these eccentric schemes, explaining that the sports centers all contain social facilities, and Hyde Park might present problems in that its royal charter goes back to Henry VIII. He says he is reconciled to the fact that only a small proportion of Britons find enough enjoyment in running to do it regularly, so he would prefer a film showing a variety of the one hundred or more sports available in the country. He gives his blessing to the proponent of slow motion, especially with geriatric patients."

At lunchtime the assembly removes, with some haste, to the Great Hall of the British Medical Association, an echoing chamber of marble columns and vaulted ceiling, adorned with flags and coats of arms. Uniformed waiters circulate through the crush dispensing three shades of sherry. "This is testimony to the drawing power of Dr. Bannister," says one physician, protecting his glass of amontillado against the jostling of his colleagues. "There are twice as many attending today as there usually are."

As the members fill plates from a vast buffet and take seats at tables ranged among the pillars, Bannister floats and darts among the most influential. "I hope you'll forgive me for repeating the same old things," he says to one, "but I believe it's a matter of getting the message out to the widest audience." He deftly slips from the grasp of an elderly gentleman who is rapturous over meeting the man who renewed his faith in British force of will during those difficult years after the war, saying, "You're too kind, really. Will you excuse me? There are several people here whose attitudes I must modify." He goes off toward an adviser to a cabinet minister while the old man looks after him with longing. "Dr. Bannister captured the imagination of Britain twenty years ago," he says, "and I don't believe he's relinquished us yet."

* * *

Memories pass into myth. Scattered across the downs and coal yards of England are dozens of cinder tracks upon which the locals now swear Bannister ran the first four-minute mile. A jogger being teased today is as likely to be compared unfavorably with Bannister as with present British record holders Steve Ovett and Sebastian Coe.

Bannister was special, so overwhelmingly applauded that it seems evident the style of the man and his accomplishments must have filled some deep need of his time. Derek Johnson, the Olympic silver medalist at 800 meters in 1956, was a contemporary. "His every ingredient touched the British psyche," says Johnson. "He embodied the trust the nation places in the university and professional classes. He appealed to the tradition of amateurism—the idea of pursuing sport on one's own terms, of keeping it in perspective. The mile itself had certain hypnotic properties then—four laps, to be done in four minutes—and finally, he just looked good running. He was tall, with that long stride, and always moving with a degree of suppressed anguish."

Anguish was essential in an era when running was characterized by unrestrained sentiment. "The art of running the mile," wrote Paul Neil, covering the Bannister-John Landy "Miracle Mile" for the first issue of *Sports Illustrated* in August 1954, "consists, in essence, of reaching the threshold of unconsciousness at the instant of breasting the tape. Few events in sport offer so ultimate a test of human courage and human will and human ability to dare and endure for the simple sake of struggle." Bannister seemed to lend substance to such heroic judgment by collapsing a few yards past the finish in his major races, but the reason for this was not inherent to a well-run mile—he did not train enough to withstand the strain of racing, a fact he now freely admits. Yet at the time Bannister's own prose contributed to the view that a fast mile was an act of extreme passion. "It was intensity of living, joy in struggle, freedom in toil, satisfaction at the mental and physical cost," he wrote in 1955 in his book *The Four-Minute Mile*. "Whether as athletes we liked it or not, the four-minute mile had become rather like an Everest—a challenge to the human spirit." The statement contains his acceptance of the public imagination, his willingness to carry vicarious hopes. Describing the actual running of the historic race on Oxford's Iffley Road track, May 6, 1954, he wrote: "I had a moment (with 300 yards to go) of mixed joy and anguish, when my mind took over. It raced well ahead of my body and drew my body compellingly forward. . . .The only reality was the next two hundred yards of track under my feet. The tape meant finality—extinction perhaps. . . .The air I breathed filled me with the spirit of the track where I had run my first race. The noise in my ears was that of the faithful Oxford crowd. . .The faint line of the finishing tape stood ahead as a haven of peace. . . . .The arms of the world were waiting to receive me if only I reached the tape without slackening. I leapt at the tape like a man taking his last spring to save himself from the chasm that threatens to engulf him."

This vibrant description caught the public fancy, but a good many athletes who had experienced similar circumstances if not similar transports, cringed. "I was in charge of preparing the track for that run, and I did it well," says Derek Johnson facetiously, "but if I'd known the rubbish that was to come out of that, I'd have let him catch his spikes."

Today, of course, Bannister's best clockings have been surpassed hundreds of times. And as it seems possible that women will be running the four-minute mile before this century ends, reassessment has set in. Harry Wilson, the British national distance-running coach, says, "I think it's bloody silly to put flowers on the grave of the four-minute mile, now isn't it? It turns out it wasn't so much like Everest as it was like the Matterhorn; somebody had to climb it first, but I hear now they've even got a cow up it."

Says one of Wilson's charges, Steve Ovett, "I think the idea of four minutes as a barrier had held people back. Bannister was a romantic about it, but it's just a time, isn't it?" Just a time to Ovett, certainly, who ran four minutes at age seventeen (and who in 1980 would break the world record with 3:48.8).

However, it could not have been wholly the passing magic of the four-minute mark that made Roger Bannister material for legend. His wondrous appeal must have had something to do with the kind of man he seemed, the philosophy he symbolized.

In his books he traces an unhappy childhood, that of a shy, studious boy for whom failure was excruciating. Running and winning the annual junior cross-country race at Bath Boys' School was a means to acceptance, to not being called a grind. "I am sure that I was not a better runner than the others, in the sense of having more innate ability. I just knew I had to win for the sake of peace."

Bannister began his study of medicine at Oxford when he was seventeen. Fired by the example of Sydney Wooderson, who held the mile and 880 world records before the war (4:06.4 and 1:49.2), he trained once a week (in later years half an hour a day) and took to heart the traditional Oxford sporting values of self-reliance and moderation. "I think we are sometimes wrong to criticize ambition," he wrote, "if we can shelve it when the right moment comes and not become embittered because of failure. He coached himself. "The human body is centuries in advance of the physiologist. . . . Improvement in running depends on self-discipline . . . acute observation . . . judgment. . . . If a man coaches himself, then he has only himself to blame when he's beaten. My ideal athlete was first and foremost a human being who ran his sport and did not allow it to run him."

* * *

Norris McWhirter, who edits the *Guinness Book of World Records*, met Bannister at Oxford in 1947. They are now godfathers to each other's children. Coaxed from his office and a welter of telegrams claiming new world records, McWhitter unwinds in the Robin Hood Pub, Enfield. "Very restless, the world of records," he says. "The tallest tree grows another foot, the longest mustache another inch. This morning we heard a Texas company has drilled a hole 5.9 miles deep." McWhirter, who was a sprinter, apparently loves his work. He notes that the *Guinness Book* has sold more than 21 million copies. "Behind Spock, but we'll overtake him by the Montreal Olympics. Ah, it's Bannister you want to know about? Born 23 March 1929, Butler Road, Harrow; father Ralph a civil servant in the Exchequer and Audit Department; one of 104 neurologists in Great Britain; a consultant in neurology at St. Mary's Hospital and at the National Hospital for Nervous Diseases." At length the facts give way to a more personal description. "I'm an expert on extremes, you see. Most people who are the best at something have one contorting drive. The exception is Roger Bannister. He is the most unneurotic person I know. He trained hard, at least for those days, but nothing was twisted; he enjoyed his sport. As a matter of philosophy he took his running only to the point where it ceased to enjoyable. Even at Oxford medicine was at the core of his life." McWhirter smiles mysteriously for a moment, remembering, then brings all of his twenty-one years of broadcasting experience to bear in the telling of a story.

"In 1951 Roger did some physiological research under Dr. D.J.C. Cunningham of Oxford, attempting to determine whether pure oxygen or a mixture of air and oxygen was better for a body under stress. They had a treadmill—absolutely remorseless, this machine. It was the equal of running up Everest in six hours; anyone would break. You had to breathe from great gasbags and they had blood guns which sprang a blade into your finger to measure lactic acid levels as you labored on. You poured sweat, your spine turned to rubber, and driving up the incline there was the most extraordinary effect of your chin and knees meeting in front of you. Near the end there was blood all over, and when you broke, you staggered and rolled off onto a mattress, trying to hit the 'off' switch as you went down. Roger himself ran to breaking on at least eleven occasions. Compared to that, the four-minute mile was like a day off. The point, of course, is that this had nothing to do with sport or improving performance. It was medicine."

As chairman of the Sports Council, Bannister has of course been interested in the medical aspects of sport, and he has become a prime moving force in the war against anabolic steroids, the artificial hormones used by many weight lifters and field event men. In October 1973 he announced that a research team led by Professor Raymond Brooks and funded by the Sports Council had developed a radioimmunoassay screening test for steroids. Immediately, he called for the International Olympic Committee to officially ban steroids, which it did on May 6, 1974.

But all is not serene. Because the benefits of steroids (essentially strength and muscle bulk) are said to continue for some weeks after the drug has passed from the body, it would seem possible for a shotputter to take steroids during a season's training, quit a week or two before the Olympics, and pass the screening test. To prevent such occurrences the IOC has said it hopes the various international sporting federations will institute season-long spot checks. But such programs are not yet mandatory, raising the specter of the ban being unevenly enforced around the world. Consequently, British weight men, fearing their country will comply while others will not, see Bannister's zeal as having done them in. "The East German sports machine is based on drugs," says shot-putter Mike Winch, himself a qualified research biochemist. "You're not going to catch them with any spot checks when it takes six weeks just to get a visa into the country. All this is going to do is make it impossible for the Western athletes to compete equally."

Winch points out a further danger. "A screening test is just that; it determines only that there is a steroid in the blood or urine. Then they have to use what is called a gas-liquid chromatography/mass spectrometry examination to find exactly which steroid it is, because if it happens to be testosterone, the natural male hormone, they cannot say it isn't the subject's own, so he cannot be disqualified. What are weight men going to do? Experiment with pure testosterone, naturally, which in terms of side effects, like liver and prostate damage and atrophy of the testes, is much more dangerous than the artificial anabolic agents."

One prominent British athlete, who admits he used to take steroids, says, "Bannister has been gullible in assuming that all sports administrations want to eliminate these agents. It's not Roger Bannister's duty to protect me; it's my duty. I don't condone or condemn steroids, but if we want to compete, they seem here to stay. We do need medical supervision for safety. Bannister could be of some help instead of simply being aghast. As it is, I'm ashamed he's English."

In the cool dimness of the Robin Hood, Norris McWhirter reflects on the controversy. "We are speaking of agents that can turn a one-hundred-sixty-pound man into a two-hundred-eighty-pound shot-putter. I'm sure Roger feels agents such as these distort the human body, not glorify it, and I agree. In a competitive world we have Gresham's Law, which states that bad currency drives out good. We can see this working in many areas. Criminals start to carry guns, so the police have to have them. Pornography has to become more and more gross in order to compete, until eventually you reach the bottom of the sink. Most athletes wouldn't consider using steroids, but are driven to out of their desire for self-expression and success. They want to keep pace. Thus the nature of the world requires us to choose whether the freedom to contort oneself is more important than the freedom to compete equally without being forced to contort oneself. It is one or the other."

                              *   *   *

Christopher Brasher set the pace for the first two and a half laps of the four-minute mile and later won the 1956 Olympic steeplechase. Now a successful journalist he has kept his ties with Bannister and introduced him to his present sport, orienteering. If the occasion demands, however, Brasher can be bluntly honest about his old and close friend. "He has erred in saying the steroid problem is broken because of this new test," Brasher says firmly. "It's obvious that the test will be circumvented unless there is worldwide, season-long monitoring by Olympic Committee doctors, a measure no one seriously contemplates."

How does he account for Bannister's repeated assurances otherwise?

"To a degree, Roger is deceiving himself. He did the same in his book." Brasher says, as a case in point, that despite Banister's assertions of independence, he did have a coach, Franz Stampfl, who was "mighty" for six months before the 1954 breakthrough. "Chris Chataway, Bannister and I trained with Stampfl two or three times a week. Stampfl planned the whole race. He rode with Bannister on the train from London to Oxford on race day, convincing him that he was capable of 3:56 and that even in the wind that was blowing he would do under four."

In his book Bannister minimizes Stampf's influence, writing of that train ride: "I would have liked his advice and help at this moment, but could not bring myself to ask him. It was as if now, at the end of my running career, I was being forced to admit that coaches were necessary after all." Asked or not, Stampfl spoke, and encouraged Bannister to an all-out effort. There is almost no further mention of Stampfl in the book.

"As Roger saw it it wasn't a falsehood to omit him," says Brasher. "He had labored through eight years of preparation, all of it inspired by a dream of self-reliance, of doing it alone. When the time came, he wrote the dream instead of the reality."

There is, therefore, if Brasher is right, some irony to Bannister's words at the book's conclusion: "In real life . . . we can play hide-and-seek with reality, never facing the truth about ourselves. In sport we cannot."

Roger Bannister is among the most private of public men. The trailing observer finds him inexhaustibly polite through the gauntlet of receptions, prizegivings, teas, and football cup finals at which his presence is demanded. Cheerfully distant, he is a master at remembering new acquaintances' titles, universities, and interests. Reciting these, he constantly introduces his questioners to one another.

Those fortunate enough to see him at home, however, find him open—and complex. Edwardes Square, in the Royal Borough of Kensington and Chelsea, faces onto an iron-fenced, four-acre block of birch and oak, lilac and green where Bannister jogs for twenty minutes in the evenings. This particular Saturday morning a white camellia blooms in the dooryard of No 31. Bannister, in an old sweater, leads his callers through a narrow hall—where resides the *Sports Illustrated* Sportsman of the Year trophy for 1954—into a comfortable sitting room. There is a photograph, of the young Bannister shaking hands with Churchill, a phrenology chart on a ceramic skull, an attractive blue oriental rug, a Diego Rivera picture of a bending nude. It is a room that speaks of education, taste, and (a feeling inescapable in all but the newest British houses) tradition.

His visitors are interested in Bannister's opposition to anabolic steroids, and discuss numerous means athletes have employed or contemplated to improve performance: weight lifting, interval training, vitamins, altitude training, "blood doping," genetic engineering. Before the list is complete Bannister's hands have flown up. "Life is about drawing lines," he says. "We must draw the line at anabolic steroids. These are not salt tablets taken to replace a natural chemical, but synthetic hormones taken to artificially improve performance. They are drugs, and drugs are a violation of the code. Many official bodies preferred to look the other way or to insist that anabolic steroids were like barbiturates or amphetamines. 'You have to have a test you can give on the day of the race or it's no good,' they said. That would be magic, not science. The problem has been to alter this thinking, to get acceptance of the use of season-long checking. Of course, there is more convincing to be done, but with the IOC announcement of the ban, we have a firm step forward."

There have been thumpings throughout the house as he has been speaking. Now his wife Moyra, a gracious and learned woman, comes to say he has a telephone call, and stays to give the visitors a glimpse at the family scrapbook. A headline from a story about the birth of their youngest child reads, BANISTER MAKES IT FOUR. A photograph shows the doctor running in a waistcoat and winning—by inches—an 80-yard fathers' race at his sons' London school in 1965. "The boys forced him into it says Moyra, and indicates the father who was second. "The poor man had a heart attack that evening and died a short while later. Roger wrote to the headmaster and said they must never again have an all-out fathers' race." There is a photograph of Moyra's father, Per Jacobsson, who was chairman of the International Monetary Fund, with Eisenhower and one of Roger receiving a cup from the Queen.

Moyra had no consuming interest in sport while she was growing up (Norris McWhirter has remarked, "When they met she had some vague idea that Roger was the first man to run four miles in a minute"), but has been involved in government commissions on social policy and shares Bannister's near-evangelical conviction that sport must be spread across the land. "Everyone has these needs," she says. "It is scandalous that there are so many urban areas with no opportunities for physical expression, none at all. It's almost sad that . . . well, after the war the bomb sites were absolutely heaven for the children. Due to the English climate they were soon overgrown with greenery and flowers. All that's been built over. All that escape has been taken away. Any mother who's got to raise children in a confined space knows the need. The thing cries out to one."

"It's known now that the rate of one's neurosis is directly related to the height of one's flat in those vast tower blocks," says Roger, slipping back into the conversation. "The sad thing is that architects are still allowed to put up projects with no places at all for children to play, let alone adults. It's a crashing mistake."

Bannister sits, glum for a moment.

"When I said the total requirement for sport in the United Kingdom was 350 million pounds, the government thought I'd got the naughts wrong."

He is cheered by the arrival of his two youngest children, Charlotte, ten, and Thurstan, thirteen. Charley, bright and straight-forward, swings her feet under her chair not from nervousness but because it feels good, and at once takes charge of the conversation.

"Thursty is running in your old shoes today," she says explaining that Thurstan has run a mile race in the afternoon.

"How well do you do?" the slender blond boy is asked.

"Very," says Charley.

"Rubbish," says Thurstan, who finally owns to a 5:21, much better than his father's time at the same age.

"Unfortunately there is no track at my school," says Charley, implying that if there were, she'd put them all to shame.

"Her speciality is backward flip across the carpet," says Roger.

The two other children, Clive, who at fifteen is bigger than Roger, and lovely seventeen-year-old Erin, enter. "Clive is a rugger," notes Roger, "and Erin a sailor with ten years' experience in dinghies."

The album is still lying open, setting off an animated discussion of ancestry. "We go back to 1066," says Clive. "The battle of Hastings," says Charley. She brings in the family pedigree, a cascade of names in black script below a purple peacock. Bannister, it turns out, is the Anglicized form of the Norman Banastre. "My family comes from Lancashire," says Bannister. My father did run a bit—to and from school—but only one race, which in fact he won. I always remember that he had a gold chain, and on it a real gold medal."

The main family sport is orienteering. "A group of friends gather three or four times a year," says Roger. "The winners of the last event have to set the course for the next."

"Then we all come home and have a huge party," says Moyra. "The Duke of Norfolk has an estate not far from our cottage south of London at Arundel near the sea. Turning inland you can run for miles over the downs. Last time there was snow, a glorious day. Great strange cattle loomed up out of the snowy mist. We lost one family completely."

"You have checkpoints," Roger explains, "each with a compass bearing and a clue. You find as many checkpoints as possible in an hour and a half. You'll cover five miles if you don't go astray."

"Of course there are enormously intellectual people who still curl their lips over the sporting scene," says Moyra. "Bernard Levin of *The Times* for one."

"This is the result of the misapplication of school sport," says Roger. "People made to feel failures. This is why *variety* is to be welcomed—for breadth of opportunity. I think everyone ought to play a team sport at school. Although I was unsuccessful at rugby and rowing, I nevertheless learned a great deal. They provide a setting in which you can encounter defeat and injury, cope with them, develop responsibility for others."

"I agree," says Moyra, "but girls want some social future in their sport, I should imagine, and here the girls' schools have taken over a red Indian war sport [lacrosse]."

This leads to a comparison of men and women as athletes. "I believe there is a fundamental difference in innate competitiveness," says Bannister. "The aggressiveness of the male is what finds expression in the high-risk sports such as football and mountaineering. You know, after football, boxing is the sport British men rate most highly."

"Oh, do they *still*, Roger?" says Moyra with choleric distaste.

"We don't know what contribution hormones make, but I would guess they play as large a part as cultural conditioning in determining the competitiveness of an individual, male or female." Asked how he would account for such magnificent competitors as Mary Peters, Britain's 1972 Olympic pentathlon champion, Bannister says, "Very rare."

"The boys simply *welcome* the battering associated with rugby," says Moyra. "Even the little one is extraordinarily brave, and his hormones haven't started pumping around yet."

"That's the benefit of sport," says Bannister with force. "All the confusion and turmoil of adolescence is thrust into the background when you compete. The essence of sport is that while you are doing it nothing else matters, but after you stop, there is a place, generally not very important, where you would put it."

That is, there is a place where Roger Bannister would put it. "There are countries where success at sport is used to justify the nation's way of life," he says. "But this leads to success at any price. It means using scientists and doctors in the effort and requiring sacrifice of great chunks of the young lives of athletes. I see that as going a step too far."

Thus Bannister seems to resist giving full consideration to the progressive inroads of science into sport. Physiological and psychological research aimed at identifying potential champions, he feels, "simply make it no longer sport. But I am a tolerable physiologist, and I don't believe research will ever predict whether X or Y will win a race. Performance is physiology combined with mental capacities, and every individual combines them in a unique way. It would be a total mess if you could forecast who would become a champion; what would be the point of an athlete's continuing? I hope, as I said in my book, that frightening day will never come."

Bannister looks around at his children, who obviously give him enormous pleasure. He settles further into his chair. "You know, when I wrote that book the feelings were fresh. I still could feel the pain and urgency of adolescence. Now I am old. I don't know what it's like to be young any more."

But Roger Bannister is not old. He remembers what it was like to pour his life into his sport. Above all he is a man of his era and its expectations. He always has conceived of sport as a preparation for life, and so must stand uncomprehending before such obsession as expressed by shot-putter Mike Winch: "Today, for a world-class athlete, the decision, the sacrifice, have to be absolutely total. You are creating yourself as an athlete. Sport *is* your life."

Bannister still symbolizes the ideal of keeping one's life "undistorted." If, as it seems, the idea of total sport is in the ascendant, Bannister must now also represent that inevitable distance, unbridgable, between the cool appraisal of sport as social benefit and the fires of self-creation. In a world described by Gresham's, Law, Bannister's dream must be increasingly hard to live.

—July 1974

Postscript:

In 1975 Bannister nearly lost his life in an automobile accident in which he broke seven ribs. One ankle was so severely damaged that he no longer runs. In that same year he was knighted by Queen Elizabeth II. The IOC has never insisted upon season-long steroid testing, so its ban is still unevenly enforced.

Muscle and Blood

A year later, a chance came for American runners to assess the efficacy of science in assisting and even predicting performance, the issue upon which Bannister had such firm opinions.

All told, we were twenty world-class distance runners, Olympic marathon champion Frank Shorter and Steve Prefontaine among us. We were gathered in Dallas on a January day in 1975, not at a track or a corn-stubbled cross-country course, but in the warmth of the Willow Bend Polo Club, to be spoken to intently over prime sirloin, to have our suspicions allayed. Here were scientists—blood men, muscle men, mind men, the best in the country—asking permission to photograph, probe, exhaust, bleed, and work all manner of other discomforts upon us. All, of course, in the interest of science.

We had a right to be suspicious. We knew that research had been going on for decades, the literature advancing glacially along the library shelves, and still no one had explained why Jesse Owens or Bob Hayes or Valery Borzov could run 100 meters faster than anyone else or why Shorter dominated the marathon. In brief, exactly what factors of blood and nerve and chemistry allow one human muscle to be faster, stronger, or more enduring than another?

As science had not supplied much of an answer to this question, coaching knowledge developed through trial and error. The sport of track and field has been advanced by stubborn crackpots trying such deviant methods as flopping backward over the high-jump bar or running 250 miles per week in training. Athletes, the beneficiaries of such progress, tend to identify with the crackpots.

Many of us were reluctant, too, because science seldom had acted in our interests. Blood had been taken from some of us in 1971 under the pretense that it was part of the U. S. Olympic Committee exam necessary to enter the Pan-American Games. The last man in line, Marty Liquori, refused, was permitted to join the team anyway, and so proved that the rest of us had been deceived. The blood, it turned out, had gone to a private study, the results of which were never made known to the athletes.

But here was Dr. Mike Pollock, a candid and earnest man, director of the Institute for Aerobics Research, saying we had reason to hope for better. He explained that research had developed ways of isolating and measuring those systems that combine to produce excellence in distance running. Tests of muscle tissue, body composition, cardiovascular function, biomechanical efficiency, and psychological traits had been developed which seemed to show a complex but decipherable pattern. To prove the usefulness of what had been found, we were to submit to the most comprehensive study ever done on world-class distance runners, then run a six-mile race to compare test results and racing performance.

"Will you be able to predict the winner?" asked Prefontaine.

"We're sure not making any guarantees," said Pollock, "but we'll take a shot at it."

"This I gotta see."

We were to be blooded early. Muscle biopsies were scheduled at the aerobics institute after dinner. "The secrets of differences between athletes reside in their adaptation to training," said Dr. David Costill of the Ball State University Human Performance Laboratory. "The major adaptation, we now think, comes not in the cardiovascular system, as we used to believe, but right in the muscle cells or fibers." Dr. Costill showed slides of muscle tissue taken in previous biopsies, identifying the two kinds of fibers everyone has in voluntary muscle—the "slow twitch," which is used for long-distance work, and the "fast twitch," which contracts more rapidly and is used mainly for short bursts. The fiber types have different chemistries, and the proportion of fast and slow fibers, genetically fixed throughout one's life, was thought to be as much as 90 percent one way or another. Different sorts of running, Costill had found, exhaust the two types of fibers and their fuel (glycogen) differently. Hard bursts drain it from the fast twitch, long runs from the slow. It stood to reason that sprinters would be endowed with more fast-twitch fibers, distance runners with slow-twitch, and this Costill hoped to confirm.

A point of philosophy seemed unavoidable here. If Costill found that the best distance runners have at least, say, 70 percent slow-twitch fibers or that the best sprinters have an equally lopsided share of fast-twitch cells, the results would be applicable at once to helping beginners select which events to train for, but they would also be a blow to that school of exhortation which has held, loudly, that you'll never know how good you are unless you try. It *will* be possible to know, not that someone will be a champion but that great numbers of eager kids will not.

To put at ease those of us who had not had the operation done before, Costill explained that an area on the outside of the calf would be anesthetized. A quarter-inch incision would be made and a special needlelike instrument inserted into the muscle, where it would snip out a cross section of a number of fibers. "This is to give you an idea of the tiny amount of tissue we extract," he said, and onto the screen came a picture of about six pounds of perforated liver.

When order had been restored, Costill reassured us that the bit of muscle lost would be regenerated within a month or two. "We've sampled some runners twenty to thirty times, and, they're running better than ever."

"They're lighter," said Prefontaine. "I'm leaving."

In fact, he went first. Mike Manley, the Olympic steeplechaser accompanied him and returned, excited, to tell us about it. "Pre thought the alcohol prep they rub on your leg before starting was anesthetic. 'More, more,' he kept saying. 'I can still feel it.' Then when the real anesthetic needle went in, he hollered, 'Wait! I can still *feel!*'"

Prefontaine, the most visibly defiant of an aloof breed, was a man who developed his loyalties on his own terms. Having been so much in demand for five years as the country's best distance runner and holder of American records at four distances, he had become sensitive to being used for the benefit of others. As the Dallas weekend wore on and he got to know the researchers, one could see his commitment growing. But coming out of the biopsy room he said, "I wouldn't do *that* again. It wasn't when they cut the skin initially, but when they cut inside, when they dug it out."

After the last man had limped away, Costill observed that runners were far less squeamish than any other group. "They're best at this because they are good at controlling their bodies." He agreed with the runners' view that simply knowing what to expect is the key to overcoming discomfort, not any sort of innate high pain threshold. Inuring oneself to the pain of running hard is a trick born of practice, not something given or denied at birth. "The threshold concept is a cop out," said Prefontaine.

When Costill's analysis was complete, it was clear that we had substantiated the fast-slow twitch theory. Gary Tuttle, a rapidly improving long-distance runner from Ventura, California, proved to have 98 percent slow-twitch fibers. Olympic 10,000-meter runner Jeff Galloway had 96 percent. Men whose best races called for more speed turned out to have the cells for it. Three-miler Paul Geis of Oregon was 79 percent slow, 21 percent fast. Prefontaine, a miler, was 77 percent slow, 23 percent fast.

So can we now sample a child's muscle tissue and judge the stamina of the adult? Not quite. Every runner's fiber ratio fit the expected pattern but one. Don Kardong, an amiable sixth-grade teacher from Seattle, one of half a dozen Americans ever to break thirteen minutes for three miles and a good marathoner (indeed, Kardong would finish fourth in the 1976 Olympic marathon), had only 53 percent slow-twitch fibers. "But his slow fibers were large," reported Costill. Strangely, Kardong is not known for a blazing finish, while Galloway, calling on but 4 percent sprint fibers, is dangerous over the last lap. Thus, judging a distance runner's prospects solely from his or her endowment of slow-twitch fibers is no sure thing. But the average for the best men distance runners in the United States is 79 percent slow, 21 percent fast, a finding that certainly lengthens the odds against athletes with sprinter's gifts becoming accomplished distance runners.

Each participant in the Dallas study was lodged with a member of the Aerobics Activity Center. It was late that first night when I limped into the home of Harriett and Calvin Cooper. I was to fast until the following day's blood tests, so there was little to do but sit wanly for a few minutes and go to bed. The anesthetic was wearing off. My calf was stiffening and beginning to throb. As Harriett showed me to the guest room I sensed a stickiness in my lower pants leg. I drew up the cuff and found a rather rapid crimson stream flowing from the taped incision down into my shoe.

Perhaps it is kinder to pass over the ensuing few seconds of clamor and faintness. In the bathroom, brief pressure stopped the bleeding. Once into bed I remembered I'd promised to call home. I picked up the extension on the night table and heard Harriett, her voice filled with maternal compassion, say, "He's wounded, and they won't let him *eat*, and the poor man is already so skinny I don't see how he can stand . . ."

In the morning Mike Pollock set about finding exactly how skinny or "lean," as he graciously put it—the finest runners are. Tenderly, Pollock and his assistants, John Ayers and Ann Ward, measured our narrow, naked dimensions. Then, with chilly calipers, they determined the thickness of our skin and subcutaneous fat at assorted locations.

After our lung volumes were measured on the spirometer we were weighed underwater, sitting in a bosun's chair hung from a scale into a murky green tank. We were requested to blow out all the air we could and slowly bend beneath the surface, waiting in warm suspension until we heard a tapping, the signal to arise. Manley came up dripping, to be told he weighed twenty-five pounds underwater. "That's as dense as we've ever seen a runner," said Ayers.

"That's what my wife has been telling me for years," said Manley.

In a while the word on our percentages of body fat began going around. Previous studies had predicted very fit male runners would be 6 to 10 percent fat. Yet Manley registered 7.5 percent and Gary Tuttle 1.3 percent. "The formulas that are generally used to determine body fat from skinfold measures turn out to overpredict for leaner people," Pollock said. Later he would come up with a new formula based on two simple measurements: thigh skinfold and shoulder width. "This can help the coach," he said. "He can use a fat caliper and assess the progress of his athletes toward the world class kind of leanness, which we now know is between 2 and 6 percent fat."

Once measured and weighed, we were wrapped against the wind and chauffeured to Dallas Medical City Hospital, a shining new facility rising above leafless gray oaks, its corridors hung with Navajo rugs and posters from the Whitney Museum. In a room illuminated only by an oscilloscope's eerie orange glow, beneath a confusion of electrode, wires and murmuring attendants, lay Jim Johnson, the 1974 AAU steeplechase champion, a pale, still, little form. Above him a massive white-coated technician pressed an instrument resembling an antique telephone receiver to Johnson's chest. This was part of the echocardiograph, a sort of miniature sonar that can plumb the internal workings of the body with sound and, by, measuring the echoes, produce pictures of a beating heart, complete to the thickness of valves. The information appeared on the screen as cloudy orange patterns, like geologic strata, each blotch carrying a message for trained eyes. "A wonderful thing," whispered one of the attending doctors. "So much information. And it's absolutely noninvasive."

After a time Johnson was unhooked, sponged, dried, and led, blinking, across the hall. I took my place on the bed and a couple of technicians began affixing electrodes—that strangely soothing process of daubing selected spots with a gel that enhances electrical contact, pressing on the little suction-cup electrodes, taping them over and carefully gathering the wires into a cable. For this examination they shaved the inside of my calves and attached wires there as well. Lying in the gloom, still having had nothing to eat since the afternoon before, I found myself relaxing, giving myself over to the researchers in a kind of trusting peace. Allowing my head to fall to the left, I saw the scope's running orange ribbons changing in thickness in time with my pulse. I wondered, if I were left to watch these pictures of my heart's performance, whether I could somehow begin to consciously manipulate them, to will the function of my heart. I know one marathoner, John Farrington of Australia, who can depress his heartbeat to as low as twenty per minute. (The average marathoner's pulse at rest is in the forties. The average man's is sixty to eighty.)

Before I could see any change, however, I was unhooked and directed across the hall to another bed, another careful wiring, this time in a lighted room. It was explained by the doctor in charge that this was vectorelectrocardiography, plotting signals from different electrodes against one another on coordinates. The end product is a piece of graph paper with a loop on it. The experience was that of lying quietly while the doctor, dressed in a hospital gown, incanted over the little computer that did all the work. "I love this machine," he said, hugging himself. "I simply love it." He did a little dance.

Later we had still more electrocardiograms taken while running on a treadmill. When the results were in, it was found that ten of the twenty runners showed abnormal or equivocal EKG findings either at rest or after stress. "I'm not sure what they mean," said Dr. Larry Gibbons of the Aerobics Center clinic. "Some of the resting abnormalities would be worthy of concern and a follow-up if one of you just walked into a doctor's office for a checkup without explaining that you're a world-class runner. Once you told him that, he'd probably realize that the voltage evidence of hypertrophy would be normal, not the unbalanced hypertrophy of a sick heart. But most intriguing are the five men who showed abnormalities while running hard. We really didn't expect to see that."

Said Dr. Kenneth Cooper of aerobics fame, "This will be a classic study because we can now say these irregularities are a normal world-class-athletes phenomenon."

(It would be nice if the word got around. All runners have heard of cases where fit athletes have been hospitalized or ordered to quit because of an anomaly on an EKG. Kerry O'Brien of Australia, a former world-record holder in the steeplechase, was told by Swedish cardiologists that he had an inverted T-wave and should discontinue running. Later he found he had had the same condition since 1968 and that it had not affected him in his races.)

Then it was time for our first real effort: the test for maximal oxygen consumption, conducted on Mike Pollock's treadmill. In this test one is fitted with a helmet, which holds a mouthpiece securely against teeth and gums. A flexible tube carries breath to a row of gasbags ranged along one side, below banks of instruments. The treadmill is situated on a platform, so high that the runner's head would strike the ceiling were it not for a small recess directly above. The unfamiliar weight of the helmet and the enclosed surroundings produce a claustrophobic sensation. Once accustomed to the machine, we did a submaximal run-seven minutes at ten miles per hour, then accelerating to twelve miles per hour for another five minutes—while the instruments recorded our oxygen uptake, our heart rate, and EKG.

During a brief stop, we sat panting, dripping sweat while blood samples and blood pressures were taken. Then we got back up and went off at eleven miles per hour, the treadmill increasing in slope 2½ percent every two minutes. The pace was not difficult, but when the incline steepened, it rapidly became work. After six minutes, when the old feeling of barely controlled panic came on and one had to keep a vigilant will, it was hard, far harder than running on a track, because there was no observable progress, nothing moving past, nothing ahead to shoot for, just a black, indifferent wastebasket. I went 7½ minutes, and as soon as I was off I knew that I hadn't approached my best. Afterward, most runners were unusually quiet, washed out, without any of the glow that comes after a race well run, or even after time trial. Shorter hated the test and stepped off after seven minutes, saying later, "You know how Pollock teaches you hand signals (to keep people from shaking their heads and ripping the tubes out of the machine)—well, at the end there I was ready to give him a hand signal everybody knows."

Prefontaine, as ever, was the exception. On the treadmill he was transformed. He drew his arms up high, hooking with his elbows as he ran, visibly fighting the machine, raging against it for the final minute. He ran not with the kind of unseeing inward acceptance of pain that the rest of us showed, but beetle-browed, furious. He complained at the prick of the needle as he sat heaving afterward, but quickly rose in an astonishing good humor. "I feel stimulated, invigorated from that," he said. "I feel ready to run, more than I have in weeks." A week later he would run a 3:58.6 indoor mile at College Park, Maryland, but now it turned out that he had done something far more important for the scientists.

"Prefontaine's oxygen uptake of 84.4 milliliters per kilogram per minute is one of the highest ever recorded in a runner," said Pollock. "This is the volume of oxygen that a body is able to consume during maximum stress. It reflects the ability of oxygen transport systems, the lungs and heart and blood vessels." The average for the world-class runners was 76.9 milliliters per kilogram per minute (average normal runners: 46.5). At the low end of the spectrum was Shorter with a score Of 71.2 milliliters per kilogram per minute, a striking finding since his three-mile and six-mile times were nearly identical to Prefontaine's (12:52 and 12:51.4, respectively, in the three-mile).

This discrepancy Pollock attempted to explain by noting that the runners seemed to fall into two groups, which he termed middle distance and long distance. The middle-distance runners were those whose best races were at six miles or less; the long-distance men were marathoners. The prime example of the first group, Prefontaine, held most American records through 10,000 meters but hated to run, even slowly, for more than twenty miles. The archetypal long-distance runner was Shorter. Comparing the two groups' scores, Pollock found a clear difference. "The long-distance runners use three to four milliliters of oxygen less than middle-distance men at all speeds. In terms of oxygen consumed, they are significantly more efficient." Why? What allowed Shorter to keep up with Prefontaine, even though he used 16 percent less oxygen at the various speeds tested? Here, finally, it seemed research was entering an area that promised to improve performance. Discover what Shorter's compensatory quality was and there was a chance it would be learnable.

"Unfortunately, we haven't the slightest idea how to account for it," said Pollock, but he reasoned that efficiency had to be gained in one of two ways. "The long-distance runners either get more work out of what oxygen they do take in or they run in a manner that doesn't require as much energy. The one would be chemical, inside the muscle cells. The other would be biomechanical, a question of coordination."

The biomechanical inquiry was up to Peter Cavanagh of Penn State, an energetic young Briton who bears a likeness to Edgar Allan Poe. "Essentially, we're studying the elements of style," he said to us. "We need measurements of your running movements and of the forces that cause them. Runners use energy to fight wind and gravity and for accelerating and decelerating their limb segments. What we'll do is ascertain from your measurements the weights and centers of gravity of your running equipment, then photograph you running on a treadmill at different speeds while you wear a biaxial accelerometer. We're interested in how much energy you're wasting."

Cavanagh's test was the most spectacular of the performances expected of us, first because eventually we were to reach a 4:15-mile pace, and also because the two synchronized cameras shooting one hundred frames per second required banks of blazing lights, and finally because we ran without our shorts. Moreover, to facilitate analysis of the pictures, black spots were painted on each runner's shoulder, elbow, hip, knee, ankle, foot, and cheek as well as on the chest, abdomen, forehead, and chin. As soon as testing was begun in the Aerobics Center lounge, signs appeared on all the doors: FILMING, NO ENTRANCE. "Apparently Dr. Cooper didn't want to offend the delicate sensitivities of Texas ladies with the sight of subjects in their jocks," said Cavanagh. Signs or not, each time someone was on the machine a hushed crowd gathered. "It felt like a scene from a Fellini movie," said Don Kardong. "The running near-naked with all the people staring, the strange black spots . . ."

The runners' unfamiliarity with the test was one of Cavanagh's main concerns and, in fact, Geis was clearly uneasy on the treadmill, while Philip Ndoo of Kenya and Eastern New Mexico (on whom white spots, had to be painted) actually fell off.

After months of analysis Cavanagh isolated several areas of mechanical interest. One had to do with trunk acceleration. "Each runner has his own pattern, of course, but some are very consistent and symmetrical, stride after stride," he reported. "Others are consistent but asymmetric, and a third group is inconsistent never quite finding equilibrium. This is the most promising area for giving feedback to runners. Eventually we'll be able to show a man his patterns on the spot as he runs, and he'll be able to work for consistency."

A second key finding was foot placement. "Viewed from the front, we watched where the runner planted his foot in relation to the midline," Cavanagh's report read. "Some crossed over. Prefontaine, especially, crossed his right foot to the left side. We found that amazing." Prefontaine's competitors found it less so. As a track man runs half his races on a left-turning curve, crossing the right or outside foot may be an advantage. Prefontaine ran curves more smoothly and closer to the curb than any of us.

Finally, the researchers addressed themselves to long-distance runners efficiency. Frank Shorter seemed to waste little energy, but others of high oxygen efficiency had biomechanical flaws. "In this we haven't been too successful," said Cavanagh. "It may be more appropriate to look to subcellular data for answers."

That brought the question back to Costill and, in effect, to where we began. "Frankly, I'm stumped," he said. "I just can't explain how the finest marathoners can be so incredibly efficient." Clearly the direction research will take is into the inner workings of the muscle cells where mitochondria and enzymes manage the production of energy from fuel and oxygen, but Costill held out no hope for a quick solution. He spoke of painstaking experiments requiring cell-by-cell analysis. "We've got it narrowed, but I don't know if we'll ever explain all the complexities of human muscle adaptation," he said. "It might not be such a wonderful thing if we did. It would certainly disappoint the ninety-nine percent who would find that no matter how they tried, they could never become champions."

On the evening of our arrival, Bill Morgan, a psychologist from the University of Wisconsin, had circulated personality inventories—lists of questions related to one's levels of guilt, self-confidence, and satisfaction. Three years before, through a combination of psychological and physiological data, Morgan and several others had predicted nine of the ten wrestlers who would make the 1972 Olympic team, so he had our attention. In the hush before we began, steeplechaser Doug Brown whispered, "Who's going to read the questions to Geis?" Paul, giggling, clapped his hands and took on an expression of vacant delight. He had just made a perfect 4.0 for the quarter at Oregon.

The results of the tests actually went some way toward explaining such behavior. "World-class runners have a psychology similar to world-class wrestlers or oarsmen," said Morgan later. "They are all lower than the general population in neuroticism, depression, anxiety. This suggests that one prerequisite for success is a psychological profile characterized by stability, by desirable mental health. Runners are stable to the point of being aloof, even defiant."

In a private talk each runner had with the psychologist Prefontaine gave Morgan a taste of defiance. Asked for short answers to three simple questions (how be began running, why he continued, what he thought about in races), Prefontaine grew impatient with the seeming shallowness of the interview. Before it concluded he had delivered a spontaneous lecture on what running was for him: "A race is a work of art that people can look at and be affected in as many ways as they're capable of understanding."

Later Morgan speculated that this allowed some insight into why Prefontaine sometimes did not satisfy himself even with a winning, record-breaking race. "He was trying for something that only the participants might be able to understand." Because Prefontaine was never more articulate on the subject than he was with Morgan, his races must speak for themselves.

Yet there was method behind Morgan's exasperatingly simple questions. In asking what we thought about in a long race (the single question runners hear more than any other), he was looking for something he had noted before: a way of dealing with the prolonged pain of running hard. In Boston he had worked with distinctly non-world-class marathoners—men slower than 2½ hours (the U.S. best is Bill Rodgers' 2:09:55). "I found that these men all used a cognitive strategy to dissociate the pain," said Morgan. "For example, one an will imagine himself building a house—from drafting the plans, pouring the foundation, doing the plumbing, the framing, every shingle. As the race ends, he's admiring the landscaping. Another mentally puts on a stack of Beethoven records and runs the whole way to the changing symphonies. Another, whose father was an engineer, becomes a locomotive up Heartbreak Hill."

Morgan thus came to study the finest marathoners with great expectations. None were fulfilled. "Even when I probed, asking, 'Do you have ways of dealing with the discomfort?' they only said things like, 'If I'm feeling bad, I try to push a little harder because the other guy must be worse off.' Not one world-class runner used a strategy to dissociate or distract himself from the pain."

A related finding was that at twelve miles per hour on the treadmill a control group of good college runners did not read their bodies well. They said they felt less stress than their oxygen consumption and heart rate indicated—until right before they collapsed. By contrast, world-class runners described levels of fatigue that accurately paralleled their physical states.

An explanation for all this, which appeals to runners, is that the imperatives of racing well call for a certain degree of attention to pace, form, tactics, level of fatigue, and liquid intake. Anything, including self-deception, that distracts a runner from the task at hand will be a detriment to performance. In its nuances the pain may be saying something that can help win the race. Rather than distract themselves, the best runners learn to listen.

Finally we gathered at Loos Stadium for the six-mile race that, theoretically, would affirm the predictive value of the previous tests. The day was clear and cold. Frank Shorter and I sat out of the wind and decided the psychological variable was the most slippery. "I felt the competitive urge stirring when I got up this morning," he said, looking at the empty stands. "It must have been rolling over to go back to sleep."

Prefontaine originally was not to run, having a hard race a few days later, but after his treadmill performance he chose to do two miles with us as an exhibition. Geis, mournful and anxiety-ridden with a sore knee, did not start.

The first mile was fast, in the vicinity Of 4:30. By the time Prefontaine stepped off the track at two miles and the pace slowed, some of us had become aware of another factor that was skewing the predictions: impending diarrhea. At nine laps I leapt the fence, found the men's room under the stands, and rejoined Manley and Brown as they completed three miles. At four minutes, Brown dropped out with the same problem. Ahead, the pack ran behind Shorter's pace until Gary Tuttle broke free with a mile and a half to go and won in a creditable 28:00.4, barely ahead of the late charge of Jim Johnson and Don Kardong. Then came Shorter, Galloway, Ndoo, and Manley.

And the predictions? Since most of the more sophisticated data couldn't be analyzed in time for the race, the scientists made an informal choice based on maximum oxygen uptake, percentages of body fat, state of training, and apparent motivation. Tuttle, who was second only to Prefontaine in consuming oxygen and led us all in leanness with his 1.28 percent fat was in fact first choice. Yet, with his first words after he regained his breath, Tuttle cast some doubt on whether his performance was the result of simple physiology. "Dr. Cooper gave me a copy of his aerobics book," he said, "and wrote in it, 'You have the makings of a champion.' I figured he knew what he was talking about. This whole week has been a fantastic confidence builder."

To Galloway it had seemed a long race. "The old Olympians (Shorter, Galloway, Brown, Moore, and Manley) didn't do so well today," he said. "It seems like we were worn down more by the week's tests than these hungry guys."

Afterward Prefontaine and I were taken to the home of his host, Ronnie Horowitz, where we were made to sit on a couch and were brought a postexertion bottle of champagne, cheeses, and fruit. We sipped quietly for a while, and then Horowitz said, "It may well be true that the most intelligent and congenial of all athletes are runners."

"You hit the nail right on the head," cried Prefontaine.

"With certain exceptions."

The bubbles appeared to rise into Prefontaine's nose and he sneezed.

As we dripped and stretched in the Horowitz sauna, I asked Prefontaine whether he had found the study rewarding. "Yeah," he said. "I'd like to come back sometime when I'm in really good shape and put that oxygen uptake mark way out there."

"But was it a good idea?" I asked.

"It was good that the scientists figured Tuttle to do well," Prefontaine said. "They're on the right track. But it's good that there is still room for people to dream, too. I don't know. Science is one thing, but when you're the guinea pig it can get stale pretty fast." He confided that each evening before bed he had been served a split of Veuve Clicquot and a pear or some grapes. Now, after the sauna and a plunge in the icy swimming pool, he would be taken horseback riding and to dinner at the club and fly home the possessor of an Oleg Cassini sweat suit, courtesy of Horowitz. Straight-faced, he said, "This thing sure would have been tough without the hosts."

—May 1976

A Final Drive to the Finish:
Steve Prefontaine

Five months later, in May 1975, Prefontaine tried to sleep on the plane from San Francisco to Eugene, squirming in his seat, closing the window shade with a snap, cracking his head against the fuselage in an apparent try at denting a hollow there. He closed his eyes for perhaps thirty seconds and then he was squirming again. He had not run as well as he had hoped in the two-mile in Modesto the night before, although he had won in 8:36.

"I went through the mile in 4:13," he said, "and then I just didn't seem to want to run very hard any more. I was lethargic. I still am. I feel like quitting training. Maybe I want to devote my energies to something positive, something I can see bearing fruit."

Prefontaine seldom spoke of his motives, and when he did he always included that "maybe"—as if he, like the rest of us, could only observe himself and wonder at this strangely engaging, obstreperous, fidgety creature.

"I talked with a lot of other athletes at Modesto about the AAU's damn moratorium rule," he said. A few days before, the AAU had announced a policy for forcing the country's best trackmen to compete in international meets against the Soviet Union, against Poland and Czechoslovakia, against West Germany and Africa. An athlete who declined a spot on the national team or who did not run in the national AAU meet would be suspended for one year if he or she competed abroad during certain moratorium periods before the AAU championships and the international meets.

"In July there are only about ten days when the moratorium is not in effect," said Prefontaine. "That screws up my whole competitive schedule."

More to touch off his celebrated fulminations on the subject than for any enlightenment, I asked him what was wrong with competing on the national team against the Russians and others. He looked at me as if I were a traitor to my class.

"Where are the best runners?" he said, coldly. "Emiel Puttemans is Belgian. Brendan Foster is English. Rod Dixon is a Kiwi. Knut and Arne Kvalheim are Norwegians. Lasse Viren is from Finland. Does the AAU have any of them on their wonderful televised schedule? Hell, no. For me, running against the Poles and Czechs would be like running against high school kids. And I hate all this gung-ho, all-for-the-red-white-and-blue attitude that the AAU spouts. If that's important to some people, fine, more power to 'em. But, damn it, I wish they'd leave me alone to do what I want to do—run against the best."

As he spoke, frustration rose in him. He seemed caged, vulnerable. He had organized a month-long visit to the Northwest by eight Finns, and then had experienced a series of withdrawals by athletes and promoters. The crowning blow had been a telegram from Finland saying Viren, the Olympic 5000- and 10,000-meter champion who was to race Prefontaine in Eugene, was injured and would not come.

"I'm not so competitive as before," Prefontaine said. "It's wearing me down holding this tour together. Maybe the negativism stems from not being able to count on big races. One disappeared with that telegram. With the AAU rule others aren't likely."

In the week leading up to the meet last Thursday night in Eugene, where Prefontaine would go against Frank Shorter at 5000-meters, I happened to talk with several men who knew Prefontaine well. Jon Anderson, an Olympian and the 1973 Boston Marathon champion, said, "He's not like other distance runners. He's not quiet, not introspective. He can't relax. A fifteen-mile run in the woods makes me kind of mellow and satisfied. All it does for Pre is make him mad. Most distance runners find expression in easy running; we take comfort in that kind of personal experience. Pre's kind of running is always hard and straining and fierce."

Anderson felt Prefontaine could not be understood without reference to the demanding, elemental life of Coos Bay, Oregon, the logging and shipping town where he grew up. There are codes there, governing social acceptance among the stevedores and lumbermen, and chief among these is success at sport. It took Prefontaine a while to gain that acceptance. When he first went to grade school he knew more German than English because his mother spoke German at home. He was taunted for his backwardness. He once said, "Kids made fun of me because I was a slow learner, because I was hyperactive, because of a lot of things." Then, in junior high school, he discovered that he could run well; all it took was being able to stand the discomfort of effort. The need to measure up, as demanded by Coos Bay, turned into a need to surpass. "Running gave me confidence," he said.

A long-abused ego burst out in a cockiness that was usually forgiven because boasts of what he could do were followed by proof. He set a national high school record of 8:41.5 for two miles, and at the University of Oregon he won four NCAA three-mile championships and three cross-country titles. He ran the mile in 3:54.6. He held U.S. records at 2,000 meters (5:01.4), 3,000 meters (7:42.6), two miles (8:18.4), three miles (12:51.4), 5000 meters (13:22.2), Six miles (26:51.4), 10,000 meters (27:43.6).

Yet he had not won when it meant most to him. In the 1972 Olympic 5000, he ran his last mile in about 4:05, but Viren, the winner, did 4:01.2, and Mohamed Gammoudi, who was second, did 4:03. Prefontaine, staggering at the finish, was passed a few yards before the line by Ian Stewart to lose the third-place medal, too. In 1974 he set three American records in Europe, all in losing races to Knut Kvalheim and Rod Dixon. "When he's in a race with someone who is capable of beating him," said Anderson, "I think his thoughts, or the kind of man he is, make him press too hard."

Given the kind of man, the defeats were met by increased resolve. Early in 1975 he was offered the largest contract in the short history of the professional track circuit, $200,000. He turned it down. Until the Europeans were well and honestly thrashed, he said, "What would I do with all that money?" Yet he displayed little of the traditional distance runner's feeling for austerity. "I like to be able to go out to dinner once in a while. I like to be able to drive my MG up the McKenzie River on a weekday afternoon. I like to be able to pay my bills on time." With a sense of humor more lascivious than droll, he relished low tavern life ("Envision a satyr," said Shorter). He delighted in describing the ruinous modes of recreation practiced in Coos Bay establishments. "I know places you better speak low if you've been to college," he would say. "Men will come across the room and cold-deck you if you hold your glass wrong."

Two days before his race with Shorter, Prefontaine ran a brief workout under the eye of Oregon Track Coach Bill Dellinger, himself a three-time Olympian and bronze medalist in the Tokyo 5000. While be held a watch during Prefontaine's 330-yard interval runs Dellinger said, "That man has something no runner in my time had. We used to warm up out of sight behind the stands, and we would never have considered taking a victory lap. But Pre . . . he's like a movie star in his relationship with the crowd. He thrives on it."

Asked if he considered himself a major influence in Prefontaine's career, Dellinger said, "Well, I render advice. I don't know how often it's taken in areas away from running." Prefontaine finished his last 330 and approached us, sweaty, his barrel chest heaving, displeased with his times.

"Do you have a guru?" I asked. "Is there someone you would go to if you found yourself in a situation you couldn't handle?" His reply was thrown back, almost defiantly. "I don't have anyone like that," he snapped, and he was jogging off, shaking out his arms.

"I told him that sounding off about how strong he was was a mistake," said Bill Bowerman, Prefontaine's first coach at Oregon and his Olympic coach. "He runs an American-record 2,000 meters at Coos Bay and Viren cables that he's hurt. If he wants to get those runners over here to his lair, he's got to be more sly." Yet Bowerman had no illusions that Prefontaine could do that, could lie low and wait. "No, that's hard for him," Bowerman said. "He's too outspoken, and honest." In the act that meant the most to him, that he defined himself by—driving for the finish in a hard race—it was hopeless to expect him to hold off, to slow down. "He doesn't look beyond races," said Bowerman. "He doesn't look beyond laps."

Frank Shorter had come to Eugene as a favor to Prefontaine. His wisdom teeth had been extracted eight weeks before and then he overtrained and had been ill. But with Viren out and the financial success of the meet in doubt, he was needed. Prefontaine had clawed past him in the stretch to win a three-mile in Eugene a year earlier—his American record—so Shorter's return attracted a twilight crowd of eight thousand.

Before the race Shorter and Prefontaine lay on the grass of the infield. They spoke almost shyly with Eryn Forbes, a beautiful, angular fourteen-year-old from Portland who had recently run an age-record 4:48.6 mile. "I hope she's blessed with nonpushing parents," said Shorter after she had gone, and Prefontaine slapped the ground in agreement. They watched as Gary Barger won the mile in 3:58.8, to become the sixteenth Oregon trackman to go under four minutes. Prefontaine went over to half-miler Steve Bence, who had fallen in a relay in the Pacific Eight championships and had broken his jaw. Now, with fourteen stitches in his chin and his mouth wired shut, Bence faced his last chance to meet the NCAA qualifying standard of 1:49.8. Prefontaine bent close and spoke intensely. "I don't think I could do what you're doing," he said. "So why don't you make it worthwhile?" Bence nodded, silent, and Prefontaine withdrew to watch. With 220 yards to go, Bence had a chance but could not kick. Prefontaine turned away.

For three laps of the 5000, Shorter and Prefontaine ran behind Paul Geis, who earlier had won the two-mile; Shorter led at the mile in 4:17. Prefontaine took over the lead at six laps, Shorter staying at his shoulder, the rest of the field far back. Shorter looked tight, apprehensive. At 2 miles, Prefontaine shot ahead and churned successive laps of 63, 64, and 63 seconds, running away with the race, running through the rising shouts of his people, his head cocked to the right his brow tightly knitted. This was where he lived, and those long searing drives never failed to be compelling. Into the last straightaway he closed his eyes and swung out from the curb slightly: he ran 50 yards with his eyes shut, squeezing away the suffering. He finished in 13:23.8, only 1.6 seconds slower than his best, and as he touched the tape he glanced back at his distant rivals, and above them the clock. Soon the crowd was flowing around him, small boys waving programs, beaming matrons, girls in halter tops.

That evening there was a party at the home of Geoff Hollister, Prefontaine's associate in an athletic shoe company. All the Finnish' athletes were there, along with many of the families who had housed them. Prefontaine's parents and his high school coach were there. As the beer flowed and sandwiches circulated, there was much talk of Pre going to Helsinki, of his hospitality being returned, and much discussion of the AAU rule. Jon Anderson tried calmly to analyze the difficulty of explaining to the layman why athletes became so enraged at the AAU. "There is such a gulf between us and all those thousands of people who would give their right arms to wear 'USA' on their chest . . ."

Prefontaine broke in. "Where is the talent that I competed with when I started in 1969?" he cried, seizing on the first injustice that came to mind. "The shortage is of guys who are out of school, and can still figure ways to train and find competition. I'm twenty-four years old and Frank is twenty-seven, and we're *veterans*. That's the shame. That's what's wrong with the American system."

I found myself with Raymond Prefontaine, who seemed daunted by his son's ferocity. We talked instead about the Dungeness crabbing in Coos Bay, he carefully explaining where good catches were being made. Steve leaned near and confided to me that he had never been crabbing. "I've never been fishing, either," he added, "but for God's sake, don't tell anybody that."

Poor revelers, my wife and I left the party at eleven. Frank Shorter, who was staying with us, said Prefontaine would drive him home later, and he did at about twelve-thirty. They sat in Prefontaine's MG on the road above our house and confirmed a date for the three of us to run an easy ten miles in the morning. Shorter, an attorney now, promised to brief Prefontaine on the legal challenges that might be brought against the AAU's restrictions on free international racing. "Yeah, well, let's go over that tomorrow, when our heads are clear," said Prefontaine and he drove off down the hill.

In the morning the phone rang, waking me, and I learned he was dead. I told Frank. At eight o'clock, the day was still, full of sun and birdsong. From the radio we learned that the accident had happened only a few hundred yards from our house, and we knew Frank had been the last to see him. After a few minutes we walked down a path through a neighbor's yard to the road below. The ashes of flares were scattered in the road. On one side, beneath an outcropping of black basalt, there was broken glass and twisted metal strewn among the poison oak. There was blood on the street, a street he had run at least three times a week for six years.

We saw the accident report, which said he was dead at the scene, his chest and stomach crushed under the weight of the overtured car. His blood alcohol content had been found to be 0.16 percent, a level presumed to significantly impair driving. We always knew that the important thing about his life, that which let him perform as he did, was his prodigious honesty. Because he had never been hypocritical about his use of alcohol, the manner of his death could not diminish that honesty.

Later, after we had spoken to the news people, Frank and I ran. I believe it was a sort of observance, something that had to be done. We could not have run a step anywhere that Prefontaine had not run. As it happened, we ran softly through the woods skirting Eugene, looking up at the rugged ground under the Bonneville power lines where he did winter training. After we finished a five-mile loop, we kept on, crossing the river over a footbridge where I had once seen Prefontaine, working on a project for a film class, crouched behind a tripod and movie camera, waving at a tired runner to sprint toward him out of the cottonwoods, yelling, "Do I have to do everything myself?"

We avoided the road of the accident, coming up the hill to my house another way, a hard climb, feeling the effort, accepting it as the only link left with what Prefontaine had felt and accepted better than any of us.

—June 1975

Appointment at a Starting Line:
Filbert Bayi and John Walker

When we reached Montreal, it seemed we were not to be allowed to forget what Prefontaine might have done had he lived. The subway stop nearest the Olympic Stadium was Prefontaine Station. The sixteen-year-old cobearer of the Olympic flame into the stadium was named Steve Prefontaine. But by then the world's eyes had turned to what promised to be a classic 1,500 meters. Prefontaine himself had spoken of it as a contest it would be a privilege to witness.

Their race has already been run, countless times, in the Montreal of the imagination. Always it is the same. The Tanzanian, Filbert Bayi, is in front, beautiful and remote, running with an elegance that serves to emphasize the power of the man just behind, in the stalking position. John Walker, tan in the startling black uniform of New Zealand, his shoulder-length hair flying, has on his face an eagerness for this battle joined at last. The pace is unprecedented, 53 seconds for 400 meters, 1:50 for 800, the remnants of the field falling away to struggle for the bronze medal. The time for three laps is 2:48, assuring a new world record for 1,500 meters. Down the last backstretch Walker challenges and Bayi responds, still potent, as he was in 1974 when he won the Commonwealth Games in 3:32.2, two yards ahead of a less mature Walker, both of them breaking Jim Ryun's 6-year-old record. Now Walker hangs three yards away as they lean into the turn with 200 meters to go. His outside arm uppercutting furiously, he begins to close in once more. Out of the turn with 100 meters to go they are dead even, the formalities completed, ready to discover the best man, the best miler who ever lived.

And then it evaporates, the imagination fading out in a puff of questions: Which man *ought* to win? Which character will have best survived the myriad stresses leading up to this race, to these final yards? What kind of men are these, accursed and yet blessed with each other at the peak of their careers? To judge such things, the observer must search them out in faraway countries, must watch them and listen carefully.

* * *

Seen from above, perhaps from atop a tourist hotel, the city appears tranquil, its mango and weeping fig trees shading the streets, lateen-rigged canoes and dhows ghosting among the ships of the harbor. But the dust of Dar es Salaam is sour and burns in the chest. Garbage decomposes quickly here; one walks the waterfront through the nearly palpable stench of rotting fish. People drink orange-colored water from dirty glasses proffered by dirty-fingered vendors. Men squat in the dust, the black exhaust of buses rolling over them. It is 92 degrees. The humidity is 90 percent. The visitor is importuned often, to exchange his dollars on the black market, to buy, to drink, to ride rather than walk. "Indestructible taxi service!" shouts a man in a battered Peugeot. One sees many deformed or crippled children, because Tanzania, one of the world's twenty-five poorest countries, cannot afford polio vaccine. Recently in Mbeya, near the Zambian border, twenty-five people died of rabies within four months, yet a campaign against the disease was abandoned, reports the daily paper, "due to a lack of bullets for shooting rabid and stray dogs."

Filbert Bayi, a lieutenant in the army, is living in a small cement bungalow on the grounds of an officer training school on the southern edge of the city. The house has a red-tile roof, a hedge of thorn and lantana. Inside the walls hold Chinese pennants and photographs of Bayi finishing races. There are large trophies from Italy, England, and the United States. Across the back of a couch is draped a white New Zealand sheepskin. Bayi, wearing only blue nylon shorts, sits on the couch and stares at the floor. He is beaded with sweat, his left shoulder swollen.

"I am better, a little," he says weakly. "Yesterday I couldn't talk and I vomited. Now that the sweating has started, it is good." He holds the small of his back. "Malaria, this is my disease. If the mosquitoes bite me, I always get it. My blood is weak, I know it. This is chronic malaria. If you, a European, caught it, you could die very quickly. But if I or other Tanzanians who have built up an immunity catch it, we are in bed for one or two days. But we have malaria organisms that are dormant. If we catch cold or do something to lose resistance, we will suffer from malaria from time to time. This time was a reaction to a cholera shot. I used to get it a lot, but not so much now. I take no medicine for it."

Bayi thumbs through some running books brought by the visitor, then returns to bed.

Later, the visitor attempts to run, to test himself in the thick tropical air, doing slow half-miles with a promising Tanzanian runner named Emmanuel Ndemandoi. He finishes cross-eyed, nauseous with the heat. Yet as he stumbles into the infield he sees Ndemandoi scurrying to put on his sweat suit. Jogging, the visitor shakes out is arms, letting the wind flow around his dripping body. Feeling a dry touch, he finds himself holding hands with the young African. "Karibu," says Ndemandoi. Welcome.

* * *

John Walker stands in knee-deep water, warm little waves breaking over his thighs. He wears shorts and a blue singlet that says INSON BROTHERS APPLE WINE. The previous day he had run a 1:46.6 800 meters in Wellington, on the other end of New Zealand's North Island, and this morning had managed seven miles on the grass in the Auckland Domain (a large park), but his Achilles' tendons were sore throughout. Now he has come north of the city to the flat reaches of Long Bay. "The salt water is good for horses' legs," he says. "It's got to be beneficial." He does not wade freely but hunches forward. Beneath his feet are smooth fragments of shell, some pink like scallops. He gazes across the wind-scoured Hauraki Gulf, pointing out some of the headlands and islands that fill the confusing Auckland seascape. "This is living," he says. "If I weren't runner, I'd be a fisherman."

Slowly he walks from the sea, perhaps slightly less bent, and crosses the twisted roots of a grove of old pine trees. On the other side are hundreds of Sunday picnickers. Walker makes his way toward the friends he has driven up with—Ross Pilkington, a housing maintenance contractor and race walker, Mark Kennedy, a journeyman half-miler from Van Nuys, California, and Gail Wooten, a hurdler. As he moves through the throng he is recognized, it seems, by everyone. Tan, heavyset men with European accents buffet him with questions about the prospects for the gold medal, the bad luck of not getting Bayi out for a race. Walker is unfailingly patient with these people, but controlled, giving the same answers again and again, saying yes, if his training goes according to plan he has a good chance to win, that he'll certainly try his best, that the public ought not to be too hard on Bayi because it is the Tanzanian government which vetoed his coming. Always the cry follows as he moves on: "Good on you, John. We'll be with you." The observer develops a vague fear for him, that this innocent but constant pressing, forcing him repeatedly to ponder and discuss the imperatives of the race in Montreal, will eventually diminish that moment, remove the spark.

Walker drops to the center of a blanket, within the perimeter of Pilkington, Kennedy, and Wooten and becomes invisible, the crowd passing unaware. He puts his head on his forearms, long hair falling about his face to form a little cave, shutting out the world. Shrimp, and canned salmon are passed around, with bread and butter. The shadows lengthen. The wind mounts. Walker curls on the blanket, not wanting to leave, somehow at peace despite the barbecues sizzling around him, an argument in Croatian, red-footed gulls descending raucously upon the bread crusts.

Finally he rises. Wooten, perhaps out of curiosity, touches his heel. Walker reacts sharply, spinning away with a shout. Turning to the frightened girl, he says, "Touch anything else you like, please, but not there." Tying his shoes, he pulls so hard one of the laces snaps.

In the car back to town Walker says he is disappointed in his races so far during the New Zealand season. "But it's all right for the Olympics. The buildups never desert you." This is a reference to the peculiar cyclical training system followed by most New Zealand runners, a rigid division of the year into racing and preparatory phases. The buildup, for Walker, is eight to ten weeks of running seventy to one hundred miles per week, at the end of which he is covering eighteen miles at a near five-minute-mile pace three times a week. "Really punishing my body," he says. Traditionally, in the schedules originated by Arthur Lydiard, coach of Murray Halberg and Peter Snell, this stamina work was done once a year, through the winter. But for the past three years Walker and Rod Dixon, the Olympic 1,500-meter bronze medalist from Nelson, on the South Island, have done two buildups per year, before the New Zealand and European summers. Walker sees this compression of seasons as the key to his improvement. "We're doing buildup upon buildup, and with so many good races in between you keep from getting bored. You have something to aim for all the time."

Over a card table later in the evening, his blackjack winnings arranged in piles before him, Walker turns to the distant opponent, seemingly compelled to speak of the challenge presented by Bayi, and of how John Walker is responding. "The thing is, the world, the press want to build this up as a historic clash, but I have to look at it simply as another race. It will be hard, but all my races are hard." Walker is quick to acknowledge the influence Bayi has had on the art of miling. "Without him I'd be sitting back and kicking with three hundred to go. I lead all my races now. I'm realistic now. The only way to beat Bayi is to run the way he does." He pauses a moment, his hands tightening on his thighs. "You know, that first lap in Montreal could be a fifty-three."

Yet Walker cannot agree that the man who has transformed his event has done so out of genius. "It's not genius, it's a temperament, a steadiness and concentration, plus the natural speed to put it to use running out in front. He's bright, don't ever forget that. I've got enormous respect for him." Again he is silent, his jaw setting. "But I don't worry about him. *He* says I worry about him. He says he just runs, and maybe he does, but I wouldn't call what I do worrying. I work to a plan. If I go for a world record, I want to set it up, I want to go through three quarters in 2:53. . . ." He describes the pace in his 3:49.4 world-record mile lavishing rather more care on it than needed to make his point. Yet when asked if the contest between Walker and Bayi could be represented as the world of scientific planning vs. the mysteries and primitive intuition of black Africa, Walker winces. "No pills, a beer for lunch, parties the night before . . . I'm the most unscientific runner I know, compared with those who have to have everything just right before they can compete. And Bayi, look at the buildup he does, a hundred and thirty kilometers a week running only six days, and in that horrendous heat. He's a natural all right, but he's also dedicated and well coached. We're different people from different worlds, but I believe that in our running we're fairly similar. We love to run hard, we hate to lose. I wish people would leave it at that."

And Bayi the man? "He's a friend, a switched-on sort of guy. I think he's got more clues than the rest of the Africans. He's a sharp dresser, a dancer. . ." But again Walker lapses into the competitive obsession. "I don't think he's avoided me. Only he knows that. We expected him in Europe last summer and he didn't come, but look at the odds. If we raced four or five times on those good tracks there is a chance I'd beat him and take his 1,500 record as well. I wouldn't set it up for him, why should he set it up for me?"

Walker seems to be bearing up well under the pressure of being a world-record holder, the standard-bearer for a small country's proudest tradition. He says, "It's hurt me, the public's expectations," and goes on to tell of a year earlier, running with bronchitis to fulfill a Manurewa club commitment. "I did 4:07 and it destroyed me. I couldn't run properly for three weeks. My hemoglobin went from 16.1 to 12.8. I couldn't do a mile without walking. All because of a club commitment. And later, when Bayi and I were racing at Mount Smart and he was tired from leading into the wind and drifted out from the curb and I went past on the inside, the public accused us of a fix." Walker knows full well that the demands of his nation are insatiable. When Walker was unsure whether his tendons would permit him to race in Wellington, the local athletic chairman, Mr. Colin MacLachalan, expressed his concern by saying, "If he doesn't run it will be a sad blow and a big disappointment to the public." Yet he does not refuse interviews to reporters from women's magazines, nor does he cut down his racing schedule to protect his tendons. The reason comes slowly to light as Ross Pilkington tells of a run on the Domain, Walker hidden among a mob of other runners until they pass a crowd of children spilling out of the trees. "And John says, 'I better go to the front now,' and they see him and it is bedlam." Walker, hearing this told, smiles at the memory, an unaffected, tender expression. "They run onto the track after my races," he says, "all with their little scraps of paper. The kids' memberships in New Zealand athletic clubs have swelled three times over since the world record. Kids are running mileage because it's the sort of thing they can do without much coaching. You see kids having 'Walker-Bayi' races on the sidewalk." He tells all this in a tone of mock resignation, but his pride in it is unmistakable.

"Swollen again," he says, his band caressing the back of his left Achilles' tendon. "Feel that." There is a half-inch long protrusion beneath the rough, dry skin of his heel. "The doctor says that eventually it will have to be scraped. It's a matter of time."

"How much time?"

"He doesn't know."

Walker decides to spend the night at Pilkington's. He has a glass of fruit juice and sits in a book-lined parlor. He lowers his voice because people are asleep in the next room. "Rick Wohlhuter told me two years ago that he'd hate to be the first man to go under 3:50, yet he tried to do it twice last year. And I remember how it was, imagining it in my training, what the joy would be, the satisfaction. And then it came, and it was like nothing I'd imagined. An ordeal. Everything went flat." His next words are spoken barely above a whisper. "I wanted that record. I wanted it. Now I wish I didn't have it."

*   *   *

His gray Volkswagen Beetle roaring and trailing smoke, Filbert Bayi drives rapidly across the undulating country west of Dar es Salaam. "We are going to Kibaha, about twenty miles," he says. "We are going to the shamba of a friend to get fruit and chicken. Chicken for fresh chicken soup. Then I think I'll be all right." It has been two days since the worst of his malaria. "I didn't run this morning because my joints are sore, and my eyes are not fully opened. But after a shower I feel O.K."

One tire has a slow leak. Bayi stops for air at a ramshackle gas station. The leathery foliage of cashew trees rattles in the wind. Women in bright patterned khangas or dark Muslim dress troop along the sandy verge of the road. Upright and strong-shouldered, they carry babies, produce, axes. Bayi, in contrast, is tastefully muted in a beige knit jacket with brown trim and matching brown bell-bottoms. Farther on, he points out the site of his new house, now a pile of bricks at the end of a rocky lane. His view will be of rolling grasslands dotted with huts beneath baobab and palm trees. "Three bedrooms," he says, "and a sitting room and dining room. They are marked on the ground. But just now there is a shortage of cement."

In Kibaha, beside a functional Norwegian-built school, Bayi meets Erasto Zambi, his Canada- and East Germany-trained coach. They gaze for a moment over the school's gray cinder track. It was here, says Zambi, that Bayi trained for his race in the African Games in 1972, in Lagos, Nigeria, a race that turned out to be a revelation. "In Munich, Filbert ran in the pack and he lost in the qualifying. In Lagos, Kipchoge Keino was the big opponent, and he had said he was running his last race. Keino has a best two hundred meters of 22.7. Bayi has a 24.9, so if it comes to the last two hundred, Keino will win. I told Bayi, 'We don't expect you to win anyway; you go to your effort, and either he will catch you or he will not. He probably will, but if you have run well, you will break your best record and set a new Tanzania record.' He stayed in bed all day and awoke only half an hour before the race. He did exactly as I told him. He went away from the start so fast, people thought he would never finish." Zambi's eyes shine with the memory. "But when he got to the last turn with two hundred meters to run, Keino was far back down the straight. Filbert won. And that was when he found the idea of his way to run."

Bayi joins Zambi in the coach's green Volkswagen Beetle, "because it is better on the trails." As they jounce along a red and dusty road the passenger door constantly flies open. Zambi reaches across Bayi each time and pulls it violently shut. "Hang on," he says. The road narrows to a sandy track through lumpy plowed fields, citrus and cashew orchards, clusters of mud and wattle huts with thatched roofs, their windows covered with chicken wire and burlap. Finally they reach the shamba, a compound of small buildings housing chickens and an attendant, surrounded by groves of fruit. The bananas, papaya, peas, pineapple, and sugarcane all grow together, twining into a bounteous jungle. Bayi is excited, disappearing into the thickets at a lope, returning with great stalks of bananas, papaya the size of loaves of bread, and his prize, an armload of hard, tiny, white tomatoes. "The reason why we come to the farm is that everything is cheaper," he says. "A papaya that is twenty-five cents in town is only ten cents here." He prowls in the cane while Zambi mounts a small rise and looks onto the neighboring land. "It is amazing how things grow here," he says. "If they get enough water, it is only six months from planting to harvesting bananas. But the rains are not regular. This man has water, so his farm is rich, but those people across the valley do not. The government is trying to help. Right now they are digging one well for every twenty families."

Bayi does not come from this coastal area but from the highland village of Karatu, ninety miles from Arusha, west of Kilimanjaro. His mother still lives there with four of her eight children. "I don't know why I got this name, Filbert," be says. "The priest gave me this name. My tribal name, given at birth, is Habiye. I don't know what that means, either, but I have been teased because the word for hyena is *habiyet.*" He goes on to say that his father died before he was born and his mother soon remarried, so he was raised by a stepfather. "It is different from Europe or America, I think, how Africans treat stepchildren. There was a time when my stepbrother and I took the cows into the forest and they became excited and ran away. We came home and said the cows are lost and my stepfather beat me, but he did not beat his own son. So I thought, 'He cannot be my father.'" There is an artless grace to Bayi's English, his third language after Iraqw and Swahili, and it often takes on a certain aphoristic finality.

"When you are born, you can't know what is in front of you," he says, "and when you are grown and look back, there is nothing you can change."

"What caused your real father's death?" he is asked.

"Poisoned. They gave him poison."

"*Who* gave him poison?"

"My mother didn't tell me everything. He was traveling, selling goats and cows. Some people didn't like him." He goes to the hen house, emerging with two dozen eggs in a square metal can, and they drive to the home of the farmer, where they are ushered through a courtyard filled with quiet, staring children, and into a dim room, where it is cool. They sit on sofas with ornate lavender antimacassars. A woman brings large glasses of water. The farmer, a natty man named A. Ruben Pallangyo, accepts payment for the fruit, asking Bayi's new army assignment. Bayi explains that he has been relieved of his duties as an administrator at an officer-training school to devote all his energies to Olympic training. Before his world record at 1,500 meters, he had been a sergeant working in aircraft maintenance. "My specialty was the frame," he says with a proud little nod. Then he was given a commission. "But officers don't use a spanner, they just give advice," so his work on airplanes ceased, with regret. "I want to be a pilot someday," he says with feeling, "but there is a long way to go between technician and pilot. I hope after the Olympics I can begin to learn."

Back in the car, Bayi shouts, "Chicken. Now we get chicken." In a few minutes they draw up to an infernal scene. In a small space between houses and barns, dark water boils in oil drums placed over sooty fires. Boys carry spurting chickens from a block where their heads have been chopped off to the caldrons, and then, plucking as they go, to men seated on old tires who eviscerate and quarter the birds. Adolescent boys, so lean that the skin moving over the ridges of their abdominal muscles seems translucent, their bare feet coated with blood and feathers pack the chickens into wet plastic bags. A centipede, six inches long and gleaming black, moves along one wall. "It is not dangerous," says Zambi. He kicks it, and the sound is that of kicking a rock.

As Bayi receives his still-twitching chicken, there is a cry from a nearby hen house. "A snake," says Bayi, and he joins a knot of people shouting and pointing into the thatch of the roof at a smooth, soft, gray-brown snake that looks very much like the rope holding the roof poles together. "Don't go near," says Bayi. "I hate snakes."

"Of course it is poisonous," says a man. "All snakes in Tanzania are poisonous." That this is not true does not calm Bayi. He picks up some rocks and lobs them tentatively into the thatch. But when a man comes up with a long stick, meaning business, Bayi beats it back to the car.

Fully provisioned, Bayi and Zambi return to Kibaha for lunch in a student cafeteria. They order omelets and mtindi, a pungent milk beverage, sometimes said to be made with cow's urine, containing soft, filamented curds. Bayi eats his omelet with his fingers, saying it is perfectly proper in Tanzania to tell a waiter you know where your hands have been, but you cannot be sure about his silverware. He is asked if he ever receives offers from U.S. college recruiters. "Yes, many. I say I have army duties to fulfill. But all these colleges teach is bookkeeping, geography, salesmanship. I say, 'Do you have a school for airplane maintenance?' Then they stop writing."

A bashful youth comes for an autograph. "Why not?" says Bayi. When the boy has gone, Bayi shows a small, composed smile. "It is good. When I become old, there will come from the children other good distance runners."

The talk turns to opponents. "I like to make friends with anybody. There are athletes who do not, men who cannot accept the chance of losing, but most are good. I like Steve Williams, my best American friend. John Walker is the same way. My teammate Suleiman Nyambui and Steve Prefontaine were friends, they both loved parties. . . . Because you know you can't win every time."

He orders a cup of tea and puts in several teaspoons of sugar.

"You certainly like sweets," he is told.

"Myself, I am sweet," he replies, smiling.

*   *   *

Dr. Lloyd Drake, physician and counselor to John Walker, has a spacious home in the Auckland suburb of Papatoetoe. Just now it is filled with cables, cameras, and television people filming a documentary on Walker. Drake reminds one of a character from *The Wind in the Willows*—the Badger, perhaps. A tidy, gregarious man, he is crisply turned out in plaid bell-bottomed slacks, a lime-green shirt, and salmon tie. Walker, after stretching in the doorframe, is filmed going through a Harvard step test and relating his training of the previous day to Drake. He is perfectly natural, to the point of breaking his laces while changing shoes. Then the television people take him off to the garden and Drake discusses his Achilles' tendons.

"John is a stiff, muscular person, all power but not flexible. His soleus muscles in the calves are very fibrosed. The elasticity is going, thus putting more stress on the Achilles' tendons. So he's having massage to break down the fibrous matter, to keep those muscles supple. It is a progressive problem only so long as he tries to push harder in training. How long he can run depends on how long he races hard. At his present rate, his athletic lifetime couldn't be over three, perhaps four years. Be assured, we'll get him through the Olympics if I have to massage his legs myself."

The phone rings. Drake answers, learning that Walker's world record for the mile has finally been ratified by the International Amateur Athletic Federation, after having been held up by the old question of a pacemaker who did not finish the race. (The IAAF once had a rule requiring pacemakers to complete the distance. It was an attempt at discouraging planned record attempts.) Drake goes out to the garden, where the cameras are on Walker, sprawled on the grass, speaking of his early career. Drake pauses a moment, then crouches beside Walker. "Your mum just rang, John, to say that your world mile record has finally been accepted."

Walker looks up at him sharply. "Is that a fair bug?"

"Fair bug, John."

Walker falls backward on the lawn, arms over his head. Then abruptly he struggles up, remembering the camera. "This has been hanging on for months," he says somewhat sheepishly, as if he feels he ought to narrate the scene. "I had to have my doubts. I felt I'd run so damn hard that night—that someone else leading the first 800 was my luck—and then to have the thought of someone coming along and wiping it out with a pen. . . . Well, it's good to have it over."

Drake returns to his sitting room, glowing. He addresses himself to the sort of life Walker leads. "They live it up in Europe, do John and Rod Dixon, racing, traveling, partying. God only knows how he does it. I think he'd be better for more rest, less night life, but this seems to be his balance. If he were restricted, it might produce tensions. I can only wonder what the pressures are, running at the level he does. But when he's looking buggered, I'll ask him to get in some early nights. He'll have two or three. But its just his balance, that raw energy. He works hard, he trains hard, he plays hard. I don't want to spoil that. That's John Walker."

Walker departs and heads for Mount Smart Stadium, a grassy bowl that has New Zealand's only Tartan track. His coach, Arch Jelley, is standing on the infield, giving times as runners pass. A small man with steel-wool hair escaping from a golf cap, he has on brown oxfords, pink socks, green walking shorts, a yellow shirt. His face is weathered and given to a grin that is sharp in the corners, seeming wolfish, but Jelley, a schoolmaster, is a marvel to one used to the authoritarian ways of U.S. college coaches. He considers himself a counselor, with no leverage save the faith of the runner. "John has had a hard sort of life," he says. "He left school at seventeen and had to fend for himself in odd jobs. Once he saw he was doing well at running, he simply wanted to be the best. I don't sort of hover over him. I see him once a week or a fortnight when he's doing his buildup, more often when he's doing track work." Nor does Jelley go with Walker to races outside Auckland or nearby towns. "I think that's best, to encourage independence in runners. Eventually they've got to have that, haven't they?"

Walker stands beside his coach. "Taking a night off," he says. "Leg not the best." Jelley nods. Walker says that because of the time he has been giving to the media he hasn't been able to work effectively (he is an advertising salesman for a radio station). "My boss said, 'Don't worry about it, mate.' That's a bit better understanding than we've had." Walker drives home, passing a sign in his town of Manurewa that says BLIND PEDESTRIANS CROSS HERE. The Walker house—until recently John lived with his parents—is beige clapboard with a corrugated iron roof. The living room strikes one as similar to Bayi's, with the marble-based trophies, the sheepskin, a photograph of an 800-meter race at Mount Smart with Bayi leading Walker. There is a picture of a racehorse, Master John, whose next offspring will be called John Walker.

Leah Walker, John's mother, is a large, sometimes booming woman from whom he inherits his shape of nose and eye. Both his sisters, Leona and Sue, are tall, large-boned.

Rod Dixon and Walker will race over 1,500 meters the next night. Now Dixon and his wife Debbie arrive for dinner. They look through the program for the meet, but Walker's attention wanders. He speaks of having had a fine lunch that day. "I'm a little vague on the place and the food, but it was good company," he says. "Marvelous company."

Dixon looks up knowingly. "These women will be the death of you."

Walker lies back in his lounger and considers. With relish, he says, "Good."

*   *   *

The track in Dar es Salaam's National Stadium is of hard asphalt, which seems to have been shoveled in by hand and patted into place with the back of a spade, leaving hillocks. On the homestretch, where military parades are conducted, it is covered with a thin layer of sand. The backstretch is strewn with chunks of broken coral. In the afternoon a hand placed on its gritty, elephant-gray surface will be jerked away, burning. Surely, this is one of the worst tracks in the world. Filbert Bayi runs intervals on it five times a week.

"Yesterday he did two 300's in 38, two 400's in 57, one 500 in 1:12.5," says Erasto Zambi. "It was good because it was his first track running after his malaria. Today he and Nyambui will do 400's at varying speeds." Bayi has warmed up with a mile jog from his house and several rapid laps of the infield. Now he sits beside Zambi and takes a little rest, slipping off his training shoes. His feet show no visible veins and tendons, but are smooth, like the rest of him. His calves are the opposite of Walker's, being long and narrow. His power is in his thighs, but nowhere is the muscle clearly defined. He differs from Nyambui, who has veins standing out on his legs, shoulders, and arms. Bayi runs his fingers between his toes, picking at a callus, and slowly eases on his spikes.

There is no sense of anticipation, of hard work ready to be done. A friend asks about his plans to be married, and Bayi smiles, almost shyly. "The wedding was to have been last August, but my fiancee got pregnant and we had to put it off until after the Olympics. Instead we had a birth, a boy." One is reminded of a line by Roger Fouquer in *The Makonde and Their Culture*: "In traditional black African society the only unpardonable sin is sterility." Zambi remarks that they shouldn't cool off too much. Bayi and Nyambui rise and walk across the track to the starting point and begin, doing a 61.5 for 400 meters, then walking and jogging a lap.

"I don't think we will soon get another so good as Filbert," says Zambi softly watching the pair trudge into the wind on the backstretch like a pair of burdened old prospectors. "He is so self-disciplined. For example, he must rest every afternoon; if he doesn't rest he does very poorly. He doesn't drink, he doesn't smoke, he doesn't chase after women. He goes to bed between seven-thirty and eight-thirty every night and is up at five a.m. to do his cross-country running. Then during the day he has lunch at his relatives', where his fiancee and child are staying, and sleeps for an hour and a half, two hours. I told him, 'Why don't you get married?' He said, 'I don't want to get involved in family things until after the Olympics. I know how hard it is to keep a woman.' It is this intelligent self-discipline, so unique in such a young man, that explains why he runs so well."

Bayi's next 400, in which he draws away from Nyambui near the end, is 53.0. Zambi smiles, musing. "People say running for its own sake is too difficult. In football you run because there is always something you are chasing for, but in athletics there is nothing. It is so tough to hold a record in a world with Europeans and Americans and Australians and New Zealanders. . . . Ordinary people who know little of running say it is so hard, Filbert must have some supernatural ability somewhere. . . . I was discussing recently with a gentleman I met in the market. He said, 'Filbert has magic in him.'" The runners pass, accelerating. "It is not magic," Zambi says firmly, watching them flow over the rocky surface. They finish in 61.0. "I cannot claim I am Filbert's coach. I am just helping him. He has developed a consciousness of himself, a knowledge of what he must do. He has so many coaches—every trip the officials assign different coaches. Sometimes he has been furious at managers who didn't know what to do. I don't blame him when he says,

'I have no coach.' He knows more about what he is doing than any of us."

Bayi's fourth 400 is 56.5, his fifth 63.0. Strangely, the two runs seem identical, so balanced is Bayi's stride. To judge the pace, the observer must watch Nyambui, whose torso comes erect on the faster laps, whose arms lower and pump. Nyambui lives in Mwanza, near Lake Victoria where he is a math and Swahili teacher. He has come to train with Bayi before they embark on an early-season tour of races in the United States and Italy. Alone, he had struggled to do 64's. "You lose alone," says Zambi rather sternly. "You win alone so you must train alone. Filbert Bayi does not mind being alone, but other athletes, they say they need friends along at practice. I think he has created it, this self-discipline." He pauses to time Bayi's sixth 400, a 52.8. "Filbert was raised by his stepfather. He was treated very rigidly. African customs don't give very much liberty. Then there was his tribe—Iraqw. It is one of those that is very hard working. It is a shame in Filbert's tribe to be told you are lazy. There are those of other tribes who do not understand him, who say he trains this hard so he will get a good job, so he will get assistance. This is a wrong assumption. Filbert Bayi runs because it is in him. He always says: 'I love sport' and 'I want to run for my nation.'"

His last 400 is run in 57.0. "One thing Filbert's success has done, it has stimulated the country. Previously, one who was teaching sports—especially other than football—was considered a useless man. After Filbert's world record, people in the army, the schools, the police—if they ask time to train, they will get it. The officers say, 'Go. Be like Bayi.'"

After a recovery lap Bayi sits down. He touches his temples, complaining of a headache. There is a V-shaped scar on the inside of his left knee. "That was in Oslo," he says, where he was spiked while experimenting with running in the pack. "I learned," he says. "And if I forget I have only to look at my leg." As he removes his spikes, carefully examining a blister on a toe, another runner, a man so gap-toothed and ugly as to be fascinating, quietly places Bayi's flats before him, in the manner of a servant.

*   *   *

In a sweat suit, John Walker arrives somewhat later than expected at the apartment of John and Debbie LeGrice for dinner and a massage. He has come from a run in Cornwall Park with Arch Jelley. Both were sore, Jelley favoring a calf muscle pulled while playing soccer on the beach. Walker still aching in his Achilles' tendon.

Debbie LeGrice, a former 400-meter runner who was coached by Peter Snell, has prepared a rubbing table from a door on sawhorses, a thick woolen blanket, and a paisley sheet. Now it serves as a dinner table. She and Walker eat shrimp cocktail, steak and chips, lime cheesecake. The apartment's large windows give a view of lights scattered on the harbor. There is a rustling wind in the trees, soft music on the stereo. "Do you want to know the day of your death?" asks Walker, and relates some of the clairvoyant gifts of his grandmother, Mrs. Margaret Broadley. "She told one woman, she would discover her husband lying in the yard and, thinking him drunk, she would kick him, but he would be dead. And it happened." Debbie's eyes are wide.

The masseuse, a soft-voiced woman named Phyllis, enters, still wearing the starched dirndl of a waitress in the Swiss restaurant downstairs. Walker strips to his shorts while the dishes are cleared, then lowers himself stomach first onto the table. He appears full of tension, arching his back, his head up. "Just be very careful of my Achilles," he says. "They're still quite tender."

"Don't worry," Phyllis says gently, speaking to Debbie, who sits nearby. "I won't do anything to harm him."

Debbie hands Walker a glass of sparkling red wine. He sips and places it on a side table. Phyllis begins on his lower calves, at the sides of the tendons, smoothing on oil, rubbing upward toward the knees, her pigtails swaying.

"Why did you let your legs get in such a bad state, John?" It is less a question than a sigh.

He puts his head on the pillow, his chest swelling.

After a few minutes Phyllis moves on to his hamstrings, rubbing with both hands together, isolating individual muscles, sliding them between fingers and thumbs. She asks how he is putting up with the demands of the press.

"I don't like it, the same questions time and again. But it's a difficult situation. You can't just say no. That would create a bad press, which would probably cause me more worry than what I've got now. That ointment won't carry into the muscle, will it?"

"No, of course not. Now I want to have a go at your back, John, if you don't mind." She works carefully along his sides, up his arms to his shoulders. "Purely to relax you, this. It's necessary. You can't just punish your muscles and not give them anything back."

"You're not strong enough to really do therapy. My legs are hard, sinewy, fibery. You need power to break down the fibers."

"John Walker, you should be grateful," says Debbie. "Phyllis chopped off her lovely long fingernails today, all for your body."

Walker's expression softens. "You're beautiful, Phyllis."

She works on his deltoids, the base of his neck. He writhes a little. She asks him to roll onto his back and goes over him again, from his toes, ending by gently stroking his forehead, his temples, the bridge of his nose and his cheekbones, smoothing away his sun-streaked hair. It has been an hour and a half. He is finally limp, eyes closed, one knee up.

"Does that feel nice?" asks Debbie, herself mesmerized.

Walker doesn't open his eyes. "I don't respond to touch," he says. Then his head comes up and he shoots her an apologetic glance. "I feel a beauty, honest. Beautifully only. Do you have a bath?"

"Shower only, I'm afraid."

"I like a bath. I fall asleep in a bath and wake up with the water bloody freezing, scum all over."

He takes a shower, singing *They Call the Wind Maria*, and comes out in his sweats once more, carrying his shoes. The laces are tufted with knots. He pulls hard on them and one snaps.

*   *   *

Filbert Bayi is awakened by birds with voices like drops falling into a pool. It is

5 A.M., an hour before dawn. He puts on green shorts, sweat top, and road shoes and sets off in the dark, down a potholed road, heading south past the National Stadium, past an army camp, Quonset huts inside a mud wall, where the air is thick with the powerful ancient aromas of spiced dates, coffee. He passes a company of soldiers double-timing, looking sourly over at him. Outside of town, Bayi accelerates gradually, through an infinite number of gears, his reaching stride getting the most out of his long thighs, going hard up every hill, fast and relaxed on the descents, through low, malarial places where pink light in the East is reflected on water beneath stunted trees. He runs through villages, scattering goats. People stand transfixed as he shoots past, now running better than five minutes per mile. Cocks crow. Baobab trees and tin-roofed shanties are silhouetted to his left. To the right, hills become visible, and columns of smoke above distant fields. After thirty minutes, at a bus stop in the village of Mbagala, he turns and heads back. Traffic builds, trucks driving him onto the road's rocky shoulder. He runs the last mile to the stadium hard, then stops to stretch on the steeplechase water barrier. "In China I met old people, but still strong," he says. "One hundred years old and still doing exercises." He demonstrates with a slow, graceful pirouette. "I want to live two centuries." He laughs. "I don't like to die. I want to live."

He jogs to his home. At such times he reveals a fine bodily sentience. "You feel now without weight," he says, "very light, very relaxed." Chickens cross the bark yard. "I feel like something cold, very cold, to drink."

Over a Coke, he discusses his place in Tanzania. "President Nyerere has spoken of rights and duties. In the Western countries everyone talks only of rights, but in China, in the East, duties to your community are important. He said that Tanzania, which is poor and needs to develop, ought to emphasize every man's duty to his brothers, to do his job not for himself only, but for Tanzania. I feel this way about my running." He will never turn professional. "The best way to live is not to have problems, to be too fat. Richness . . . There are many ways you get the riches." His tone suggests that all are vexations to the spirit. "I wish not to have problems. I am a simple man."

*   *   *

The evening of John Walker's final race of the New Zealand season, a 1,500 at Mount Smart, is filled with a cold, swirling wind that has the crowd of five thousand huddling under blankets. Walker comes late, distracted. Trying to get to the meet on time, he had been clocked by a patrolman at eighty. "Halfway to the car he did a double take and said, 'Oh, Mr. Walker, why can't you do your racing on the track?' He let me off with a warning. It might have been better to go to jail. I'll be lucky to do 3:42 in these conditions." During the introduction of 1,500-meter entrants, Rod Dixon rolls his eyes as Walker is hailed as "the man you've all come to see."

Larry Wiechern, a stocky half-miler, is the rabbit, streaking away at the start with only Walker going after him. The two have 20 yards on the field at the 400, passed in 56.0. Walker trails along the backstretch the second time, then calmly takes the lead with 850 meters to go, runs a curve into a cloud of dust blown up from outside the track, and passes 800 meters in 1: 56. It is a terrific pace. The announcer, recalling that Walker was 1:55 in his record mile, says he is disappointed.

At the bell, with one lap to go, Walker looks skyward in supplication for an instant and shoulders into the wind, passing 1,200 meters in 2:54.2. Noting that splendid time, the observer is on his feet, shouting him home—and is told by people behind him to sit down. Through the backstretch and turn Walker lifts, running with abandon, finding out what is left. In the last yards he is tired, his form going. Across the line he sways out, and jogs, recovering rapidly, while word of the time comes from the announcer: 3:35.6, the equal of a 3:52.8 mile. There are events left to be run, but the crowd starts flowing out, disappointed, while the athletes on the field run to Walker, forming an applauding line along the curve as he trots back, shaking hands. They know what kind of a run it has been.

"It was bloody windy," Walker says. "My throat's burning." But he knows how well he has run and glories in it. "I'd have killed him. I will kill him."

Arch Kelley beams from within an oversized windbreaker. "I think we'd have seen the world record go under calm conditions. John is running very strongly, very determined to do a good job."

* * *

Anna, Bayi's fiancee, a shy, delicate woman, holds his hand as they walk through Dar es Salaam's tiny, chaotic airport. She is gaily dressed in orange, but is pensive, her eyes downcast. Behind the pair comes a throng of sleek dignitaries and bustling aides to see Bayi off on his trip to the United States. The luggage is taken and the group is ushered to a lounge by a customs official. Anna promises to run a little while Bayi is gone. "Crocodile pace," says Filbert. "Very slow."

"I'm not sad," she says, compressing her lips. She is asked if she will be able to go to Montreal. "I don't know," she whispers, "it is a great luxury."

She is allowed to walk with Bayi through the night to the bottom of the steps to the plane, along with the president of the Tanzanian Amateur Athletic Association, the Director of Sport for the Ministry of Youth and Culture, and half a dozen others. Bayi squeezes her hand and she steps away, brave, smiling, as the officials send him up the ramp. "We consider you a roving ambassador," says the sports minister. Bayi gets to the door and gives a flash of a backward glance, checking. Anna nods and he is gone.

* * *

The morning after the 3:35.6, Walker runs on the Domain. It is hard to warm up. Stretching does not relieve the pain. Jelley has written him a letter, and Dr. Drake has supported his advice not to jeopardize Olympic training. Walker decides not to race indoors, but merely to have a holiday in the United States. The following evening, wearing a white New Zealand sweat top made by Debbie LeGrice, he boards a flight for Los Angeles. "I'll be right," he says to gathered friends, and blithely departs amid press photographers' flashes. There are no officials in the bon voyage party, which repairs to the airport bar. Dr. Drake, growing increasingly jovial, says, "He's taking it well, the not racing. It's a measure of his determination to succeed in the Olympics." Ross Pilkington agrees. "If he's quiet, or seems to be worrying about other people, then he's crook. If he sings in the bath like he has been, he's coming right."

Leah Walker speaks of the ox she has purchased for her freezer. "Thirty-four cents a pound is not bad for a five-hundred-pound beast." She thinks of the mushrooms needed to accompany all those steaks, recalling the day John came home from running with the cry of "Give me sacks."

"He had found that little paddock at the rear of the quarry, hidden by stones, and it was white with mushrooms. He filled my window seat with them, a foot deep." She notices Debbie LeGrice quietly listening, her expression far away. "Ah," says Leah Walker, "he's like a ray of light round us all."

The observer withdraws, thinking of Bayi and Walker, the luck of these balanced and gifted men to arrive at their best together, hoping luck will hold against disease and strained connective tissue for a while longer, that the Olympic 1,500 meters may be doubly lit.

—June 1976

Postscript:

Walker's tendons held. Bayi's malaria lay dormant. But they did not keep their appointment. The black African boycott of the Montreal Games, an action initiated by Tanzania's President Nyerere to protest New Zealand's rugby exchanges with South Africa, kept most black Africans out of the Olympics.

John Walker won the 1,500 meters in a slow 3:39.2, kicking past the field over the final 300 meters.

Four years later, New Zealand joined the U.S. led boycott of the Moscow Olympics, protesting the Soviet invasion of Afghanistan. But Tanzania took part.

Bayi, leaving the 1,500 to England's Steve Ovett and Sebastian Coe, ran the steeplechase. He set a world-record pace in the final, tired dramatically over the last lap, and was passed for the gold medal by Poland's Bronislaw Malinowski. Suleiman Nyambui, who had attended the University of Texas at El Paso, was second to Ethiopia's Miruts Yifter in the 5000 meters. Their two silvers were the first Olympic medals ever won by Tanzanians.

Lasse Viren

Snow runs in blurry white trails across the road to Myrskylä. Ravens rise and dip on the wind beneath the sky of silver gray, a sky without a trace of warmth or hope. Snowfields spread to dark horizons of timber. Rust-red barns stand amid the trees, piles of golden-ended logs beside them. Smoke from farmhouses is whipped away and dispersed by the wind. People wearing wool or fur overcoats stand at bus stops along the road, slowly turning white on their windward sides. Once on the buses they shake out like collies. This is spring. This is Finland.

Throughout the Middle Ages, the Finns, who have inhabited this forested land for two thousand years, were believed potent sorcerers, able to call up fierce storms. Joseph Conrad and Jack London carried that idea into this century, and much of the rest of Europe still shakes its head at these 4.7 million people who speak in mystifying incantations and rush steaming and naked from their saunas into hoarfrost and icy lakes, laughing.

Of contemporary sorcerers, one stands alone. Lasse Viren, in perfection of that other fine Finnish tradition of running long distances, won the 5000 and 10,000 meters in the 1972 Olympic Games in Munich. In 1976, in Montreal, he won both races again, a defense never before accomplished. But the circumstances of Viren's career and character—his many poor races in non-Olympic competition, his carefully kept privacy, his mildly sarcastic way with curious reporters—have evoked a storm of accusations. It is said that his medals were won with the help of "blood doping," a misleading term for an experimental technique whereby some of an athlete's blood is withdrawn and the oxygen-carrying hemoglobin extracted and stored. When the athlete's system has regenerated the missing red blood cells in a few weeks, the hemoglobin is returned, giving the recipient a higher concentration than can occur naturally. Since distance running depends on oxygen-carrying capacity, the runner, theoretically, prospers.

Does Viren benefit from this procedure? What sort of man is he, this distant subject of rumor? To find out, one begins on the road to Myrskylä—meaning a place of storms—a town of twenty-three hundred located on a lake sixty-five miles northeast of Helsinki. You come through a thick pine wood, passing a dairy and a furniture factory, a bar, a couple of wooden churches, and a bank. A mile beyond the town, beside Syvajarvi Lake, is a low brick building that at first seems to be a little elementary school or perhaps a fire station. It is Lasse Viren's house. On the door is a small printed message, in red, which translates to "Finish smoking or it will finish you."

The door is opened by Lasse Viren, dressed in T-shirt and jeans, looking wan and sleepy on this cold midmorning. He accepts a gift of tulips and leads his visitors, once they have removed their shoes, into a sparkling kitchen. He puts the flowers into a scarlet glass vase that clashes with their pastel yellow and carries them into the living room, a large space filled with soft white leather couches. One wall is taken up with cabinets displaying cups and trays and lacquer ware and beer steins and crystal goblets and wooden drinking vessels. Viren places the tulips on a table and sags into a lounge chair, his back to large, double-paned windows that give a view of ice-locked lake and wooded ridge. This house stands on land that the surrounding counties made available to him for a very reasonable price after his medals of 1972. It was decorated by Finland's leading furniture and fabric designers. There is a bronze bust of Viren, executed by one of Finland's best sculptors, paid for by a group of business people. It is a fair likeness, and because the statue is informed with athletic energy—it is obviously Viren in competition, clear-eyed and vibrant—it looms in contrast to the boyish, swaybacked figure now slouching beside it.

Viren's voice is high and nasal because he has a little cold. He understands English but prefers, in this formal first meeting, to speak Finnish. The stresses in Finnish are placed at the beginnings of words, so his speech contains, at the end of every phrase, whispers. These seem almost a second language, a language between the lines, soft and faintly conspiratorial.

Perhaps this accentuates the enigma that is Viren. It was a misunderstanding, a language problem, he says, that inflamed the blood-doping aspersions at Montreal. In the interview after winning the 5000 meters, he had been faced with argumentative questioners and had seemed to gloat in the furor, asking in seeming mock innocence if such a thing as blood doping really was possible, never flatly denying his use of it. Now he says he thinks the translation was faulty. "I did deny it in Montreal," he says. "I meant to. I don't remember much of that interview. I was tired and the marathon was the next day. But no, I have never blood-doped. I have never experimented with it. They have never done that to me. Why are journalists always talking like that? No one does it." He asserts that if he had, he would say so, because the practice is not forbidden by Olympic rules.

Viren's wife of a year, Päivi, comes home from shopping. She is a tall, strong woman who at once sweeps up the bouquet of tulips, returning with them in a clear crystal vase. Lasse seems not to notice. He says that his honest way to winning Olympic races is intelligent planning of peak performance. He wins Olympic races because they are almost the only ones—the European championships excepted—that he cares about. For this, too, Viren has often been criticized.

"I don't care what they write," he says. "I know the expectations of people in this country. Every day they'd like a new world record. But I don't care. I am running only for the Olympic Games." For Viren, the need to be consistently excellent amounts almost to a flaw in an athlete, an insecurity that must be constantly assuaged by winning. "There are runners and there are runners," he says calmly. "Some do well in other races, some run fast times, but they cannot do well in the ultimate, the Olympics." This is expressed almost with a trace of sadness.

"The value of the Olympics remains," he continues. He does not gesture so much as he fidgets. "If you win, you're lasting. And the Games include all the best runners; they are the true world championships. I'm not the only one who thinks this way. All runners want to run against the very best. The question is not why I run this way, but why so many others cannot. Seventeen men had faster times than I did going into the Montreal 5000 meters. The question is why they could not do it again in the Olympic Games."

Viren's mystification over the weakness of the world's runners has softly turned to pride. He grins, remembering, looking smug. Päivi, opening a box of chocolates for the guests, smiles at him fondly, as at a goofy child. "The plan was to run a fast last kilometer, to keep the good milers like New Zealand's Rod Dixon and Dick Quax from being able to sprint at the end." He says no more, because obviously it worked perfectly, leading to an incredible stretch run that saw Viren, his stride unchanging, drawing away from the open-mouthed, staggering Kiwis.

Now he hooks his arms over the back of his chair, stretching out that spare (134-pound), lanky (five-foot-eleven-inch) frame. His head lolls back to gaze idly at his home's beautiful sandblasted pine ceiling, at his statue with its Caesar's tousled hair and eyes that seem to see more than those they simulate. He planned his finest hour, and had it happen. Twice. And he planned again and had it happen again. Twice more. He's right. They can't take that away from him. But to speak of peaks is to imply valleys, times of mortality. To have one's finest hour, and to know it, means the rest of one's life is decline, an observed falling away. Can a man who has achieved such excellence be content simply with memory, even one grandly cast in bronze?

Viren was born in Myrskylä. His son is the fourth generation of his family born there. He attended elementary school for eight years, worked with his father driving and repairing trucks, and spent eight months in the army before becoming a country policeman. He began running as a teenager "because as you can see"—he hunches around and looks out over the white reaches of the lake—"there is nothing to do in Myrskylä." Nevertheless, that is where he wishes to spend the rest of his life.

Over a lunch of black coffee and *lihapiirakka*, a pastry containing chopped meat, egg, and rice, Viren says, "In summer this is a wonderful place. The lake is there for swimming. There is a sauna . . ." He trails off, and is asked if the prospect of being a celebrity in a more urban setting ever tempts him. "The ideal situation in life," he says, uncomfortable in the need to speak abstractly, "is when you are free to do what you want. If I am on my way somewhere and I meet a friend, I want to be able to stop and talk, to have a coffee. You can do that here. In the city it is all schedules."

He speaks of his work as a policeman not as a calling but as a good job for a runner, permitting much time off for travel and training. "The work is varied. We cover four counties and have to do paper work and detective work and take care of traffic accidents." He has never caught a really big criminal, but then there has never been a murder in Myrskylä. He thinks there may once have been a suicide.

Viren is not politically active, saying he has no time for that, but enjoys tinkering with his orange Peugeot 504 with fake leopard-skin seat covers. In the early years of his success he was famously shy, and marathoner Pekka Tiihonen, his roommate in Munich, once told a story of Viren running down an apple thief in an orchard. Having tackled the man, he was so embarrassed that another policeman had to come up and formally say, "You're under arrest."

Viren smiles in seeming recognition as this is repeated for his corroboration, then says, "I can't remember that."

The city offices of Myrskylä display a pair of shoes—one from Montreal, one from

Munich—given by Viren in thanks for the community's support. "I certainly can't complain," he says. But when asked if he considers himself lucky, he takes on the expression of a man sensing he is about to be tricked. "Of course you need good luck, but you also must work hard. I'm no more lucky than any other runner. The main thing is to do hard work and never lose hope."

He switches the talk back to Myrskylä, to the virtues of knowing all his neighbors, of taking strength from natural, peaceful surroundings.

"But you are spending that strength in running," says a visitor. "What will happen when that is over? Will you still be happy here?"

"It's impossible to tell, isn't it?" Viren replies.

Riding back to Helsinki, the visitors talk. Rami Hannonen, a Finnish marketing analyst who has done the interpreting, is agitated, unsatisfied at this first meeting with his nation's foremost celebrity. "He seems to have hit the right balance," he says, "To run in faraway cities and still have the life he grew to love. But to not wish to go beyond that, to not be interested in anything else . . . I couldn't live like that."

Hannonen seems struck, too, by Viren's lassitude. "It doesn't seem to matter what he talks about, he never gets excited. You see no evidence of force of character."

"Well, we know that is there," the other visitor replies. "Might he not be simply a man perfectly suited for running, without great ambition or talent otherwise?"

"Yes," says Hannonen. "But I don't believe that ambition is ever cured by success."

The Virens have been massively exploited by Finland's women's magazines. Almost monthly they smile from the covers of slick, superficial rags, Päivi with the face of a thousand windblown Nordic wives pressed to the shoulder of her rugged, scraggly-bearded husband. Inside there are more pictures of them jogging or gardening or wrinkling noses at each other. Connect the dots on the pencil page and there is Lasse again. But the text of these pieces is oddly abusive. "A clown who fell down and who got up and became famous," reads one, remarking on Viren's fall early in the Munich 10,000, where he bounded back to his feet and defeated Emiel Puttemans of Belgium in the world-record time of 27:38.4.

Viren seems to cooperate in these unfunny jokes, giving the reporters the type of answer they want. Asked his secret, he replies, "The milk of a cow in heat." The result is that, like the rest of the world, few Finns have a clear idea of the nature of the man. A Finnish reporter, Juha Numminen, attempted to profile Viren for a newsmagazine. Afterward he lamented Viren's refusal to discuss politics or philosophies. "It was my worst story," he said.

* * *

Fishermen tramp the frozen Helsinki harbor, a white plain stretching away to low islands that in summer curve like whales' backs into the calm Baltic. In August the air from the forest carries a fragrance like sawdust and cream. Now it is cutting, sterile, rushing across the Arctic space. Finns seem to come to their land on its own terms, rejoicing in its sweep and hardness. "Winter," one hears time and again, "is when everything is so clean."

Only the cluttered language seems out of character with such people. Its fourteen cases and absence of prepositions confound the listener. Nothing ever seems to sound the same. But the effect is to bind these people to this land, the only one where they are understood. The experience of being a Finn is far more precise than that of being an American or Russian. The colors of Finland's flag are well chosen, the blue and white, sky and snow, water and birch, the blue eyes and the luminous Nordic complexion. Both Lasse and Päivi Viren have those eyes, a polished granite blue. These are not eyes you fall into, they are hard places, with a deflecting gloss. They have weight. It sometimes seems it must be hard to hold up a head with such eyes. "Eyes," Evelyn Waugh wrote, "pale blue, blank and mad."

There is madness in the spring, a sloppy, dirty time when more snow melts than falls, but still it falls. Helsinki sees its first crocus in May. This is the suicide season, and Finland's rate is one of the highest in the world. "It's when a few things are beginning to bloom and grow," says Hannonen. "The animals are finding each other, birds arrive, and yet the winter-wearied people are so drained, so tired. The contrast is too much for some." Finnish runners, the best and most promising of them, spend a winter month in the Canary Islands or Kenya or Brazil, but seldom run well at indoor events or spring cross-country races. They peak late in the summer, and if Lasse Viren has been good at it in selected summers it is because his whole life has been lived that way. He is a Finn.

Viren began training in earnest in 1969, when he was nineteen. For his coach he sought out Rolf Haikkola, also of Myrskylä. Haikkola was influenced by New Zealand's Arthur Lydiard, whom he got to come to Finland to advise runners and coaches. "Lydiard's ideas of how to bring runners to the best shape at the *right time* seemed ideal for us with our long winter and short racing season." says Haikkola, who is now executive director of the Finnish Amateur Athletic Association. He is a large man with horn-rimmed glasses and fine, receding hair. In 1954 he ran 5000 meters in 14:14.2, which was ninth best in the world that year. Now, in a business suit and polka-dot tie, he sits in Helsinki's Hotel Torni restaurant, where the menu lists snow grouse with cranberry purée and noisettes of reindeer baked in crust. Haikkola speaks in clear, carefully built sentences, and as the evening wears on and empty cognac snifters collect before him, he becomes more voluble.

"Lasse's problems before the Olympics were entirely different," he says. "Six weeks before Munich he ran 5000 in 13:19, so he was ready. But was he too early? We had a test run in Stockholm and he broke the world record for two miles with 8:14. He was ready. But still the newspapers said the peak won't last. So we employed a test to put Lasse's mind at ease. Most of his speed work is not done on the track but out on forest trails or soft roads and in races. He only went on the track three times all that summer. Each time was the same. He would run 200 meters 20 times and we would time him and take his pulse right after each 200. In June he averaged 30 seconds and 190 beats per minute. In July, before the two-mile record, he averaged 29.3 and 186. In August, before the Olympics, he did 27.2 and 172. So we had real proof that there was nothing to worry about. Tactics were easy in Munich because we knew Dave Bedford of England would lead fast. Everything worked according to plan."

Listening, one quickly senses how Viren could place his faith in this rational, assured man.

"Trust doesn't come from personality," Haikkola says. "It comes from being able to *show* a runner what he can do. Before Montreal we gave Lasse the same test. He averaged 28.2 and 182 beats per minute, not his best. His training had been interrupted by a month-long sinus infection that had to be drained six or seven times. So we did another test, to discover what kind of work was needed. He did 5,000 meters on grass by sprinting 50 meters and easing 50 meters, sprinting and easing, 50 sprints in all. He finished in a time of 13:32 (better than all but a handful of runners can do while running an even pace). But his pulse was only 186. In perfect racing condition he would go over 200 after such sustained stress-ease exercise. His body was not reacting to the stress in an efficient manner. It was obvious that he needed additional speed training, but there were only eight days left before the 10,000-meter heats. It was here that Lasse was different from any other runner I've known. He believed me when I said there was still time. Three days later he was quicker; you could see the difference in the action of his ankles. He was reaching his maximum sharpness."

Then there were tactics. "Before every race, just before going to the stadium, we analyze every opponent—his strengths and weaknesses and habits." Haikkola draws out a thick notebook of pages of material on all the best distance runners in the world. "No one seemed to be sure to lead for the first two or three kilometers. So the plan we made was to run the last two kilometers hard." But in the race Carlos Lopes of Portugal ran fast enough to lose everyone but Lasse, and Lasse had only to take the race from Lopes in the last lap. In the 5000, everything developed exactly as we expected.

It was only after his win in the 5000 that Viren decided to enter the marathon. Earlier in the year he had run one 25-kilometer race in Helsinki to become one of the three Finns named for the event, but he had kept open the option not to compete at Montreal until after he had run the two long-distance track races. Then he would decide, and he would run only if he thought he could win the marathon. It was not to be, but, remarkably, the day after his victory in the 5000, Viren finished fifth in the 26-mile road race, thus completing 102,000 meters of Olympic competition.

Seeming at pains to minimize his own role in Viren's accomplishments, Haikkola raises a hand and says, "Now I am going to tell you how Lasse Viren won," and begins to tick off the man's gifts. "His style is the most economical in the world. Using a computer, we found he wastes far less energy than anyone else." Indeed, Puttemans, the world-record holder at 5000 meters and a smoothie himself, says running next to Viren is infuriating. "You're running *hard* and he's floating away as if he's doing nothing."

"I think he is similar to Herb Elliott," says Haikkola, referring to the 1960 Olympic 1,500-meter champion from Australia. "At the end Lasse doesn't change his style. He just puts more energy into it."

There are internal amazements as well. "Lasse's heart is twice as big as that of any other Finnish distance runner. His pulse at rest is thirty-two beats a minute. He has an enormous capacity for transporting oxygen."

Finally, Haikkola comes to the element of faith, about which he is shy, because he is the keeper of it, but he tells of one incident that illustrates the bond between runner and coach. In 1974, Viren pulled his left hamstring muscle but attempted to continue training for the European championships in Rome. "We were in Lapland, in a training camp. Lasse had to hold ice on his leg three times a day. Once he ran too hard and the next morning he could hardly stand." Haikkola describes an outburst of frustration. "Lasse threw his running shoes right into the lake. I went to him . . ." And the listener knows that Haikkola's voice is as it was then, icy and penetrating. "'We will now stop talking about your leg,' I said, 'until after Rome.'" Viren finished third in the 5000 there, then had to have an operation on the muscle in early 1975. The surgeon said it seemed impossible that he had run on it at all.

Wisps of Haikkola's hair lift from his head and his Finnish becomes impassioned when he considers the blood-doping rumors. "When Lasse was asked about it so much he thought it was an insulting bad joke. Maybe the innuendo angered him and made him run faster. But in any case, it's absurd. If it worked with Lasse, why wouldn't we have done it with all our steeplechasers and distance runners? All those medals went to English and Portuguese and New Zealanders and Swedes and Belgians, Poles, West and, East Germans, and Americans. No one here asked how it could be possible for one man to win so much. He was just good. Nurmi, Zatopek, Kuts, they were good. But Lasse, when he wins, it is questioned."

The mention of Nurmi gets Haikkola thinking. "Nurmi was different from Lasse. Lasse is private and shy. But Nurmi was truly, terribly alone."

The father of Finland's running tradition, Paavo Nurmi won Olympic gold medals in the 1920, 1924, and 1928 Olympics, and later became a wealthy businessman, yet always remained reclusive and parsimonious. Toward the end he was bitter. "When Nurmi had his seventy-fifth birthday, our president, Urho Kekkonen, wanted to pay a call and help celebrate," says Haikkola. "Nurmi refused."

Viren has said, "Nurmi offers nothing to the runner of today," but Haikkola represents a connection between the two greatest Finnish Olympians. As a young coach he often sought Nurmi's counsel. "He gave advice, but he would never come talk with my young athletes. 'They don't know me,' he would say. His chief lesson was always this: 'If you want to tell something to an athlete, say it quickly and give no alternatives. This is a game of winning and losing. It is senseless to explain and explain.'"

There is something of that in Viren. "Normally he doesn't like to talk about sport or training. He's doing it so much he doesn't need to dwell on it. He's wary and reserved until he gets to know you. You should run with him, take a sauna with him. He'll loosen up. But you will always have a sense of something hidden in Lasse's mind, something you can never see. He is sensitive. He will be an indulgent father. But he is also hard. When he tries something, he tries to the ultimate. When he fell in Munich, his only reaction was to get up. No second thoughts, no fear. Mohamed Gammoudi, who went down with him, stayed there too long. He lost hope. Lasse Viren doesn't lose hope."

Haikkola the student of long winter preparations and shining summer peaks, influenced Viren to frame his entire career on his conclusions. "In 1972 he won the first gold for Finland in a running event in thirty-six years. The receptions and obligations and business opportunities were so great, he only slept three hours a night for months. [As a result, Viren now has a little sports-shoe distributorship that is run by a brother, Erkki, and a modest trucking venture, run by another brother, Nisse. His youngest brother, Heikki, drives a bus.] We talked. He had to make a decision. He could go for the world records that year or the next, but he was burning the candle at both ends. By Montreal he would be shot. I said choose records or more Olympic medals. He said medals. That made the in-between years easier. Races became part of his training."

Haikkola and Viren charted a plan for 1980. The astonishing thing is that it was made before Montreal. "It was important to decide before. We knew it would be easy to say 'Moscow' if he won in Montreal. But what if he didn't? It is better to make a vow in the wilderness."

*   *   *

There is a strike at the electric facility in Myrskylä, but it has a certain civility—the power goes off and comes back on every two hours. Just now it is off, so Lasse Viren's mother sits in the warmest place in her home, the dining, room. Watery sunshine streams through lace curtains onto antique oak sideboards and heavy cut crystal. Elvi Viren is a prim, pale woman with iron-gray hair, glasses, and a great many large teeth that impart to her face an arresting vigor.

"Lasse was always a peaceful boy," she says in a tone of reverie. "He was terribly shy. It was like milking a cow to get him to say anything. But everything he wanted to do he wanted to do perfectly." She smiles. "Besides working the farm here, Lasse's father drove trucks. [Johann Illmarie Viren, a hard smoker, died of lung cancer in September 1975 at age sixty; thus the force of the placard on Lasse's front door.] After Lasse was three he always wanted to travel with him. He would insist that I wake him so he wouldn't miss an early morning departure. He was quite firm about it. And when he began running races at school, it was the same. There were times, when he was working for his father, and they would be out unloading trucks until eleven o'clock or midnight, but still Lasse would go run. We said to him, 'It couldn't possibly do any good to run this late.' He would say only, 'I must.'

"That was when he was eighteen. He quit mechanical trade school to train more. He left everything else because of running. Yes, we worried. If he wasn't any good he would have given up a lot. But then we thought, well, he *must* be good if he is training so much, and besides he was a wonderful son. The neighbors always said if something happens to you, we'll take care of the kids; and then they'd all bid for Lasse."

Then came Munich. There were premonitions. "Lasse's father saw him in a dream the night before the 10,000 meters. Lasse came to him and said, 'I am going to win.' Before the 5000 his father spoke in his sleep. He said, 'Where can we find a plate big enough for both of the gold medals?'" Elvi Viren says she herself gets a feeling whenever Lasse is winning. "It's like a rush of blood to your head," she says. "Like blushing."

Such feelings have been necessary because she attended neither the Munich nor Montreal Olympics. Thus she was at home on the most glorious day in Myrskylä history the day of the 10,000 gold in 1972. "At first I thought this can't be true," she says with a laugh. "A hundred roses came in one box! And then hundreds of boxes!" Two roses remain in the dining room, gilded. "People cried and the reporters came and tramped through the house, and every Christmas, even now, people see the reruns on television and they call and send presents."

* * *

Doctor Pekka Peltokallio is a huge shambling man whose gray-blond hair gives the impression that someone has dumped a bowl of lentil soup over his head, where it quickly froze. He is good-humored and expansive, alarmingly so, for as soon as the visitor is seated, the great doctor lurches at him, and rips off his shoe and sock to demonstrate how he repaired an ankle injury of Viren's. "The tendon actually slipped over the point of the ankle bone, *here*," he says running a fingernail among delicate muscles and cords and nerves. "We had to make a little groove in the bone below *here*, to ensure it wouldn't pop out again."

Peltokallio gives Viren a thorough examination annually, then sees him once a month briefly. "Socially, we meet more often," Peltokallio says. He and the runner are close friends. The doctor reports his findings to the coach, Haikkola. He says that Viren, like all Finnish distance runners, takes a gram of vitamin E every day and a gram of C three times a day. He takes a multivitamin pill with trace minerals and bee pollen as well. He does not blood-dope.

"There can be no use in adding red blood cells if one's hemoglobin count is above 15, and Viren's is nominally 15.4 to 15.6," says Peltokallio. "That is close to an optimum level. Any less and you carry less oxygen. But any *more*—the doctor hunches over his desk and it creaks under the load—"any more and the blood becomes too thick. It can't work as well. There is a disease where the blood gets too thick. People who have it can get congestive heart failure. They can't pump it. So it is crazy for most runners to try blood exchanges."

Peltokallio has not himself experimented with blood doping, but draws his information from Swiss and Swedish studies. "The reason why people connect Finns with blood doping is that there was a Finnish sportsman some years ago—just about the time of the first experiments in Sweden—who had a hemoglobin level of 11. He tried it and improved dramatically." Peltokallio declines to mention this man's name, but other sources say he probably was Jouko Kuha, who came from obscurity to break the world steeplechase record in 1968. "It is sad that these suspicions take away from Lasse's greatness," says the doctor. "He needs no trick. Why do they single him out?"

The visitor muses that it may be a mixture of jealousy and circumstantial evidence; people cannot understand Viren's seeming inability to win non-Olympic races.

"At the beginning of May last year," says Peltokallio, bristling, "there was the twenty-five-kilometer road race here in Helsinki. Cold weather. Wind. Lasse was not well, with an allergy cold. But he was only four seconds off the world record. Is that a bad race?" He sits quietly for a moment, then growls, "The world has no shame. They can't prove that he did it. So they make me try to disprove it."

He returns to Viren's miraculous physical gifts, relating how because of them he was almost told to quit running. "After his cold he had a really bad race, worse than the worst. He felt awful. I thought he might have pneumonia, so we took a chest X-ray. His lungs were O.K., but the X-ray showed his heart in sharp outline. We compared it to an X-ray taken a couple of months before and there was a huge difference. His heart had grown by about a third. There seemed no way that transformation could take place just by training. He had a grave problem. Four heart specialists came in, and all agreed. Then one, who had sport in his background, said, 'Are we sure both these X-rays were taken in the same phase of respiration? If he was holding his breath in on one and out on the other it might make a difference.' Now we thought this was grasping at a straw. But we took new X-rays, one in, one out, and sure enough the difference was there. Normal people don't do that. The best runners show a tiny difference, but nothing like Lasse's. It's an absolutely unique phenomenon.

Lasse, as is his custom, endured this unnerving inquiry with patience and trust. "You know, when we first began working together six years ago, Lasse wasn't really the ideal patient. He was so shy he seemed to brood, walking blocks without saying anything, never taking part in social activities. But he's improved with becoming successful. And now that he's married he's even better. In fact, I think he's nearly perfect."

*   *   *

Lasse Viren walks through slush in his driveway until he reaches the bare road. Then he begins to run. It is a quarter to six in the evening in late April. The sun floats through a roiling cloud, filling the damp air with bursts of misty rose and gold, igniting the greens and browns of the forest. Viren runs a mile on the paved road, then takes a hard left onto a lane of packed granite sand, a luxurious surface for running because the melting snow drains right through it. The moment he treads on this, Viren seems to expand, like his heart when he inhales. He takes off his leather ski gloves. He points out ancient farm buildings. The road rises through the forest, in places covered with packed ice where the sun never reaches. He knows the terrain intimately; knows, for example, that the lake beside his house is sixteen meters higher than the one beside the town of Myrskylä. He notes which farms still keep a cow and which have given in to modern ways. He tells which neighbors have an excess of visitors in the summer. He points out snow-clogged trails he runs in the summer. The two runners come to a fork. "One way will be nine kilometers, the other fourteen," he says. He lets his visitor choose, saying it makes no difference to him, although at present he is running only half of his usual 150 miles per week. They take the fourteen kilometer route. Among the pines rest huge granite boulders left by the Ice Age glaciers that scraped away most of Finland's topsoil. Some remains. In hollows the road becomes gritty chocolate mud. Viren runs easily with his rather stooped stride at about a 6 minute-per-mile pace, pleased that his ankle isn't bothered by the uneven ground.

The sun sets and the air grows colder. A wind comes up, Viren puts his gloves back on. In the last few miles the surface water begins to glaze; mushy snow becomes ice, crackling underfoot. Returning to his house, he stretches in the driveway and Päivi comes out to tell him that the electricity is off again. Viren, who has promised his guest a Finnish sauna, and whose sauna heater is electric, is prepared for this. He leads the way across the road to the home of a neighbor who has a wood-burning sauna. His black and white cat, named Tappila ("Spot") leaps ahead. "The cat loves to go to sauna." he says.

"The cat does?"

"Yes. She insists. It's hard to get her out."

"She doesn't take a shower afterward, surely?"

"No, but she licks herself for an hour."

The sauna is in a shed on a hillside. Tappila circles and declines to enter. Viren shrugs, strips off his moist running clothes in an anteroom and goes in. He climbs to the top of a tier of benches and sits on a checkered linen cloth, his head near the ceiling, where pitch has extruded from the wood in large amber globules. The temperature is 185° F.

For the visitor the sauna is like a run. In the beginning it is pleasant to sit and sweat and talk, but as the heat begins really to penetrate, as Viren tosses a cupful of water on the shimmering red stones and steam fills the room, it is like a race. There is the same unease. Thought becomes random, hard to control. The time before relief is permissible seems to stretch out of view. A small window, curtained, with four tiny panes, gives a little light. The dim scene out the window is of icicles on nearby branches, the cat crouched on a snowbank. It cannot be that cold so near. It becomes irresistible to think of how it will be to emerge, faint and heavy, and sink into cool water, the heat draining away, passing out like a vaporous spirit. Then the routine will be repeated, cultivating the demon and expel him with simple snow or a dive into the pond. When one comes finally from the recovery room, the Finnish night is found to be a balmy evening, the snow about your ankles no more than goosedown. And so the winter passes. Surely the sauna is a nurturer of hope through these long, cold silences.

Lasse Viren isn't a staunch sauna man. He does this only about once a week, and now leaves first, washes, and goes to thank his neighbor for the favor. Soon he is back in his own candlelit kitchen, sipping black coffee and chewing on sweet pretzelly bread. He is asked questions that have come to seem important to the visitor. "What made him decide to sacrifice everything for running? Was there a real moment of decision? Is there a psychological aspect to peaking? These do not seem unusually vague or analytical, but Viren shrinks from them, squirming. "I just wanted to run," he says. "I had no goal. It is perfectly normal to run at midnight when you are eighteen without having a goal. Then I trained for the European Championships and then the Olympics. But when did I decide this and that? Why? I can't remember." He speaks in a whisper. "I can't remember."

His discomfort is so clearly evident that it makes his guest ashamed. Running cannot be verbalized for Lasse Viren; it is not something to be dwelt upon and picked apart. Viren's rationale lies back there on the crusty roads, back among the pines and granite boulders, or out on the Tartan of Olympic stadia with astonished praise raining about him.

Seeing this, one feels a protective urge. Such a man cannot by himself make himself understood. He will either be maligned by all those who see his silences and awkward deflecting jokes as crude screens for secrets or he will be thought dumb. He is neither rude, nor dumb. And yet it suddenly seems by far the wisest life that he stay near his roots, that he live, shielded, in Myrskylä.

As the visitor makes ready to leave, Viren brings out an icy little glass of clear fluid. Its bouquet is that of the jars hospitals keep thermometers in. *"Pontikka,"* he says slyly, and explains that, this is Finnish moonshine, made of rye and potatoes, illegal and widespread. (Viren being a policeman, the following demonstration will be termed instruction, not entertainment.)

The visitor sips. Even as the chill drink touches his tongue he feels trickles of flame beginning on the tender parts of his lips, chapped by the run. In his throat it bursts into a flare. He gasps. Viren rocks back in his chair, giggling with delight. Such appreciation must be rewarded, he says, and rushes to get a little bottle for the visitor to take with him. Lasse and Päivi walk out to the car to say good-by. The road away from Myrskylä is an inch deep in new snow, as yet unmarked by the passage of any vehicles. Viren warns the driver to be careful. Still he laughs, his arm around his strong wife, smiling through the snowflakes at the discomfiture he has caused.

–June 1977

Postscript:

In his best race in four years, Viren ran fifth in the Moscow Olympics 10,000 meters, then dropped out of the marathon after fifteen miles. Subdued on the day following the 10,000, his mood seemed dominated by relief. "It is good to have it done," he said.

Bill Rodgers

The Olympics have treated no one as kindly as Lasse Viren. Then there are those they abuse. Ron Clarke was one, and Jim Ryun. The runner whose reputation is least dependent upon Olympic success surely is Bill Rodgers.

Rodgers' marathons go one of two ways. He wins without distress, finishing minutes ahead of the best runners in the world, as he did at Boston in 1975 and 1979 and in the New York City Marathon in 1976, recording the three fastest times ever by an American 2:09:55, 2:09:27, and 2:10:09.6. Or he may run as he did at Boston in 1977. That race began at Hopkinton on a sunny morning redolent of cut sod and apple blossoms. Around him, Rodgers saw couples kissing, enjoying the sensual bloom of fitness before the ordeal. The start was a ragged, noisy stampede of 2,000 runners, in which Canadian Olympic marathoner Jerome Drayton was kicked and nearly trampled. Once they were on the road, there was no shade. Along the course the watching crowds were deep, totaling perhaps a million people, many of them listening to an account of the race on portable radios. At Wellesley, the halfway point, Rodgers and Drayton were alone in the lead. The commentator on WBZ was appallingly ignorant, identifying Drayton as defending champion Jack Fultz for mile after mile, enthusing over the "terrific weather for running," while the marathoners were glancing ruefully at the sky. Rodgers began to run with his head cocked slightly back, seeming to acknowledge the spectators' cheers, but in fact it was a posture of early ruin, a realization of the sun's supremacy. "It was deadly truckin' in that heat," he said later.

Drayton pulled away after fifteen miles. Rodgers shrugged, slowing into what a friend recognized as his "survival stride." At the top of Heartbreak Hill, the twenty-mile point, Rodgers stopped. "The old gut had gone," he said. "And besides, there were bigger crowds down the other side." Crowds that wouldn't understand.

Drayton won. Irritated by the race officials' traditional nonchalance about providing water and coherent intermediate times, he batted away the laurel wreath, "the crown of thorns," as Rodgers calls it. Rodgers caught a ride to the finish, walked to the Eliot Lounge, a favorite watering hole, and had a drink with his wife Ellen. Back at the twenty-mile point, on the crest of the hill beside Boston College, where in 1961 two-time Olympic marathon champion Abebe Bikila sat down to rub his freezing legs and so lost his race, the pack was still passing, another thousand people with miles to run, repeating images of froth and chafe.

With runners still on the course, Rodgers had showered and was sitting wet-haired and relaxed, on the corner of a bed in his hotel. "From now on at Boston, I'll decide at the starting line whether it is cool enough to run," he said, making a vow he will not be able to keep. "If it's hot, I'll simply walk away." All marathoners suffer in temperatures above the 60's, but Rodgers suffers more than most. Conversely, he is supremely energized by what many consider stiffening cold. "No gloves," he says, "no good race."

On the street below, runners tottered on. Rodgers went to the window and turned away. "I don't believe there is dishonor in dropping out," he said softly, "but in a way they are guttier than I, to run through that ugliness and pain."

*   *   *

Bill Rodgers grew up in Newington, Connecticut, near Hartford, where his father is the head of the Hartford State College Mechanical Engineering Department. His mother worked as a nurse's aide at Newington Hospital, and it is from her, Rodgers believes, that he received his extraordinary energy—as a boy be spent hours running after rabbits and squirrels in the woods—and a profound sympathy for the handicapped and retarded. "I'm involved with people who've been zapped," he says, as though involvement itself were an affliction.

During high school summers Rodgers worked as a porter in the hospital, then attended Wesleyan University, where no one seems to have noticed that he bears a resemblance to the young John Wesley, founder of Methodism and an inveterate visitor of the sick and imprisoned. Upon graduation, in 1970, Rodgers was granted conscientious objector status, doing his alternative service at Peter Bent Brigham Hospital in Boston. "I was dirt in that hospital," he says, his tone milder than his words. "I had one of those top level jobs washing dishes, emptying bedpans, taking bodies down to the morgue." It was a disturbing time. "There were lots of nasty, horrible cases; don't make me describe them. It bothered me most that here were people dying among strangers."

Rodgers had run a 4:28.8 mile in high school, then ran and roomed at Wesleyan with Ambrose Burfoot, who then won the 1968 Boston Marathon. After college Rodgers had quit training, and even had begun smoking. "I had had no commitment to fitness or real competition," he says. "Running was always associated with fun."

Now it became escape. "Running gave me an outlet from that stultifying job," he says. At first he worked toward the modest goal of finishing ten miles—125 laps around the Huntington Avenue Y track. Then he was fired from his job for attempting rather clumsily to organize a union among the hospital orderlies. "For a year I couldn't find another job," he says, "so I ran fifteen miles a day." He lived in a tenement, on food stamps. His first marathon was Boston in 1973. "It was a torrid day," he says. "Jon Anderson (also a conscientious objector, who washed dishes at a San Francisco area hospital) won. I dropped out at twenty miles, same spot as this year. Seeing Anderson run 2:16 in that heat, I knew I'd never be a top runner. It was impossible."

The next year, having changed clubs and come under the coaching of Billy Squires of the Greater Boston Track Club, Rodgers placed fourteenth in 2:19:34. His breakthrough was a second place in the national AAU 20-kilometer road race in the autumn of 1974. The following spring he was a spectacular third in the World Cross-Country Championship in Morocco and, on a perfect day, broke Frank Shorter's record for the marathon by 35 seconds with his 2:09:55 at Boston, an average of 4:57.3 per mile.

Throughout this sudden rise, Rodgers was working at Fernald School in Belmont, Massachusetts, a state institution for the retarded, and studying for his master's degree in Special Education at Boston College. At Fernald, he was in charge of a ward of eight retarded men, an experience that forced as much self-discovery as the grimmest of marathons.

"You go in and one of two things happens," Rodgers says. "You reject them or you want to help them. The first time on ward duty was intimidating. They were like babies, but huge. There was the paradox of grown people needing so much care, the messes of food and elimination, the seizures. I didn't like it, but it was satisfying to work there. These people get nothing from life. They're rejected by everybody, even their families. Yet the smallest things make them happy. Working there, you had to recognize your own streak of cruelty. There are times when disgust overcomes reason. I once let a guy lie in his soiled bed for a day because I was sure he had done it on purpose. My supervisor made me ashamed; it wasn't my job to reject or punish, for any reason."

Rodgers speaks fondly of his work at Fernald, of an autistic child who all day addressed the wall in monosyllables, but who, once Rodgers reached him, turned out to be quite intelligent. Rodgers tells of running by the school after he had decided to work full time on his master's and of going in to say hello. Yet these recollections don't have point-serving conclusions. The remote little boy, never improved enough to leave the institution. Of those Rodgers returned to visit, he says, "Some recognized me, I think." He falls silent. Then unbidden, gives voice to the root of his attachment to these people. "You have to always realize that that could be you."

For two years, Rodgers taught emotionally disturbed children, a far different proposition from teaching the retarded. "E.D.s are not happy," he says. "They're smart enough to know what a rotten break they've got. They have real problems, and you can't teach them anything until those problems are solved."

Rodgers' young charges were raucous, manic, nearly unreachable souls. Daily he had to break up fights, sometimes finding himself with fistfuls of hair. Some authorities recommend a teacher not work with such pupils for more than three years at a stretch, lest the teacher turn permanently misanthropic. In 1977 Rodgers quit to enter the sporting-wear business and to devote more time to training. "I'll get back to them," he says with a trace of apology, as one noting the inevitable.

When he is preparing for a marathon, Rodgers trains roughly 170 miles a week, which he does by running twice a day, usually fourteen miles in the morning and ten at night, with intervals on the track once a week. He is a boon to the sport in Boston because of his success, more so because of his accessibility. He loves company in training and gentles his pace to whatever the slowest man or woman in a group can keep. This makes for ease of conversation. When he runs with Vinnie Fleming (fifth at Boston in 1977) and Randy Thomas (third in the 1977 AAU 10,000 meters), there is much retelling of races—talk that seems random at first, but gradually reveals a philosophy. Rodgers says he was appalled when Jos Hermens of The Netherlands ran a tactical race against Miruts Yifter in the World Cup 10,000 meters, allowing the Ethiopian to save his kick. Hermens said afterward, "He would have beaten me no matter how fast I set the pace." Rodgers says, "Nobody should win by intimidation. I ran suicidal in the Olympic Marathon because of Lasse Viren, (Rodgers knew he had little chance because a foot injury had curtailed his training, but nonetheless set a hard pace for the first thirteen miles). It wasn't right that he get an easy ride out of it." Viren finished fifth, Rodgers fortieth, certifying his pattern of boom or bust.

Rodgers competes a lot. His schedule has called for as many as thirty races a year, including seven marathons. He, has won New York in 1976, 1977, 1978, and 1979, Boston in 1975, 1978, 1979, and 1980. Friends say he is acutely conscious of the rapidity with which he suddenly became world-class, that he regards his ability as a gift, and is afraid he might lose it just as suddenly. Conceivably for this reason he is driven to race as much as possible now that he is at his peak. "I do have a feeling that once you take a break from running good marathons, something happens," he says. "It takes so long to come back. It's the scariest thing." He cites England's Ian Thompson, the 1974 Commonwealth Games marathon champion (2:09:13.2) and 1974 European champion, who failed to make the British Olympic team in 1976.

"Every time I bomb out, I have to come back," Rodgers says. "I have a feeling after a bad race that my next one will be good. Of course, after a couple of good ones, I get the feeling I'm going to bomb out. Yin and yang." Five weeks after 1977's debacle at Boston, Rodgers won the Amsterdam Marathon in 2:12:47.

Rodgers and friends are training on the bike paths along the Charles River at noon. As they sometimes do, they jog a few blocks through busy traffic to the Eliot Lounge, where—startled businessmen looking up from their martinis—the bartender Tommy Leonard greets them with shouts and "sea breezes"—two parts cranberry juice to one of grapefruit. When the refreshed runners have gone, Leonard, a thickset, passionate man who has run twenty-three Boston Marathons, waxes eloquent on Rodgers. "You should have seen the shrug act," the bartender says. "Breaking four records in one race (Rodgers in August 1977 ran a U.S. record 12 miles, 1,351 yards in an hour, and also set U.S. records for 15 kilometers (43:39.8), 10 miles (46:35.8), and 20 kilometers (58:15.0) along the way), and every lap, hearing the time, he would give an amused shrug. His golden hair was flowing in a rose sunset. He was even lapping his pacers, for God's sake. It was beautiful. A mist came over my eyes. It was just my most poignant experience in running."

It happens that Rodgers' wife Ellen is sitting within earshot and growing restless. "For romance," she says, "I'd rather go see Elvira Madigan." A former art teacher, Ellen has one green eye and one brown, and a Liv Ullmann look of clear good sense. She runs twice a day herself, not to race but simply to keep in the rhythm of the household. "When we were first going together and he would leave to run, I thought, 'He'd rather do that than be with me?'" Now she is, for want of a better word, his agent, lamenting and occasionally countering his inability to say no. "I thought he had learned his lesson. He actually wrote Amsterdam after Boston and said no, he would not be there. Then they called and pleaded, and he said yes." She says this with such loving forbearance that one concludes that she is Rodgers' greatest gift, a buffer between him and the draining demands of TV documentaries, coaching clinics, charities, and two races per weekend. At the conclusion of one Boston Marathon week, she had a cold sore on her lip from so many kisses from strangers.

The Rodgers have built a spare, elegant new house in Sherborn, Massachusetts, but for years lived in Melrose, ten miles north of Boston, on the second floor of a dark green three-story frame house. There were the flags and trophies common to the walls of runners, and a butterfly collection, but the most affecting thing about this house was its apparent existence within a gravitational vortex. Pens and teacups slipped off tables, you rushed involuntarily from the kitchen when you only meant to stand, or found yourself with one foot poised above the living room threshold, unable to move further. Barring occult explanation, this seemed to have been caused by a settling of the interior of the house which created downslopes from the outside walls.

Rodgers spends much of his time in the kitchen, eating. He will sleep ten hours a night, if permitted, but even so will rise at 3 A.M. for his fourth meal of the day, raiding the refrigerator which always contains a pitcher of apricot nectar mixed with flat ginger ale, quart bottles of cola, chocolate chip cookies, and mayonnaise, which he will eat straight out of the jar with a tablespoon. "Sometimes I wonder," he said one such morning, yawning, heading back to bed, "whether I run high mileage so I can eat like this, or do I eat like this so I can do high mileage?" Whatever the reason, his dimensions are 5 feet 8½ inches, 128 pounds, and size 9E feet, "and flattening."

Awake, Rodgers is always on the phone to friends who call from all over the country with results, plans, hopes. He tries to hang up, but so gently that he rarely succeeds.

"That was really an, uh, interesting guy," he says to a friend in a respite between callers.

"Sounds like a euphemism to me," says the friend.

"Why, do you know him?"

* * *

It is a dreary, rainy morning in early autumn. Rodgers had run thirty miles in training the previous day. Now, wearing a trim green and white sweat suit, he sits in a conference room with a director of the National Wheelchair Foundation and three John Hancock Insurance Company public-relations people, two of them unselfconsciously smoking up a great blue cloud. The windows on the 46th floor of the Hancock Building give a misty view of Back Bay, the Charles, and MIT. The point of the meeting is to ask John Hancock to sponsor the National Wheelchair Marathon, run concurrently with the Boston race, as a symbol of what the handicapped can achieve. Rodgers speaks briefly of his respect for wheelchair athletes, noting that many paraplegics were athletes first, having suffered spinal damage from injuries. "Bikila was one," he says, with reverence for the name, then sees that it means nothing to these jowly, bland, brown-suited men. "The two-time Olympic gold medalist in the marathon," he explains softly. "Ethiopia . . . paralyzed from the waist down in an automobile accident." Rodgers gazes at his thighs as he speaks.

The senior PR man, who has an eloquent frown that at once conveys charity, good wishes, and rejection, lists the reasons—previous budget commitments, too few people in the race, little publicity "rub-off"—why Hancock cannot sponsor the event. But he is willing to set up a subsequent meeting with other likely sponsors, maybe even pledge a thousand dollars.

"That would be a terrible life," Rodgers says, once out on the street in the rain, jogging. "To have to say so elaborately every day why you couldn't spare more than a grand."

Rodgers occasionally refers to himself as a radical, and that is surely true, to the extent that his concerns often run counter to the self-interest of our species. By example, he calls for understanding of the poor, the retarded, the disturbed, the crippled, and dying: "There, that could be me." What is extraordinary, what is truly radical about Bill Rodgers, is the inclusiveness of his concern, extended evenly to the smokers, the bosses, the denyers, to insensitive hospital wardens. Bill Rodgers is sympathetic with everyone.

Even in racing, an activity that would seem the essence of self-assertion over weaker competitors, Rodgers is at pains to remove the element of rejection of others. In perhaps his finest race, the 1976 New York City Marathon, Rodgers felt that the competition was irrelevant. Something else drove him. "I remember going over the Verrazano Narrows Bridge after the start and finding myself very serious," he says. "I remember checking my form, holding my hands just right to be perfectly efficient."

For a time Rodgers ran near Frank Shorter, who had taken the Olympic silver medal 2 months before. Shorter's stride was the more fluid, his feet falling more softly, yet Rodgers' was the more beautiful. There can be something hard in Shorter, a scornful quality, especially when he is out front and applying pressure. But Rodgers' blond and open-faced, simply ran faster, ghosting away with a look of amazement. "I wanted to stop near the East River and go to the bathroom," he says, "but there was something working that day, an imperative to get the thing done right." He finished three minutes ahead of Shorter. "And of course there was Mayor Beame shoving the crown of thorns on my head." Rodgers resented the fuss. "It's over," he said to the mayor. "Somebody had to win. It just happened to be me."

—October 1977

Postscript:
Rodgers' running business is booming, but his marriage has ended.

Yesterday's Child:
Mary Decker

On August 4, 1973. Mary Teresa Decker was five feet tall and weighed 89 pounds, counting the braces on her teeth. She was also the best female half-miler in the United States. On that afternoon she found herself sitting with her teammates at lunch in a hotel dining room in Dakar, Senegal, on the westernmost tip of Africa. The meal was spaghetti; the mood was uneasy, for in the evening the U.S. team would compete against the best African track and field athletes.

Suddenly conversation ceased, except for whispers. A stately file of tall black men had entered the dining room. They wore shining white robes, densely embroidered. As they proceeded between the tables, it was seen that some of them carried roses. They stopped before Mary Decker and stood motionless and solemn. She shrank into her chair.

The leader motioned that she be given the roses. Then he identified himself as an aide to Monsieur Abdou Diouf, the prime minister of Senegal, and said that, because it had come to His Excellency's attention that on this day Mary Decker became fifteen years old, he had sent a gift. Whereupon the aide bowed and placed before her a heavy bronze sculpture of an African soldier on a horse. It was, the emissary intoned, from the prime minister's private collection.

Decker turned crimson and lost all capacity for speech. Her teammates rose and sang a ringing "Happy Birthday" as the prime minister's men withdrew. Later she would win her race easily and be comfortable in the stadium's applause, but now Decker sat in embarrassed turmoil, staring at the bronze, fastening on its pitted surface, the result of long burial. Quietly she began to cry.

Mary Decker now keeps the statue on her mantle along with the medals she won on that 1973 tour of Europe and Africa. She has never discovered the sculpture's history or its age. She has never tried, because for her it is a personal symbol of her exalted and vigorous youth, a youth which, given all that has befallen her since her African adventure, seems dimly of another age.

*   *   *

Mary, the daughter of John and Jacqueline Decker, was born and spent the first ten years of her life in Bunnvale near Flemington, New Jersey. Her father was a private pilot and a tool and die maker. "The atmosphere was dominated by my mother," says Decker, "my father is a very quiet person. My mother is a very unquiet one."

By the time Mary was twelve her parents had come to the brink of a divorce. "They stayed together for the sake of the kids," she says. "It was the biggest mistake they ever made besides getting married in the first place. They were never close, as long as I can remember."

Thus, although she recalls life with her brother and two sister as being friendly, there was reason enough for her to seek acceptance outside her home. Friends have always been extraordinarily important to Decker, and her need to please them is strong.

In 1968, when Mary was ten, the Deckers moved for eight months to Santa Ana, California, then to Huntington Beach, and two years later to Garden Grove. Decker began running at eleven. "It was out of boredom," she says. "In the sixth grade my best friend and I were sitting around one Saturday saying 'What can we do?' We had a flyer from the parks department and saw there was a 'cross-country' that day. We didn't know what 'cross-country' was. We went down and found out it was running. So we ran. My friend dropped out. I won by a long ways. I don't remember its being very hard."

Decker went on to win a countywide race that year but was sick for the state age-group meet. Nevertheless, she already had attracted the eye of Don DeNoon, a race walker who had recently become women's coach for the Long Beach Comets club. After training with DeNoon for two years, Decker set a thirteen-year-old age-group 880 record Of 2:12.7 at the Mount San Antonio Relays. That same year she ran a 4:55 mile. Such times showed spectacular promise, but DeNoon's expectations were without limit. He and Mary's mother formed a demanding alliance. Besides doing hard speed work on the track every day, Decker was raced constantly. When she was twelve, she competed in the Palos Verdes Marathon one day and ran the 400 and the 880 in an age-group meet the next. The following Saturday she ran a 440, 880, mile, and two-mile. The day after that she had her appendix out. "Have you been under any unusual stress?" asked the doctor.

"There was no pressure at first," Decker says now. "I enjoyed running and I always did everything my coaches said"—for that was how approval was to be won—"but when I began running well, everybody seemed to know what was best. And everybody told me something different."

The late Steve Prefontaine, convinced that Decker was America's greatest middle-distance talent ever, worried about her guidance. "Pre called me every week or two, as a friend," she says. "Sort of a paternal friend. He said, 'Stand up for yourself. Don't run so many races.' I just ran what I was told to run. He was trying to look out for my best interests. I know that now."

In 1973, at fourteen, Decker was eligible to enter open races against the best women in the country. She ran bests Of 4:37.4 in the mile and 2:02.4 in the 800, was second to Wendy Knudson in the half-mile at the national championships, won the Pan-Pacific Cames 800 meters in Toronto, and toured Europe and Africa. When the summer was over, she cried as she saw her new friends disperse. She went home to Garden Grove, caught her foot in the spokes of her bicycle, and cracked a bone. She was in a cast for six weeks, and when she resumed running, it was at the same frenetic pace.

In February 1974 she set the indoor 880 world record of 2:02.4 in San Diego. In July she won the U.S. vs. U.S.S.R. 800 meters in 2:02.3, but decided not to race in Europe. "My parents were finally divorcing, and I was in the middle of that." The entente between DeNoon and Decker's mother had also broken up, and Decker entered a soap opera period of family strife and injury and revolving door coaches.

In the fall of 1974 she was running on the fire trails in the hills near her home when she felt a pain in her ankle. X-rays showed nothing, so she flew off to compete in Japan, where she was able to run only one of her four scheduled races. On her return to the United States, a second set of X-rays showed a stress fracture. Decker spent another six weeks in a cast. Looking back, she feels it was a vulnerable time. "I grew from five feet and ninety pounds in late '73 to five feet six inches and a hundred fifteen by the beginning of '75," she says. "I didn't know what to do with all this *body* I had," She giggles at the sound of that. "I mean in my running. My stride changed. My center of gravity changed. The stresses were different. I was ripe to get hurt."

In the Sunkist Indoor meet in January 1975, Decker developed fiery pain in her shins. "I rested. I had all kinds of therapy. I tried efferent shoes. I only ran on the grass. Nothing worked." The Olympic year of 1976 dawned and Decker was practically a cripple. "I knew by then that I couldn't make the team. I had gone beyond caring about that to just longing to run, no matter how badly. I thought I'd have to run in pain all my life."

The summer after being graduated from high school, Decker went to Denver with a friend. "While the Olympics were on, I didn't want to be around people who knew me," she says. "All the question, the constant, 'Why aren't, you there?'" She visited Boulder, twenty miles to the northwest and hard against the Front Range of the Rockies. With its calming mountains and friendly University of Colorado students, it was the sort of place that promised refuge to a troubled Californian. She began working at Frank Shorter's sporting store, where all the staff runs. Decker could run only with a viselike pain. "I was born to be a runner," she says. "I simply love to train. So it was a drag when the others would say 'We don't have to worry. Mary will hold down the store. We can go run.' When she could, she trained a little with the University of Colorado women's team. "She seemed pretty spacey sometimes," says Coach Rich Castro, "but when you talked about something of high priority to her, like running, suddenly she was all business." Castro took a chance and offered Decker a scholarship. She enrolled in January 1977. Without ever training at much more than a lope, she won the Big-Eight indoor 440 and was third in the 880. "On guts alone," says Castro. "She did it for the team, but, Lord, was she sick afterward, and of course every time she ran fast, the pain blossomed."

A doctor in Denver had a go at her. Radiographic studies showed what appeared to be dozens of tiny, imperfectly healed stress fractures all up and down her shin bones, so she had to endure ten more weeks of casts. When she was released, the pain was back in two days.

It must not be thought that Decker suffered all this in bitterness. Always an open, spirited person, given to infectious laughing fits, she kept her humor; it became perhaps even more manic for having no physical outlet. Shorter treasured her in his business, for her uncomplaining diligence, and for her way with difficult customers.

"This big guy, a football player, comes into the store," says Shorter, "and he has these shoes he's bought, and the toes have worn out in the strangest way. I very timidly ask how he's using them. Mary is there, smiling and curious. Finally the guy says that he's been running in reverse."

"'You what? You run *backward?*' says Mary, and she can't help it, she laughs.

"'Yes, of course,' says the guy, really earnest, really lecturing. 'You absolutely have to, to get stronger for sprinting.'

"This sets Mary on a laughing jag. She's falling over, and everything he says is just making it worse.

"'Listen.' he says, 'you can't consider yourself truly fit unless you run backward.' She starts to shriek.

"Well, what could he do to this kind of gregarious, hoppity girl? Punch her out like he would have me? Finally he just turned to water and ran out of the store."

In May 1977, Dick Quax of New Zealand, the 1976 Olympic silver medalist in the 5000 and a friend of Shorter's, trained for a month in Boulder before breaking the 5000 world record in Europe. Quax met Decker and as he heard her story he grew agitated. "I had exactly the same thing," he said, displaying parallel scars on his shins. "Surgery cured it.

"It's a simple operation," he told her. "What happens is the sheath containing the muscle, called the fascia, stiffens and can't expand as the muscle does. The surgeon just slices through the membrane to relieve the pressure. I've got photos of mine, the muscle bulging out like meat out of a sausage skin. I was back running in two weeks."

Decker found a California doctor who thought Quax's diagnosis made sense. Castro paid for her plane fare, and she was operated on in July. She was running free in August. "It was such a treat," she says. "There hasn't been even the slightest, slightest ache."

In November she finished seventh in the AIAW cross-country championships, leading Colorado to third place in the team standings. When Castro asked Decker her goals for 1978 in the 800 and 1,500, she wrote down 1:58 and 4:05 (the American records were 1:57.9 by Madeline Manning Jackson and 4:02.6 by Jan Merrill).

"Come on, be realistic," said the coach, thinking it would take at least two years to gain the strength necessary for that kind of 1,500. Then in January at a meet promoted by Quax in New Zealand, Decker ran 4:08.9. Four days later she equaled her personal best of 2:01.8 for 800 meters. In her first major U.S. race in three years, the Los Angeles *Times* Games in February, Decker broke her own world indoor 1,000-yard record by three seconds with a 2:23.8.

One reason such fast times are possible is Decker's raw speed. She has run a 23.7 220. That's nearly a world-class sprint time.

"She is a physical genius," says Quax. "All that speed and she seems to be able to run all day as well. She's got no weaknesses."

Decker confirmed that point in the Toronto indoor 1,500 in February 1978, when she met the two best U.S. milers of the past three years, Francie Larrieu and Merrill. Larrieu is an old friend who respects the devotion that brought Decker through her years of travail. "I don't know if I could have hung on as long as she did," says Larrieu. "I would have given up."

Larrieu and Decker are similar in that they confine their competitiveness to the track. Merrill is far less chummy, especially before a race.

"She won't talk to me, Francis," said Decker while warming up in Toronto. "Is she for real?"

"That's the way she is," said Larrieu.

"Aren't you kind of worried for her?" asked Decker.

Merrill and Decker traded the lead until the last two laps, when Merrill fell back. Then Larrieu came on. "With half a lap to go I was on her shoulder," recalls Larrieu. "Then Mary looked over and kind of shrugged and she pranced away." Decker won by five yards in 4:13.4. Afterward, her thoughts returned to Merrill. "Jan just never said anything, even after the race when all the tension was gone. I guess I'll just have to try harder to get to know her, because I really want to be friends. What's the fun of racing if you can't be friends?"

Carved in the lintel above the entrance to the University of Colorado library is the aphorism "Who knows only his own generation remains always a child." Decker, running past the library one afternoon recently, offered the opinion that there is much to be said for preserving at least some of the child.

"I don't want to grow up too much," she said. "As long as I can be responsible sometimes, can't I have fun?"

Decker has always been rewarded for her childlike qualities, so it is natural that she should shed them reluctantly. "She was like Olga Korbut in 1973," says Maren Seidler, America's best woman shot-putter. "Everybody's little darling. The media can cope with little girls. They love 'em because then they don't have to deal with adult women."

Thus Decker today can be characterized as two females, the serious and talented adult runner alternating with yesterday's child. "The difference between Mary-fooling-around and Mary-in-competition is the difference between Jim Nabors playing Gomer Pyle and Jim Nabors singing opera," says Rich Castro. "A complete metamorphosis."

After the 1978 indoor season, in which she got behind in her classes, Decker withdrew from Colorado. She followed a program of stamina training, written for her by Quax, in which she simply ran twice a day through the campus and town and surrounding country.

"It's the first time I've ever done any training to get strong," she said.

Decker is not fond of running alone, so her afternoon company was often Rob Yahn, a business partner of Shorter's. "I don't know what it's doing for Mary, but it's getting me in great shape," panted Yahn one brilliant day as they ran through the remains of the winter's snow, their breath like cotton before their eyes. Above them the Flatirons, precipitous sandstone formations, rose like the Matterhorn against a sky so deep blue that one realized outer space was near.

"I just hate slippery snow," said Decker. "The balls of my feet get sore from trying to grip the ground." Her stride at a 6½ minutes a mile pace was lovely and loose with a little flick of the ankle as she lifted each foot, an action that soon had the backs of her legs soaked. When crossing intersections, Yahn ran in front of any waiting cars; Decker went behind.

A blue Mustang full of kids shot past, fishtailing on the melting snow, throwing slush on the runners. "I hope they go in the ditch," said Decker. She pointed out a brick and dark glass house that belonged to Linda Ronstadt. At the highest point in the run, there was the sweet aroma of piñon woodsmoke and a view to the southeast, where Denver lay hidden under a veil of brown smog that looked especially poisonous from this clean and hard-won vantage point.

Arriving back at her apartment Decker deftly spit beside the door before entering. She lived with Kathy Woodbridge, also a middle-distance runner. The place was filled with surfing pictures and huge grasping plants. Decker loves to sit in a hot tub after a day's running, sipping cocoa laced with peppermint schnapps. "I really am a California girl," she called from the sloshing bathroom. "I'm always shivering up here."

As soon as she began to run well in the winter, offers came from several colleges to transfer. "I don't want to name names but yes there were inducements that were against the rules. Money, cars, an apartment. Rich Castro knows about it, and we both think it's a shame. At the stage women's programs are at, recruiting is a waste of money. Maybe it always is. What we need is development, better coaching, greater participation."

She came from her bath dewy and radiant, putting on sticky lip gloss that filled the room with the smell of overripe strawberries. Decker's body language is a soliloquy of adolescent twists and stretches. Thus it was unnerving, when she rested her cheek in her hand, to examine her fingernails, which looked like elegant meat hooks caked with dried blood. "The shade is called rosy brown," she said firmly, with a trace of a pout.

Judging from the dozens of telephone numbers written near the phone, Boulder's young men found her irresistible. But, she confided, too many developed ominous symptoms of seriousness. "They get persistent, and I make excuses and make excuse and they don't take the hint. I know it's kinder to say how I feel and be done with it, but it's hard, and I don't want to make enemies. So, instead, I make more excuses."

Decker and a close friend, Nancy Gregorio, who was a girls' basketball and track coach at Thomas Jefferson High in Denver, stood in the Colorado field house, watching the annual Potts Invitational indoor meet. It was Mary's duty to present the awards to the victors. "Man, are you going to kiss 'em?" asked Nancy.

"It depends on who they are," said Decker airily. She was drawn away for instructions and Nancy turned to a companion saying, "You know, Mary has talents that she'll never tell you about. She macraméd all those plant holders in her apartment; she's a seamstress and a clothes designer. She even sews her own swimsuits."

"Nancy, are you blabbing again?" But Decker could only scold for second; she had to give the high-hurdles winner his medal. He was tall and stood so high on the pedestal that he was too far up to kiss, unless he should bend over like a swimmer on the starting blocks, so he got a handshake.

"And she's an artist," continued Gregorio. "She does displays down at the store and did one oil painting that was so good it was stolen. And Mary loves all the team. She invites everyone for dinner, even the outcasts."

"Wait a minute. Outcasts?"

"Well, you know. Even the little, sick ones. She's really 'fondly,' really affectionate. I get cross-eyed when she talks to me, she's always so close." (This is true, and, perhaps a small warning is in order. Should the reader ever watch a track meet with Decker, she speaking excitedly near your face, then turning her ear for your reply, the temptation will arise to whisper into that ear. If that temptation is not resisted, Decker's shoulder will instantly jerk up violently. "I'm sensitive!" she will cry showing gooseflesh on her arm. Sensitive like that can break your jaw.)

Decker's last award of the evening was to the winner of the half-mile. He got a kiss. It was nicely done with Decker performing a little pirouette, twisting away as he opened his eyes. He experienced a moment of dizziness, putting a hand on the shoulder of the runner-up to steady himself.

Decker missed only one day of running in the spring of 1978. That was a Sunday in March when she went cross-country skiing with John and Vickie Cossick, also Shorter associates. The first stop was a country store where Decker bought a sack of candy bars, five discus-sized chocolate chip cookies, and six sugar-free root beers. Then they all drove into the mountains, past old silver mines and feathery gray aspens rising like smoke above snowy hillsides. Across Berthoud Pass, elevation 11,314 feet, the high-country spruce were gothic. Distant ridges were burdened with snow cornices. The party skied over the gentle terrain of Devil's Thumb Ranch a training ground for the Olympic cross-country ski team.

Decker had only been a downhill skier before, but she caught on quickly to the different techniques of cross-country. Soon she was bounding up the hills past astonished middle-aged skiers who had thought that ski touring was a relaxed, contemplative endeavor. Going downhill, Decker let loose a soul-stirring screech, beginning at about high C and rising out of the range of human hearing. "Her nickname is 'Eek,'" a teammate had said, "because on the bus she screams with joy and pentup energy about every half hour. We try to get her to do it out the window."

Decker seemed to feel no fatigue on the trails. However, later, at a rustic lodge, sipping wine and studying pretty ski suits she suddenly went limp, her forehead corning to rest on the cool wood of the table.

She dozed on the drive back to Boulder, perking up when Louise, Shorter Frank's wife, invited her in for a sauna. Lying on the uppermost bench, she pointed out a fresh scar, high on her left thigh. "Muscle biopsy," she said. "I turned out to be sixty-two percent fast-twitch fibers, thirty-eight percent slow. But in a comparison of total area, it was fifty-fifty." This seems to mean that she has a fine balance between speed and endurance muscle fibers. A perfect miler. Analysis of Decker's muscle chemistry shows little training adaption. "She is capable of increasing the anaerobic and aerobic capacities of her muscles," says Ken Sparks of the Human Performance laboratory at the University of Colorado. "This means better performances are possible." That finding supported Shorter's gut feeling about Decker's potential: "She is the best U.S. Olympic hope in any women's track event."

It was suggested to Mary that her forced absence from serious running may have been a blessing. "I know," she said. "Wouldn't it be horrible if I'd kept racing and was burned out by now? This way my hunger to run and my physical peak will be nearer the same time."

At dinner with the Shorters, Mary and Frank compared notes on New Zealand, discussing one rather lecherous physiotherapist in particular. "I had stiff calves, so he rubbed them very nicely," said Decker. "Then he moved on to rub everything else that was rubbable. I couldn't believe it."

There was an edge in Shorter's voice. "That's maybe what you ought to try to learn," he said. "To believe it."

Later, Shorter waxed protective. "Her coaches exploited her, her mother exploited her, recruiters are trying to lure her to schools that would exploit her, and now that running has spawned an industry she's getting offers to use her name on clothing. The contracts read like articles of indentured servitude. She's smart; she hasn't fallen for that, so I don't know why I'm getting so worked up about it. She has that energy, and that transparent need to I please. People see that and they play on it. I guess I wish she wouldn't let them."

Decker pondered this. "I don't think I'll ever be the way Frank wants, sort of the mistress of my destiny," she said, "because I don't want to hurt other people." She was quiet for a moment. "If it comes to hurting someone else or hurting myself, I'll hurt myself. I don't know how to explain that, except to say I've been hurt so much these last four years."

Decker has indeed been torn and broken to excess. Besides all the plaster and sutures expended on her legs she fractured her skull in a motorcycle accident with her father when she was twelve. That resulted in a year's therapy and a scare when she ran too soon and began hemorrhaging. Twice, in 1977 she was in automobile accidents, once catching a soft shoulder and rolling her car four times. She was unhurt. The other time she was a passenger in a pickup truck that became entangled in a six car crash on an icy mountain pass. "We were mashed beneath a jackknifed semi," she says. "I was only bruised, but the guy driving was hurt. There was glass in his arm. I couldn't get him out. And the cars were still hitting us. If you're not moving, I'm not staying here,' I said. But I still had a cast on my leg." She tells it as if it were a funny story, but her eyes are blank and hot still seeing the looming machines.

Such a burden of injuries may explain some of Decker's determinedly high spirits, her acute sensitivity. It may account too for such things as the tumbleweed story. "The Colorado women's team was in a bus, going over the prairie," she says. "There were black clouds and a wind, and suddenly here were all these tumbleweeds, thousands of them, as far as you could see, running across the road, bumping into us, scratching against the windows." The others on the team, delighted, cheered and laughed. Then they turned to Decker, who was ashen and shivering, frightened to tears. Even now Decker is incapable of fully explaining her fear. "Please don't think me a crybaby," she says.

Decker does not dwell on the somber. If a theme recurs in her conversation, it is reverie. She returns often to the details of that summer when she was fourteen— how shot-put world-record holder Al Feuerbach carried her luggage in Germany; how she was protected from the unseemly advances of Italian men by a quartet of wonderfully menacing black sprinters. "I remember the first time I ever got drunk, ooh," she says. "Francie fed me gin and tonics after the Pan-Pacific Games. The chaperones said, 'Mary looks so *tired.*' I got to be a team captain in Russia, but I was too small to carry the big flag, so I got a little flag." Her voice, describing this, is not the child's, but that of a tender older sister. "I remember in Africa there was a dispute over some ticket arrangements and some of our black guys left early in a huff. I was interviewed by the Senegal press, and they asked, 'Are they prejudiced?' 'How could they be?' I said. 'They're all black like you.'" She closes her eyes, suppressing a smile. "I remember a time on a beach in Africa, when all the weight men were seeing how high they could throw me. And body surfing with Mac Wilkins. Afterward the pavement was so hot on my feet that he carried me back to the hotel on his shoulders." Thus delivered from the sea by the great and gentle discus thrower, she received her roses and bronze statue from the prime minister. "It seems now that I saw all of that through a window," she says. "It would be fun to go back and do it for real."

—May 1978

Postscript:

In the following two years, Decker went back and did it all again, finding unchanged the major themes of her life: her prodigious energy and devotion to running, her continuing vulnerability. She broke the world record for the mile twice, cutting it to 4:21.68 in New Zealand in January 1980, then took the indoor 1,500 meter and half-mile records (4:00.8 and 1:59.4). She won the U. S. Olympic Trials 1,500, then finally broke 4:00 for that distance with 3:59.43 in Europe following the Games the U.S. team was required to boycott. Her performances were more remarkable because she gave them between several serious injuries. In 1978, her shin pain necessitated a second operation. A torn muscle in her back, suffered in a fall in Zealand, wiped out half her 1979 season. After her 1980 indoor records, she weathered several weeks of plantar fasciitis, and at this writing she is recovering from surgery on an Achilles' tendon and a third shin operation.

Now married to marathoner Ron Tabb, living in Eugene, Oregon, Decker contemplates no slackening in her drive to improve. Compared to the pain of injury, the discomfort of effort seems but a joy to her. "Honestly," she said after running 4:17.6 for the mile in the Houston Astrodome in February 1980 (a time not acceptable for a record because of an oversize track), "it's almost like the faster I go, the easier it becomes."

Henry Rono

One need not wander the shambas and high plateaus of Kenya or Tanzania to come upon wonderful African runners. In 1978, it seemed an Oregonian had only to look across the road.

The lawns and rhododendrons of the Oregon State campus in Corvallis are dewy this spring morning in 1978 as Henry Rono runs softly past. The day before, this twenty-five-year-old Kenyan who attends Washington State had won the 10,000 meters at the Pac-8 championship meet finishing in 27:46.6, the fastest time in the world so far this year. That is an extraordinary record, made as it was with no competition save a stiff wind that blew up each of the twenty-five homestretches, but it pales beside two of Rono's previous efforts. On April 8, in Berkeley, California, he ran the 5,000 in 13:08.4, to shatter the world record of Dick Quax of New Zealand by 4.5 seconds. Quax had set his record in 1977 by shaving 0.1 of a second off the mark established five years earlier by Emiel Puttemans of Belgium. Then, on May 13, before 200 people in a rain-soaked relay meet in Seattle, Rono ran the 3,000-meter steeplechase in 8:05.4, removing 2.6 seconds from the world record of Anders Garderud of Sweden, which was set in the Montreal Olympic final. In response to Rono's records—and it is safe to say they will not be his last—the world's runners have been fairly unanimous. "It makes you want to quit," said Frank Shorter, on hearing of the steeplechase.

Later this day, Rono will come back to win the Pac-8 5,000, so this morning's run will not be difficult. "We will go slowly for an hour," he says. "To just sweat a little, to get out the beer we drank last night with our pizza." Though his companion is comfortable in shorts, Rono wears the bright red sweat suit of Kenya. "We are starting late," he says, shaking his wrist, upon which hangs a heavy digital timepiece. "Joshua Kimeto timed me with my watch yesterday, and I don't know what he did. He changed the program, and it didn't wake me this morning until seven-thirty. Usually I run at six-thirty."

Joshua Kimeto, the two-time NCAA 5,000-meter champion, is Rono's teammate at Washington State and a tribemate as well. Both runners are Nandi, the tribe of the renowned Olympic champion Kipchoge Keino. Members of the Nandi are clearly recognizable by the absence of their two middle lower front teeth "They are not 'knocked out,'" says Kimeto. "They are *removed*." This is done for reasons of tribal identity and health. If a Nandi contracts lockjaw, he can be fed through a straw. And, as the remaining teeth tend to move into the gap, there is more room for wisdom teeth in the back. "I haven't seen a dentist since I was ten," says Kimeto.

As he runs Rono begins to sweat freely, though his pace is gentle. He keeps to the shade beneath the fir trees. "It is good weather here," he says. "Like in a forest. The place I come from is seventy-six hundred feet elevation. You can't run easily in that place, the oxygen is so rarefied."

That place is Kiptaragon village in the Nandi Hills, in Rift Valley Province of Kenya. Rono, who is five feet nine and weighs 139 pounds, turned twenty-five on the day he set his steeplechase record. He has run seriously only since he was eighteen. "At school I played soccer and volleyball," he says, "and I kept in my mind the idea to run later. One day in 1971 I heard that Keino was coming with other athletes to appear at a place near where I lived. He was from only three miles away, but I had never seen him, so I went. The place was a little stadium and there were many athletes there. The announcer asked Keino to put up his hand so we would know who he was, and I saw him."

"Did you speak with him?" Rono is asked.

"No. There were many people around him. The mayor of the place gave him a cup to carry, and the people who wanted to talk could put something in it, like a nickel. I stood by myself above in the stadium and watched." Rono pauses. "From that time I was a runner."

In that decision, Rono was not unlike most runners—the vow to begin is usually solitary and silent. Rono has gone on to combine his natural shyness with an unbending independence. He began running on his own, and though he spoke with other runners about training, he never had a coach in Kenya.

"My first understanding was that you could not become a distance runner quickly," Rono says. "I began gradually, not doing too much. To build my mind I started with the steeplechase."

Almost against his wishes, it seems, he was soon running very well, winning school races, and running an 8:30 steeplechase over barriers, but without a water jump, in 1972.

The ages of schoolboys in the Rift Valley are not as standardized as in the United States. Rono graduated from high school in 1975, at age twenty-two. "In 1960, when I was seven, my father was working on a farm, driving a tractor, pulling a plow," Rono-says. "It was the kind with many disks. A snake came up in the tires and onto the front of the tractor. My father jumped back and fell. The disks ran over him and killed him. They cut his throat and across his chest." After that, Rono lived with his grandmother and tended cattle, and that was why he started school later than he might have. The matter-of-fact telling of his father's death evokes thoughts in Rono's running companion of the culture of the high plains of East Africa. It seems a place at once elemental and near to death, and yet sumptuous. Its people develop a realism, a clarity of judgment about such things as pain and effort, that is difficult for Westerners to share. As a distance runner, Rono has no illusions, which is good, because the case has been made that it is our illusion that we can go no faster that holds us back.

Rono went into the army after he completed secondary school, but disliked military inflexibility. Washington State was recommended to him by the brother of Kip Ngeno, who had run the high hurdles there. And in the fall of 1976 Rono turned up in Pullman after the African boycott forced the Kenya team to depart the Montreal Olympics.

That fall he won the NCAA cross-country championship. Injuries and illness dogged him through his freshman track season, but he placed second in the NCAA steeplechase, ten yards behind his countryman James Munyala of the University of Texas at El Paso. What Rono was capable of began to be clear when he was in Europe that summer.

"In Germany I trained with Mike Boit and one day we ran a 1,200-meter time trial. Mike ran the last lap very fast, but he isn't quite so good on the turns and I gained on him there and finished only one yard behind." Rono's time was 7:52. "Mike was very surprised. He said, 'I think you can run a mile in 3:52.' Later, when I ran a flat 3,000-meter race in 7:41, I told Mike, 'If we can find a steeplechase, I will break eight minutes.'" Eight minutes, for the steeplechase is the sort of barrier no one had seriously considered. "We could not find one for me," Rono recalls. "It is possible that the promoters did not believe me.

They are believers now. The 5,000 record took care of that. "I had run 13:22 in bad weather the week before that race," says Rono. "I had a secret plan for the record, but you don't know how you will run. You know from other races, maybe, that you ought to be around a record, but you cannot *know.*"

That race in April started slowly. Running with Kimeto and WSU teammate Samson Kimobwa, a fellow Kenyan who held the world record of 27:30.5 in the 10,000, Rono hit the first 400 in 67 seconds. He wanted 63. "Usually that would upset me," he says, "but for some reason I was calm. I felt 'Well, I can run a sixty-one and make up for it.'" After three laps, Rono took the lead with a burst. "The thing that was good, I looked back after a hundred fifty yards of hard running and saw that I had pulled far away from Samson and Joshua and I knew this was to be a fast race." Passing the mile in 4:17, Rono was still accelerating. "It is better, I think, to begin easily and get your running to be smooth and relaxed and then to go faster and faster." Rono ended his record 5,000 sprinting. Then a month later he set the steeplechase record.

"I am very flexible in the legs," says Rono. "The steeplechase is easy for me." Indeed, the steeplechase sometimes seems God's gift to the East Africans. Amos Biwott and Ben Kogo of Kenya won the gold and silver in the 1968 Olympics. Keino won in 1972, despite nearly falling several times. Ben Jipcho was second in Munich and later lowered the world record to 8:14.0. And now Rono.

The steeple is different from flat races. Each barrier has the oxygen-sapping effort of a short sprint. "People living at altitude develop a greater oxygen-carrying capacity," says Kimeto. "That allows them not to go into oxygen debt over the barriers." It also allows for repeated hard bursts in the midst of flat races. East African-bred runners are remarkable for their ability to run uneven pace. Rono trains to take full advantage of that strength. In one workout this spring he ran a 7:57 for 3,000 meters by sprinting down each backstretch and striding the balance of each lap

"We can control every race," says WSU Coach John Chaplin, a blunt, sometimes caustic man who is passionately devoted to his athletes. "With our ability to surge, anything you—the opposition—do is wrong. Go with us and you're in oxygen debt. Stay back, and *adios*, were gone."

Chaplin believes in breaking races open. "My rule is if you let things go to the final sprint, it's usually the *worst* guy who ends up winning. That's because he's so psyched up that if he's even *near* the lead, he's going to go bananas. Waiting and kicking may work in the 1,500 where the whole field can stay close, but not in the distances.

Chaplin loves to palm himself off as a hayseed sprint coach. "Distance runners?" he says. "I don't know what they do. I just send them off into the wheat fields." He knows exactly what they do. The Kenyans have gravitated to WSU because it is a school offering sound courses in practical subjects that are in demand back home. Rono majors in industrial psychology. Kimeto and Kimobwa study agricultural economics.

"Everybody graduates," says Chaplin, "and it's hard work. They haven't got time to be killing themselves running." So Rono runs only eighty to ninety miles a week, doing brisk roadwork in the early mornings and intervals on selected afternoons.

Chaplin is seen by his charges as more of a partner than a watch-wielding taskmaster. For example, in those interval sessions, which usually add up to three miles of hard running, it is Rono who decides how fast they shall be.

"I run as I feel." he says. "If I feel very good and am fit, I will run twelve 400's in sixty seconds each with a two-minute rest. If I am not good, they will be slower." Sometimes Rono announces he is tired and stops in the middle of a workout. It is to Chaplin's credit that he trusts and encourages his runners to make such decisions, because if there is a key to Rono's success, it is his sensitivity to his body's requirements for work and rest. "You don't need a coach when you know what you are doing," says Kimeto. Rono, perhaps better than any other runner, seems to sense the optimum stress, when to go harder, when to relax.

These are incommunicable things; the principle is not. The Kenyans at WSU, who are intelligent, distinct individuals, provided by their culture and their coaching with a profound sensitivity to the demands of running distances, have been perceived by many coaches as a flock of transient starlings, identical in maroon and silver, descending upon our delicate native species.

Even some runners have a hard time coming to terms with the Kenyans gifts. Craig Virgin, who while at the University of Illinois, was the first American finisher in eight NCAA championship races but won only one, says, "You get discouraged. It's hard to keep your pride. But the runners who race against WSU most often, those from the Northwest, speak of the experience as a privilege. "Nobody runs tactical races better than the Kenyans," says Rudy Chapa, of Oregon. "I'm learning from the Kenyans. I wish I could run with them more."

Few rivalries can compare with that between WSU and Oregon in the distance races. Lindgren, the late Steve Prefontaine, John Ngeno, Paul Geis, and Kimeto had through 1977, won eleven of the past twelve NCAA 3-mile/5,000 titles (six for WSU, five for Oregon). Runners from the two schools took the first eight places in 1978's Pac-8 Conference 5,000.

Chaplin glories in this rivalry and fans it often, saying, "the people of Eugene are wonderful, rabid fans, [Oregon Coach] Bill Dellinger is a real friend, and Oregon is a fine university, but they have a terrible homer down there [Eugene Register-Guard sports editor Blaine Newnham] who cannot bring himself to mention the WSU runners without saying they are Kenyan and implying we are somehow tainted by that."

Chaplin seems to have a point. For instance, Newnham's column on the Pac-8 meet mentioned "the Kenyans" five times without even noting their school at all. "They [the Oregon runners in the 5,000] were there," he wrote, "should Henry Rono have dropped out or Kenya suddenly declared a national holiday, or something."

Chaplin's indignation at this sort of thing spurred him to a drastic countermeasure at the 1978 Oregon-WSU dual meet in Eugene. Rono had been running a world-record pace in the steeplechase. After the mile he glanced up to see Chaplin waving his coat. "I slowed him down, says Chaplin. "I didn't want to have him break a world record in Eugene and have them say it couldn't have been done without their track, not after the complaining about our foreign athletes."

Rono and his teammates would just as soon not get into this. As it is, they feel beset with the consternations of culture shock, mostly because of U.S. stereotypes of Africa, which make it out to be a continent of teeming, starving, rebellious savages slaughtering each other in desert and jungle, all supervised by Idi Amin. Rono is forever explaining that things aren't all that bad.

"Even Mary Decker, who has been to *West* Africa, asked why I wanted to live in a place where there were no jobs and no food," Rono recalls. "I said, what part of Africa do you mean? There is plenty of food in the Rift Valley."

Kimeto says in astonishment, "Lots of Americans, if you say you like it here, they think you don't like it at home!"

"That's a thing I don't understand," says Rono. "Who does not like home? If I tell you that you have a fine house, does it mean I live in a poor one?"

Rono is a gentle person, and gaining rapidly in social confidence, but still can be thrown off balance by such things as the pretty girl who, on being told of the Nandi reasons for his missing teeth, said, "Well, while you're in America, have you thought about having a bridge put in?"

"Is it that bad?" asked Rono, suddenly afraid he was unintentionally giving offense. Studying newspaper pictures of his 5,000 record, he asked friends whether the gap in his teeth was really noticeable. "Leon Spinks has been a blessing to Henry," says one of the friends. "Sort of an upside-down Nandi."

Rono has adjusted almost too well to Western food, relishing pizza and quiches to the point of having to watch his weight. He has yet to think of shrimp and shellfish as appetizing. "We feed that to the dogs in Kenya," he says, nicely.

All four of WSU's Kenyan distance runners are from the Great Rift Valley. All ran against each other in high school. Cheruiyot is of the Kipsigis tribe and Kimobwa is Sabei. But all are members of the Kalenjin group. When the runners relax, they talk of their shared history and of the need for change to make a better future. They talk of their country's economy, of the research needed to help the transformation from subsistence farming to commercial agriculture, of the proper balance between agriculture and wildlife management. Only with prompting does the talk return to running. Asked about worthy opponents, Rono thinks first of Ethiopia's Miruts Yifter, then Tanzania's Suleiman Nyambui, Nick Rose of England, and Marty Liquori

"Those are the guys," he says, "when we run together, we are all very tired at the end."

Mike Boit, who is a graduate student at Oregon, has said that when he returns to Kenya to teach or become an administrator, he will have no more time for running, that building the nation will consume all his energies. Kimeto says the same. Rono, however, smiles and says, "I don't feel like Mike and Josh. I want to run. How many years is it until I am forty-five? Twenty. I want to keep that in my mind."

"Henry has a great interest to run," says Kimeto softly, because he is speaking of a mystery. "That is what drives you, more than talent or training, and that is given differently to each of us."

Of future records, Rono will say little, but a tight-lipped grin attests to more secret plans. "I think I can run eight minutes for the steeplechase sometime. I think I can say that, but I don't know about the 5,000." Rono makes no promises save one, implicitly, that he will do his best.

*   *   *

Two weeks later, Rono's best was put forth in such a way that the sports historians were rocked.

"What we are witnessing is not taught, and it is not learned," said Bill Exum, the 1976 Olympic track manager from Kentucky State. "It is a mysterious gift, and we have never seen a man more blessed with it than this one."

The man was Rono running to a 50-yard lead in a qualifying heat of the steeplechase in the 1978 NCAA championships. His stride smooth and precise, as if his legs weighed nothing after 3,000 meters, 28 barriers, and seven water jumps, Rono crossed the finish line in 8:18.63, breaking by 6.2 seconds the meet record of the University of Texas at El Paso's defending champion James Munyala.

Rono's run seemed such a blithe squandering of energy that even John Chaplin's eyes were wide. "Maybe his sore foot [bruised three weeks earlier in his world-record 8:05.4 steeplechase] hurts more when he runs slowly," said Chaplin, who had given Rono no instructions to go wild.

"I ran fast for my thinking," said Rono, breathing easily, "for my confidence."

Four hours later, after a nap and a shower and nearly an hour's warm-up, Rono took the track again for a 5,000 meter heat. By his own choice he was entered in the steeple and the 5,000 and 10,000 meters, and naturally had grumbled about the need for heats. "His foot is taped," said Chaplin. "If he goes poorly, that's O.K. We're in no position to win the team competition, so frankly I'd rather he just ran the steeplechase and skipped the rest."

But to run the steeple final, once he was entered in the 5,000, Rono had to run the 5,000 heat. That was because the NCAA has a rule requiring "honest effort" in preliminaries, the penalty for dogging it being disqualification from later races.

In the heat, Rono transformed honest effort into glorious dementia. After a lap in 65 seconds he burst down the homestretch with the wind and hit 2:06 for the half-mile. Into the next homestretch he lifted yet again, his elbows rising behind him as he accelerated, and completed that lap in 59 seconds. A 63 brought him past the mile in 4:08, the most extraordinary first mile in 5,000-meter history. Still he looked calm and eager, not bearing out but running two inches from the curb on the turns, which, like a thoroughbred, a runner will not do if he is tired. His arms, when he was not blasting down each homestretch were carried in effortless rhythm; his stride was mesmerizing in its fluid power. The Eugene crowd rose to him and began clapping and stamping in time with his footfalls. These were moments of awe, a sense of privilege to be witnessing this unexpected, truly profligate display.

Rono ran past two miles in 8:33, slowing, but still a vision, an image all runners would carry in their mind's eye if they could. One spectator, seeing the joyous effort on Rono's face, said, "I wonder where he is right now."

A hundred yards behind, though yards ahead of the rest of the pack, was Joshua Kimeto. He had said earlier, "Running is a kind of play, I think. When you are moving well, you feel like a spectator enjoying this movement of your own. If there is a great crowd with you, you are moved." Running thus disembodied, Kimeto felt, was when one reached his ultimate. "But if you start thinking of the number of laps to go or the time or how tired you will be at the end you will start getting tense and then you will lose the rhythm, and when that stops you can't go anymore."

If this is true, if the essence of running well is running for the moment—and Rono was running well—he could not think of saving himself.

But semantics intrude. Surely it was not play as Rono passed three miles in 12:56 and stretched into a rakish sprint to the finish, the crowd howling him home. He hit the tape unseeing, in 13:21.79, to take the meet and field records of the late Steve Prefontaine.

John Chaplin was left trembling. "He's lost every marble he owns!" he cried. "He's *mad* now, because his foot hurts him a little, and he gets irritated and runs a fast lap to test it and gets caught up in the crowd and runs two collegiate records in the *heats*. The best distance double in history in the *heats*. I've had good kids before. I've had world-record holders before. But I've never had anyone like this." He paused, then said softly, "Maybe the world has never seen anyone like this."

When the 10,000-meter final arrived, Rono was not in it. Then his teammates Joel Cheruiyot and Samson Kimobwa were tripped in a collision after two miles. A grateful Mike Musyoki of UTEP and Kenya took what was given, winning in 28:30.91. "I expected to see Rono," he said. "But I wasn't disappointed not to see him."

That evening, the night before the steeplechase and 5,000 finals, Rono dined with a friend and made himself out to be a sloppy steeplechaser. "I am too high above the barriers. My trail leg is weak. They say I use the wrong leg to lead with." Reminded that Chaplin had slowed him in the dual meet with Oregon, Rono said, smiling, "I won't look near the coach tomorrow. I will show the people how I can run." There seemed in him something shared with Prefontaine, who had relished the crowd and let it drive him. Rono is far less demonstrative than was the Oregon runner, but he appears to be as sensitive to a congregation's wishes.

The day came hot and dry, with a significant wind up the backstretch. Rono started the steeplechase slowly, first staying behind Richmond's Hillary Tuwei for a kilometer, then racing ahead, then easing. "Break away in the middle," Chaplin had told him. "No one can follow you." After a mile Rono broke cleanly from James Munyala, who had moved into close company with him. Rono had trouble gauging his steps and had to chop before several barriers, but sprinted the last 200 with great bounds. "Nice job," said Chaplin.

"Nice and easy." The time was 8:12:39, six more seconds sliced from the old meet record.

Rono lay for a few minutes in the trainer's tent, sweat streaming from his body, then slowly walked the perimeter of an adjoining grassy field, his head down. When he returned, Chaplin walked beside him. "I don't think I want to run the 5,000," said Rono. There was relief in Chaplin's eyes.

"But I want to help the team," said Rono.

"You've done enough."

−1978

Postscript:

Enough for one day, perhaps, but later in the summer of 1978, Rono ran 10,000 meters in Vienna in 27:22.5 and 3,000 meters in Oslo in 7:32.1, both world records, giving him four for the year. In 1981, Rono improved the 5,000 record to 13:06.20, ten weeks after he had taken his degree in psychology from WSU.

Grete Waitz

Again to Scandinavia. Summer woods, dripping and fragrant. Trails of sand and sawdust, smooth from the rain, lead through blueberries and and fern, rising over smooth humps of granite. The ridges, carved by glaciers, run north and south, with lakes between, their waters dark with conifers' shadow, evoking Norse legend. In the mind's eye the remains of Grendel lie wedged beneath sunken logs and stones.

The trail goes for miles, its severity of rock and evergreen drawing the runner on, farther and farther from Oslo. So long as the day is cool and wet, few people are to be seen, but with the midmorning sun appear elderly couples in walking shorts and tea dresses, backpackers with dogs on leads. The slanting shafts of light sometimes fall upon bare girls, glowing brown behind veils of fireweed. Graying, wiry runners trot slowly but with radiant purpose, as if they don't mean to stop until they reach Trondheim or Stavanger.

With such terrain and a tradition of rigorous sport, it seems a wonder that Norway has not produced more fine runners than it has, but, of course, for five months of the year this land beneath snow. Then the trails are used for cross-country skiing. Runners, if they don't simply quit and ski through the winter, must go to the hard and treacherous road.

Grete Waitz does. Those are the days when she rises at five hours before the northern dawn, and pushes out into the cold and wind. "Don't run with her in the morning," says Arne Kvalheim, a former Olympic 1,500-meter runner and now an Oslo city councilman. "She runs too fast. A 5:45 mile pace right out the front door." Then during the day Waitz teaches physical education, Norwegian and English to secondary students at Björsen School in one of Oslo's tougher neighborboods. The light has again failed by the time she joins her husband Jack, an accountant, for her evening training, which may be an hour of repeated charges up a snow-swept hill, weighted by two or three sweat suits, seeing no more than a stride or two ahead, her breath snapping in the ten-below-zero air.

"There is no sense of sacrifice," she says, "except sometimes in the summer. When it is warm and sunny, it's hard for me to run. I'd rather go on a holiday instead. But in the winter, I go early to bed, I get up and run. I like it, the way I live, but I find I can't explain the satisfaction to people who do not run."

Perhaps the way to start is to mention the achievements founded upon all that cold, dark work. Waitz has won the world cross-country championship the last four years, by 30 seconds each time. In July 1979 she ran 3,000 meters in 8:31.8 a time second only to the 8:27.1 world record of the U.S.S.R.'s Ludmila Bragina, and she won the 1977 World Cup at 3,000 meters, the longest regularly contested track race for women. On the road, Waitz has covered the popular 10-kilometer distance in a world-best 30:59, which is 45 seconds better than any other woman. In her first marathon, the New York race of 1978, Waitz broke the world record by more than two minutes with her 2:32:30, a time that showed but a hint of her true potential.

Knut Kvalheim, Arne's brother and the Norwegian men's 10,000-meter record holder, is the man who got Waitz interested in her first marathon. He believed in 1979 that if conditions are right, she can run in the vicinity of 2:25. Statistics support him. A ratio of other good marathoners' times for the 10,000 meters shows that they all slow down by a factor of 8 to 10 percent in the longer race. Granting Waitz the liberal rate of a 10 percent slower pace than she maintains over 10,000 meters, she still figured to complete the full 26-mile, 385-yard marathon distance in 2:25:07. The element that has allowed Waitz to so embarrass prior long distance records is her speed, not necessarily raw sprinter's power—that she doesn't have—but an ability to sustain a high percentage of her maximum pace over all kinds of distances. This she developed in a ten-year career as a middle-distance runner, and she has taken her records by such margins in part because she is the first international class woman miler and 3,000-meter runner to attempt the 10,000 and marathon seriously.

Waitz was born Grete Andersen in Oslo in 1953. Her father was a manufacturing pharmacist, and her mother worked in a grocery shop. "I always liked sport," she says. she had gone from handball to gymnastics to track before she was twelve. She ran the sprints at first, rising to "the longer distances" Of 400 and 800 meters when she was fifteen. Her chief inspiration was a neighbor, Terje Pedersen, who in 1964 was the first man ever to throw the javelin more than 300 feet. "He was my hero, says Waitz now, smiling at the memory. "I joined the same club, I wanted to please him so much.

"As a child I understood I was better in the 800 than the 400. As I trained I got no faster, only stronger. By 1972 I was running the 800 and 1,500, and I saw I was better in the 1,500, so I trained more and more but still got no faster, just stronger."

In 1974 she was third in the European championship 1,500, by then fitting the classically frustrating mold of a solid miler without a kick. The next year she set a world record of 8:46.6 for 3,000 meters, but as the Olympics did not include even that modest distance (about 240 yards short of two miles) for women, she was forced back to the 1,500, where she made the semifinals in Montreal but not the finals.

Until 1978 Waitz's career developed much as those of earlier women runners whose natural gifts were in the direction of endurance, but who found no chance for full expression on the track. A close parallel is Doris Brown Heritage, of Seattle, five-time world cross-country champion between 1967 and 1971, who was forced to run 800 meters in the 1968 Olympics because at that time it was the longest race permitted to women. Brown Heritage finished fifth in 2:03.9. At the peak of her fitness, Brown Heritage incorporated training runs of as much as thirty miles in her routine, and surely would have run a marathon in the low 2:30's, but women didn't run marathons in 1968.

Ten years later women did, having embraced the distance by the thousands, and so when it occurred to Knut Kvalheim and Jack Waitz that Grete for once ought to discover what she could do at a real distance, there was New York's invitation. "It came at a good time," says Waitz, "after the European championship, when I was getting back into some distance training, but I really came because I had never seen New York City. I had no idea how I would do. I'd never run more than eighteen miles in training."

Always an intelligent runner, Waitz carefully followed the pace of West

Germany's Christa Vahlensieck, the record holder at 2:34:48, and let brave and ambitious American Marty Cooksey run to a substantial lead by ten miles. Across the Queensborough Bridge, with miles to go, Waitz struck out after Cooksey, caught her on the long pull north on First Avenue, and carried on through the Bronx, Harlem, and into Central Park, driving herself the way she had learned on the track, her face impassive, her eyes often directed at an angle slightly above the road in a manner suggesting supplication, her attention fixed on the alarming pain the pounding was creating in her thighs. Though she ran the second half of the race four minutes faster than the first the finish came just in time.

"I couldn't have gone much farther," she says now. "I couldn't run for three days afterward. I even had trouble walking. Maybe I ran well because I didn't know how terrible it is, the pain after thirty kilometers. Now that I understand what a marathon is, maybe this year I will run slower."

Maybe, but it is hard to imagine Waitz slacking off once she has committed herself to a race. Her career and her life reflect a harsh set of imperatives. "I'll never stop running, but the hard training and competition call for intensity. Once you know international racing, you can't just ease off a bit. It has to be one or the other: as hard as you can, or just for fun."

Jack Waitz, whom Grete married in 1975, believes that she might have quit if she hadn't discovered road racing. Grete allows that she had difficulty with "motivation" in 1974 and 1975, but credits Jack himself with being the key to her continuing. "If not for him I wouldn't be running today. He's interested, he's there to discuss training and tactics, he picks me up in the wintertime. If he should choose only to sit inside beside the fire and I have to go out running. . . well, I would not do that."

Grete is a private person, "seeking the quiet," she says. "Especially coming home from a whole day of noisy children," but out of the calm interior she is careful to preserve comes a fine independent resolve. "She isn't easily molded. She wouldn't have thrived in any more structured system," says Jack, thinking of the Eastern European ways of total sport. "Hers must be as normal a life as possible. She is very bright, she always got the best marks in school and was the youngest applicant accepted for the teachers college. She prepared for teaching as carefully as for running, and it is just as important to her."

The opportunities posed by the running boom are so compelling however, that Grete took 1979 [and 1980] off from teaching "to travel, to say yes to lots of invitations in the U.S., Australia, Czechoslovakia. You can always work as a teacher but you can't always run." Such is her devotion to her own way that she refuses the stipend offered world-class athletes by the Norwegian Amateur Athletic Federation to help with training expenses. "If I accept the money, I cannot help it, I feel pressured to pay it back in good results, she says. "Now I run for myself and I feel free."

One thing Waitz has decidedly not been free to do is display her talent and training before an Olympic audience, unless of course, she cared to return to the struggles of the 1,500 meters. In 1979 the brothers Kvalheim (along, with half the population of Oslo) discussed Waitz's plight, Arne maintaining, "If she changed her training, I'm sure she could run the 1,500 in 3:54." (The world record at the time was 3:56.0 by Tatyana Kazankina of the U.S.S.R.) Knut said, "I can understand her feeling, that she has gotten to be the best in the world at her natural distances. So why should she be expected to sacrifice that to run something too short for her? Let the international officials come to their senses and put in a 5,000 meters for women, at least."

Waitz, considering these points of view, agreed. "I probably could get near 3:55 with a year of intensive speed training. But I believe you will need to run a 3:55 just to make the final in the Moscow Olympics. If I had never been in an Olympics, I would try for the 1,500. But I have been in two Olympics, and I have decided I won't do all that kind of training; that I don't like to *maybe* be in the final. I have found my way of training, and I want to stick to it. So, since I cannot feel right about going to an Olympics with no chance to represent my country as best I can, I shall not run in Moscow."

Waitz was without illusion that the IOC would be quickly persuaded to add the distances to the Games. "It won't be easy. The arguments have all been tried. I think for many people anything new takes getting used to. In 1973 when we first ran the 3,000 here in Oslo, lots of journalists said it was terrible, it wasn't pretty to see women getting tired. That changed when I set a world record in it in 1975. Everybody loved it then." Indeed, in 1979 when Grete ran the Norwegian cross-country championship, held on the grassy hills near the Ostensjovann bird sanctuary, 3,000 people came out to watch her win, and 1,500 promptly went home satisfied, ignoring the men's race.

Waitz is hailed by her road-racing competition as an inspiring view of what is to come. "She's teaching us what it is to train like serious athletes," said Patti Catalano, who by 1981 would be the American-record holder at all four distances from five miles to the marathon. In her concentration, her cool grace, her coiled-spring hardness, Waitz is a riveting symbol of uncompromised excellence, and the message is taking hold.

Blessed with a progressive society and encouraging husband Waitz has little sense of herself as a campaigner for the right to fully develop one's gifts. Oslo, which frequently sees world records set in its Bislett Stadium, never has had an exercise boom because its citizens have never stopped exercising. "People walk in the woods and to work, and ski in the winter," she says. "The common man is much more fit than in the U.S." Norwegians do not worship their champions so much as they respectfully emulate them. Waitz finds the mass runs in the United States, such as the 14,000-strong New York City Marathon, strangely antic, the running mania as far out of proportion as was the country's earlier indifference to running. Too, the surge to women's road running, she feels, with its emphasis on high training mileages, is not necessarily best for performances. "The main difference between me and the other girls is simply that I have more speed, more tempo. Girls training now don't do enough speed or track training. They are running long all the time."

Even though road races have proved to be her forte, Waitz remains steadfast in her judgment that track and cross-country are more important. She changed nothing in her training to prepare for her subsequent marathons. "No really long runs," she says. "Rather than the two hours at a time that others do, I prefer an hour in the morning, another hour in the evening." Her goals are private, but she will tolerate some brief speculation about how rapidly she may be able to run 10,000 meters. Thirty minutes would be a historic pinnacle, as Paavo Nurmi was never able to run that fast (he set a world record of 30:06.1 in 1924). Waitz's 30:59 was done on the road on a warm day in June in New York's L'eggs Mini-Marathon over a hilly course, and she set her own pace all the way. "It's mentally easier on the road," says Waitz, "but Jack says running in spikes on a level track on a cool evening will be faster, and running with men, it will not feel like twenty-five laps."

"Maybe 30:30," says Jack with a tender expression. "The only question is, will she ever do it?"

This seems a bow to the quiet internal workings of Grete, a willingness to wait for her resolve to crystallize. It conforms with her own assessment of herself, that she will get to these things when she is ready.

"Sometimes people look at me and because I am not always smiling and laughing they think I am sad. I'm not sad. I'm not. I'm maybe a little cool. Not impulsive, but controlled. That's the word. Controlled."

—October 1979

Postscript:

Running a carefully controlled pace, in the 1979 New York City Marathon, Waitz removed almost five minutes from her record with 2:27:33. "One of these a year is enough," she said then. Exactly a year later she came to her third New York City Marathon, and set her third world record. 2:25:42, a time that would have won all men's Olympic marathons until 1952.

Then, to her delight, in February 1981, the IOC executive committee voted a women's marathon into the 1984 Games in Los Angeles.

The Man Who United Ireland:
Eamonn Coghlan

Mist floats through the woods of Newlands Golf Club outside Dublin, making the heavily leafed trees two dimensional, dulling the muddy green of the fairways. Irish golfers are out in force this late spring morning, quietly moving about the course, peering intently after each shot in hopes of catching at least a glimpse of the general direction of the ball's flight before it is erased by the fog. Ahead, however, there is some kind of disturbance. Shouting. And running. The golfers nearest him are raising their clubs as if apoplectic. Their calls come clear. "Ah, you're a hard man, Eamonn Coghlan."

Running lightly, Coghlan smiles, for this is homage. "You're a great bit o' stuff and God bless," he hears. "Run like hell and get us a gold next year in Moscow," comes another. "Or a silver or a bronze. Anything, as long as it's for Ireland."

For four years Coghlan has carried such fervent hopes onto the track, and just now in early 1979, after demolishing the world record for the indoor mile with his 3:52.6 in San Diego and then winning the European Indoor 1,500 meter championship in Vienna, Dublin is making much of him. He accepts praise gracefully, not trying to deflect or deny it—for if an observer is moved, can that be denied? Yet Coghlan's pleasure at recognition often seems less personal than communal. When he says he is proud of what his father was told after the Montreal Olympic 1,500 in which Eamonn finished fourth—"He may not have won, but, by God, for four minutes he united Ireland," he seems simply to be sharing in the common wish that the nation prevail. Indeed, Coghlan's ties with Dublin are so close that a study of him must encompass the history and people of his native city, each illuminating the other.

Leaving the golf course, Coghlan runs down a busy road past the grounds of Belgard Castle and reaches home, half of a Georgian duplex, part of a large development of modern, white two-story houses with black tile roofs. the Coghlan residence is distinguished by a huge tree just over the wall of the garden, enabling Coghlan to pick it out from miles away.

After a fast shower, Coghlan emerges for breakfast elegantly dressed in a gray double-breasted suit, a pearl gray shirt and blue tie. He is a handsome man, saved from prettiness by the runner's tautness of skin. His eyes are clear blue and seem rather small for being set so deep. Photos of him at seventeen show the gorgeous dimpled youth he was when, on a bus to a track meet in Tipperary, he met the dark-haired woman who now places bacon and eggs and tea before him. Yvonne Coghlan, who bears a resemblance to Liza Minnelli, is calm and quiet. "It was five months to our first date," says Eamonn. "She always considered me a flirt." He wishes he could avoid the truth of that judgment, but all he can say is, "She always was the sensible one."

Less so himself, Coghlan often spent all his money on the movies with Yvonne

133

near her home in Santry, and then had to run the six miles back to his parents'
house in Drimnagh. The courtship was rocked only once. After four homesick
months at Villanova University in 1971, Coghlan came home to recover from
mononucleosis and the following fall didn't care to return. Yvonne, who was still
only sixteen, said he either went back or they were through. "He wasn't being
reasonable," she says simply. He obliged her, prospered, and they were married in
1976. In October 1978, the third member of the family was born. Suzanne at eight
months was a sober child with black onyx eyes. Her attention span seemed
inordinately long for an infant. A breakfast guest had to squirm under an unrelent-
ing gaze before her small, neat mouth broke into an abrupt grin, adorned with her
father's dimples. Both Yvonne and Suzanne were with Coghlan when he raced on
the U.S. indoor circuit. "Suzanne hasn't adjusted back to European time and doesn't
sleep through the night anymore," says Coghlan. "She's made my morning runs
quite consistent."

Off to work in his new Capri, Coghlan drives swiftly past factories and then
blocks of gray cement houses in the neighborhood of Drimnagh, where he grew
up. Near his parents' home stands Our Lady's Hospital for Sick Children.

"I was there for ten days when I was four," Coghlan says. "It was Ash Wednesday.
I remember it clearly. I was scudding a turf truck—that's peat to you—on a dare. I
climbed on when it was stopped and fell off on my head right in front of the hospital.
A bus driver scooped me up and carried me straight in. I was always a lucky little
devil." The first day of first grade, at the first opportunity, Coghlan ran home and
put up such a protest that he was allowed to stay out of school for six months, until
his best friend started. "I seem to have had to ease into these things," he says.

A triangle of green among the row houses, known only as "the field," was where
Coghlan hung out as a youth, playing football and sneaking cigarettes. "But when
the toughs from Crumlin [an adjoining neighborhood] came over with hurling sticks
looking for trouble, I was no hero. I ran."

He slows the car on Long Mile Road as it passes Drimnagh Castle School, run
by the Christian Brothers, where he received his secondary education. The red brick
buildings flank a twelfth-century Danish castle. Most of its stone tower is closed,
but the school uses part of it as a changing room. Coghlan began his daily training
by trotting across a bridge over a frog-filled moat. "The only castle in Ireland still
with a moat," he says, his gaze rising to the crumbling battlements. "More stones
have fallen. They say it would take eighty five thousand pounds to restore it, and
who's going to give that?"

"Irish education," he says, while continuing into Dublin's center, "is more or
less beaten into you. It was a tough transition when I went to Villanova, where you
had to take notes from lectures and ask questions. Here you copied what was on
the board and memorized it. Gaelic especially was taught that way. In the 1800s
the English suppressed Gaelic, and ever since we've been trying to revive it. I needed
to pass it to leave high school, but now I only have the habit of a phrase or two."

Coghlan draws up before Bord Fáilte, the Irish Tourist Board, where he has
worked as the youth and educational representative since July 1977. "I spent five
months reading brochures for study programs and youth tours, and meeting tour
operators, and I'm still not aware of all the products available," he said

Coghlan is marvelous at his work for about a dozen reasons. His celebrity, his American education, his manner are means of opening communication, but what a listener remembers is his feeling for Ireland and the Irish. He emphasizes their warmth toward visitors, the immense sweep of Ireland's history, the power of its spoken and written word, the beauty of its landscape, and just when one begins to grow uneasy with such superlatives, Coghlan confesses his frustrations with his people's complex character and in so doing lifts himself clear of public relations.

"The Irish are a hidebound breed," he says, not at all mildly. "In the country, life is parochial, people caring only to keep to themselves and their traditional ways and not taking notice of the rest of the world." He mentions novelist James Plunkett (*Strumpet City*), a Dubliner who has written that "Observers of human character, when they have turned their attention to Dublin, have isolated with remarkable unanimity the distinguishing mark of its true home citizen. . . He will share a characteristic philosophy, the essence of which is a serene and fatalistic composure." Plunkett explained this by reference to the Dubliners' habit of brooding over disappointments. "Add to this an inherited race memory and the history of his native city—that story of siege, pestilence, invasion, rebellion, fire, slaughter, persecution, and civil war—and the combination seems likely to instill tolerance and patience to an unusual degree."

To Coghlan, returned from the activism and efficiencies of the New World, the stolid traits of his people often seem lamentable. "Even though traffic is horrendous, Dublin doesn't want a new expressway over the bay," he says. "We can't construct new office buildings because they may disturb some of the old Viking city Dublin is built upon. It is wonderful to have such a past, but sometimes you have to cease dwelling on the ordeals the Irish have endured and think of the future." This perhaps sounds too strident to him, so he says, "I admit I've thought of leaving, but my heart is still in Ireland."

In his bright, poster filled office, Coghlan makes dozens of telephone calls, organizing presentations, itineraries, luncheons. His English takes on more pace, a stiffer accent when he is addressing countrymen. "When I'm in the States I'm influenced by the voices," he says, grinning. "In Dublin I revert to the way the tongue is meant to be used." John Synge, who wrote, among other masterpieces, *The Playboy of the Western World*, felt that the Irish have been notable in English literature because of the "invigorating suggestiveness" of Irish popular speech, but Coghlan finds that American slang has equivalent force. "'Airhead' makes people here smile," he says, "though 'zonked' is incomprehensible."

While Coghlan labors at his arranging, a gnomish, gray-haired man pops into his office. J. P. Murray is the golf promotion adviser to the Tourist Board, a runner and a man of clear pronouncements. "There is nothing *good* advertised on TV," he says, apropos of how valuable is the wholesome appeal of Coghlan. "Not sunsets, not fresh fruit, not rainbows. Not even women for their own sake." Murray can feel his society exerting firm pressure against being first rate. "Decay is everywhere. Insidious. Now they're reducing a natural, elemental thing like running to second rate 'jogging' or 'fun runs.'" He looks as if he's about to spit. "You never see anyone playing 'fun golf.'"

Coghlan lunches in the Old Stand, which is filled with golden light, paintings of Dublin street scenes, brass, and dark paneling. "Pub grub," says Coghlan, hacking into his lamb chops at the bar.

"You've been in the big time since we saw you last" says Seamus O'Rourke, pouring him a Harp lager.

"Things fell into place," says Coghlan easily. When O'Rourke has gone, Coghlan reflects that his life has indeed seemed a charmed one. "Things have always fitted into place. When I was in high school and my running came into conflict with the demands of hard Irish scholarship, I chose running, and through that got a good university education. Now I have a good job, surpassing most of the guys who ground it out at school."

None of this was planned, at least not by Coghlan. He says, "Lucky breaks, I've gotten them. Things like the world record, the European Indoor gold medal, those once were dreams, but if I dream anything, it seems to work out." Such a faith is calming, at the very least. "In the dark days of winter, when my hemoglobin was low and training was an ordeal, I didn't really worry. If I were to worry, I think perhaps things *wouldn't* fit into place. I let the goals come to me.

This is not to suggest that Coghlan has been exactly passive about ordering his life around his discipline. "Mates at work say on days when it's splashing out, 'Come on have a few beers with us,' and I say I can't and they say, 'Just this once,' but I know that once turns into twice and then a dozen, so I can't, and they don't understand that." His tone is flat, without illusion. "When I came back from Villanova in 1976 the comparison of American and Irish life was forced on me. It seemed in the U.S. that people wanted to do the best they could, they wanted to achieve without cutting corners, whether in sports or business. Here there is a tendency to want the most you can get for the least work." He cites the post office and dock workers' strikes of that spring. "Sometimes it seems people are looking to strike not for legitimate reasons of fairness but out of jealousy of other workers or greed. The crane operators say they won't go back without a raise of fifty pounds a *week*."

Outside, walking, Coghlan is hailed by an elderly priest with crooked teeth. He says he is from the nearby Clarendon Street Church and has a Mrs. Coghlan in the flock.

"Near ninety and independent?" says Coghlan. "Practically lives in the church? That's my grandmother."

"Is she now?" the priest says. "How fine for her to have such a grandson." This seems too syrupy to the cleric, apparently, for he concludes with, "Ah, you're trying, anyway. That's the thing, you're trying.

Coghlan watches him retreat and says with satisfaction, "This, *this* is Dublin."

He stops in at the City Hall to pick up some engraved invitations to a reception the following week, at which he is to be honored for his recent achievements. He receives the gilt-edged cards from Noel Carroll, the Dublin public relations officer, who looks leaner than when he ran a 1:47.5 880 for Villanova in the early sixties. A decade and a half later, Carroll was still the Irish national 880-meter champion and had just returned from a noon hour devoted to hard 220's at a nearby track. He shows Coghlan and a visitor around the great dome of the hall, pointing at the city motto in mosaic on the stone floor OBEDIENTIA CIVIUM URBIS FELICITAS.

"Which means if you toe the line, you'll be O.K." says Carroll, a man of easy informality. But informality is carried to a fault in the Dublin City Hall, as one learns when Carroll ducks through a little door beneath the stairs and emerges with a frayed brown paper envelope, from which he slips the first charter of Dublin, brown ink on leather, signed by Henry II in 1172, two years after the Normans overpowered the Danes. Coghlan plays with the charter's green braided thong while Carroll unfolds a great folio of vellum—a later charter illuminated with gold leaf and a painting of Queen Elizabeth.

"The first, I guess," says Carroll. Soon he is struggling to lift the city's sword and huge, three-hundred-year-old silver and gold mace. "Great symbolism here," he says pointing out the chased Irish harp, the English rose, and the Scottish thistle. "In any other city in the world these would be on display," he says. "And we do bring them out on one or two occasions, quietly, but it takes a while for people to think of them as other than hateful symbols of the monarchy, the foreign rule we fought to get rid of. The emotion still lingers. This seems to confirm Coghlan's belief that history is different for the Irish, never seeming to fade. But then the English still gently fan the embers, as in a report Carroll saw filed by an English reporter from the 1979 World Cross-Country Championship in Limerick (where Ireland's John Treacy scored a masterful victory and Coghlan ploughed home seventieth). "England won the team championship," says Carroll, easily quoting the article from memory, "but Ireland had the consolation of supplying the first individual to finish."

It is with more reverence that Carroll opens a green leather book containing the signatures of those on whom the Freedom of the City has been conferred, modern Dublin's highest honor. "There are fifty-two names, on numbered lines. Ulysses S. Grant is there, and Charles Parnell, and George Bernard Shaw, and John F. Kennedy." Coghlan's expression, examining this roster, is one of soft pride. "Lots of cardinals in between the great names," he says. "No runners, though." He seems to be cheered by this reminder that sporting conquests do fade, that athletes seldom by their art win men out of bondage.

In the afternoon, after a drive past St. Patrick's Cathedral, where Jonathan Swift was dean from 1713 to 1745, Coghlan parks near the gray stone of Kilmainham Gaol. "The leaders of the Easter Week Rising were executed up there," he says. That was in 1916, though he speaks as if it happened last year. Nearby is the clubhouse of the Donore Harriers, a bare, cold room with bits of mud on its masonite floor. Coghlan hangs his suit on a nail and is soon out running across Phoenix Park, 1,750 acres of moist woods and fields surrounding Arus an Uachtaráin—the Irish White House.

"I do about seventy percent of my running over soft country," he says "I think it's best not to pound your legs on the hard roads any more than you have to." In this off season between indoors and out, he runs ninety miles a week of stamina work, alternating days of hard surges over hills with days of more gentle effort. This is an easy day, but Coghlan still constantly changes his speed, as if answering some internal spring that gets wound too tightly, by an unvarying pace.

Cruising down a long row of huge trees, he says, "See the crooked trunk, fourth from the end? That's where I started my first race, when I was eleven. I'd just joined the club, and the officials said I couldn't run the mile cross-country, I was too young, too new. I cried until they let me in and then I won. I can still see the shock on those faces."

A couple of miles on, Coghlan plunges down steep trails through thickets. "This is Furry Glen," he shouts. "On Sundays we'd go for cat and mouse chases in here with Gerry Farnan, my coach then and now. Miles and miles and loved it all." Then and now. "The idea was to enjoy our running, not. to be slogging away so hard we'd be tired of competing by seventeen. Gerry has no use for people who slog kids."

Coghlan churns over the tops of steep green moguls, part of what he calls the "Munich Lap" because his first hard training came here, as he tried to get a qualifying time for the 1972 Olympic 1,500. He was nineteen then. Coghlan missed by a tenth and then took up his Villanova education in earnest.

The line of Irish runners at Villanova began in 1948 with Jim Reardon and continued with the likes of John Joe Barry (The Ballincurrie Hare), Ron Delany, the 1956 Olympic 1,500 meter champion, Noel Carroll, Frank Murphy, Donal Walsh, and John Hartnett. Now that Neil Cusack and Ed Leddy have performed well at East Tennessee State, Niall O'Shaughnessy at Arkansas, and Treacy at Providence, an Irish runner of promise senses he has a choice, but Coghlan's only dream was of Villanova. "I thought it was going to be the greatest thing since sliced pan," he says. "But it wasn't easy. I was homesick at first, and Jumbo Elliott [the school's almost magically successful coach since 1935] wanted it hard, academically and athletically. The guys I met in school were a tremendous help, genuine friends, not at all like the mouthy U.S. tourists in plaid slacks from which I'd formed my stereotypes of Americans. Jumbo coached the team like a 3:30 to 5 business, like the heavy equipment company that made him a millionaire, and there were no board meetings. Jumbo was the boss. We'd warm up and then learn our day's workout. It took a while to understand Jumbo even a little. He wanted to do all the thinking. It was his job to get us ready. It was our job to run. Guys who didn't understand that didn't do well. Those who did, and accepted it, and went with him did fine."

Coghlan was a good accepter. In 1975 he ran a 3:53.3 mile behind Filbert Bayi's 3:51:0 world record in Jamaica. His natural speed and a dramatic talent for acceleration late in a race were honed with thousands of 440's on Villanova's outdoor board track, and with races on the U.S. indoor circuit.

"I could never have achieved the same goals if I'd stayed in Ireland," he says. "I was pretty raw when I arrived. I still smoked until I got the scholarship. And suddenly I was thrown in with guys like Ken Schappert, Hartnett, and Marty Liquori. It was hard even to train the way they did. But inside there was a flicker of certainty. I had won in the Irish juniors. In a couple of years I won in college and then in the NCAA championships. Then on the next plateau, international competition. The point is I wouldn't have gotten there had I not been exposed to those various levels. Each plateau took a new adjustment and gave new confidence. Now I can run with anyone in the world, even though the sensations of racing are a exactly the same as they were when I was fourteen."

Deep in the park, Coghlan surges up a wooded slope, scattering a herd of deer. "It's great here today," he says. "But you can hate it sometimes. I always cringe inside when people say running comes naturally to me, that training is nothing but an uplifting joy. That's not why I race well. I'm competitive. I always have been—not necessarily to be first, but to do the best I can." He runs slowly across a half mile of soccer and hurling fields that were Dublin's eighteenth century dueling grounds. "It's something in me, deep down that makes me different in a race."

The difference lies in Coghlan's kick, the late move so explosive it cannot be countered. It is an act requiring calm husbanding of reserves during the race, then a sudden blazing release. "Coghlan perfectly balances these extremes. He is the potent sprinter waiting within the patient distance runner. There are men who can carry a kick longer than Coghlan—England's Steve Ovett is the best just now—but none who detonate as he does. He won the 1976 NCAA 1,500 from UTEP's Wilson Waigwa and Oregon's Matt Centrowitz by not beginning to sprint until the last 50 meters. In his semifinal at the Montreal Olympics he came out of the pack off the last turn and, within 20 meters, moved out to a five-meter lead, coasting in with a happy smile.

Then, the evening before the final, he was nervous. "I spoke to Gerry Farnan and said I was just going to follow John Walker and go in the last straight. Gerry was content with that, and I felt better. I went to bed and fell right to sleep.

"In the morning Jumbo called. He said that with all the faster half-milers in the field, like Rick Wohlhuter and Ivo Van Damme from Belgium, if the pace was slow I'd have to run their speed out of them. I'd have to lead. I think the bottom fell out of my confidence right there. I remember warming up, unable to keep from watching everything Walker and Van Damme did. I should have been concentrating. I was new to this last plateau. I went to the line confused."

Dave Moorcroft of England was in front at the 400 Meter mark, in 62.5. "Frustration set in," says Coghlan. "I led after 500 meters. As soon as I was in front I started praying for someone to pass me." The 800 was 2:03.2, the pack compressed within three strides. "It was a horrible realization," Coghlan says, shaking his arms at the memory of those moments. "They were kickers. Instead of running it out of them, I was running it out of me."

Walker challenged on the third lap, less a decisive move than one to establish a position to kick from. "I held him off, held him off," says Coghlan. "That was wrong. I should have just readied myself for one last burst." Walker went by in earnest with 300 meters to run, and the race was on. Van Damme went by. "I held off Wohlhuter on the turn, but when I hit the straight the zip was gone," Coghlan says. Van Damme moved out to challenge Walker. Coghlan found the inside blocked by Paul Heinz Wellman of West Germany, the outside by Van Damme. "I had nowhere to go. I began to lean, but it was too early. I lost momentum before the line. Wellman passed me for the bronze medal. I had lost the gold by three tenths of a second. As far as I was concerned, it was the end of my career."

The following weeks were for Coghlan the closest to purgatory he cares to pass. "I tried to be brave, but I was hurt in a way I had never been. All the omens had seemed right, all my dreams had been for success. I went back to the Villanova campus and was afraid to face anyone. I walked across the street to avoid the question. He looks across at his running companion. "You know, fourth is the absolute worst place to finish in the Olympics."

"It took weeks, but I got over it," he says, perhaps too blithely. "Maybe it was a good thing to have happen because you learn what it's worth, the medal. And it's not the world. I visited Walker last year and I said, 'Hey, John, where's that medal you won off me?' And there it was on the wall, just a medal with a bunch of other medals."

When he returned to Dublin after graduating with a degree in management, Coghlan submitted the training he had been doing at Villanova to Gerry Farnan's review. Farnan felt that Elliott's program, which was based on 400 yard intervals, certainly had given Coghlan speed but not the stamina to sustain it. Farnan added weekly 20-mile runs and vigorous 3/4- and 1½-mile intervals over hills. "Gerry likes things done right," Coghlan says, "but he prefers to stay in the background. In training he knows me, through and through. If I'm down and don't want to run, he'll know whether there is something organically wrong or whether I just need to get going." Coghlan has granted the same decision-making powers to Farnan that Elliott demanded "I don't want to agonize about how everything ought to go. We have a talk every three or four weeks and adjust the schedule as seems best." Thus Coghlan resolves the eternal tension between thought and action by a division of labor, leaving the coach's contemplations unclouded by the runner's fears, the runner's efforts unburdened by doubt.

It works, as proved by his 3:52.6 indoor record. Coghlan speaks as if that run may have lifted him to a yet loftier plateau. "There was some question in my mind whether I'd ever run a 3:53 again. I'd done it in 1975, then 3:53.4 in 1977. Running it indoors has given me a real confidence."

After a shower, Coghlan drops by his parents' home, where he sits down to a quick cup of tea beside the coal fire in their small medal- and trophy-cluttered parlor. Mrs. Kathleen Coghlan, his mother, has flashing russet hair. Before she has time for pleasantries, the doorbell rings and in rushes Father Andy Sheehan, a runner, singer, and the priest who christened Coghlan's daughter.

"Ah, I was watching you struggle away down there in the limerick mud," he says to Eamonn, laughing at the recollection of the World Cross Country Championship weeks earlier. "That's why I missed the Music Society meeting." Father Sheehan reveals that he has taken delivery of a new Kawasaki 650 motorcycle, his second in a month. "Can you imagine? Some bugger *stole* the first." The conversation turns to Eamonn's beginnings, which in a neighbor's view were not auspicious. "She said he looked like a skinned rabbit," says Mrs. Coghlan. "Long and thin and red." She is firm on the point that she never pushed Eamonn into running. "It was a God-given gift, is the way I look at it," she says.

"Which would be lying dead now if he didn't put forth the effort," says Father Sheehan. He cannot stay long because he has a race this afternoon and confessions at seven and eulogies to prepare. "The parishioners are dying like flies," he says and exits, displaying electric blue socks beneath his black broadcloth. In the sudden vacuum of his passing, he seems an appropriate addition to an Ireland that let Swift run its cathedral.

Then the room is filled once more, this time by William Coghlan, Eamonn's father. A man of immense warmth, he is an electrical contractor. Asked if he has any big jobs going, he says, "No, just little ones. Just things I can do myself. Who wants to be a millionaire? The money only brings worries. Can money put a good family around you, the likes of Yvonne and Suzanne? I'm richer than all the millionaires I know." Eamonn beams approval.

William Coghlan for four years has been the president of the Irish Amateur Athletic Federation, the national governing body for track and field. "It can be mutually embarrassing," Eamonn has said of having the governor and the governed in the same family. "If I complain publicly, am I complaining about my father? And if he makes a point in a meeting, is he saying what's best or what's best for his son?" The runner has come to appreciate the problems of the official, and the official those of the runner. "Now that he knows how forcefully the Irish people are behind him," says William Coghlan, walking Eamonn and a guest to the car, "Eamonn should spend six months in the States, racing the best people, to prepare for Moscow. That's because the official idea of sport can be discouraging here. It seems that I am always lecturing other officials that it is not they who are important but the athletes."

It is Coghlan's practice three or four times a week to have a massage from Barney Crosbie who is a physiotherapist to rugby teams and the occasional runner, "because he's a loner," says Crosbie, "as I was for twenty years." Crosbie has a firmly set down-turning mouth and sixty or eighty mobile wrinkles on his forehead. He rubs Coghlan with "putcheen," a mixture of barley moonshine and olive oil. Coghlan has turned his head while the table and seen Crosbie taking a swig of the stuff for inspiration. "They use it on horses and dogs so it must be good for humans," says the masseur, coughing.

Crosbie and Coghlan enjoy an affectionate contentiousness, based on Crosbie's remarkable assertions. "No world records are set after ten P.M.," he says. "After that the muck of the air comes down on you. After three A.M. the muck of the air starts to lift and you're lifted with it."

"But, Barney, I ran my world record after ten at night." "Now, that was *indoors*, wasn't it?," says Crosbie with a tone of dismissal. "Another thing. You'll do yourself harm if you train when it's below freezing."

"But I do it all the time, and I've never had any problem."

"You're a lucky man."

Crosbie says that swimming and running don't mix, and that "endurance comes from running seventy or eighty naked miles a week, but *stamina* comes from sprinting."

"Stamina?" says Coghlan. "I disagree. Sprinting just sharpens my speed."

"Ah, as soon as I open a hole you have a post to stick in it. I'll tell you why I never was a coach, even though I studied all this for forty years—because I would always fight with my athletes."

"Ah, Barney, you would," says Coghlan with a soft smile. "But it's a great pair of hands you have."

As they part, Crosbie's farewell is, "Come a day and, go a day and God send Sunday."

Come Sunday and Coghlan has his twenty-mile run with clubmates. This morning it was with Paddy Keogh, a hard-muscled bus driver in his late thirties who runs twenty miles every day. "And never won a thing," says Coghlan with respect for the man's love of simply covering the country.

"I run because if I didn't I'd just end up in the boozer," says Paddy cheerfully as they set off against a cool, wet wind, heading for the hills that rise behind Dublin. For a while they chatter about obscure club politics, training, and how the devil appeared at the old tavern, visible above them, where the Hell Fire Club met. "He came as a black cat," says Coghlan in seeming earnest. "Blew a hole right through the roof." Coghlan's Irishness includes a certain faith in what might be called divine justice. "I could never fake an injury to get out of a race promise," he has said. "If I did that, I'd be afraid I'd actually get the injury I faked." Or what might be called superstition.

On the steepest pitches the only sounds are the runners' soggy footfalls and their blowing as they work at the hill. Stone pasture walls give way to thickening pine woods and then vistas. They turn onto an unpaved track. It is clean and cool this morning, and Coghlan slows to better enjoy the landscape. Dublin below is hidden by clouds. He speaks of his growing stamina, saying that runs like this were once devastating labor but now are exhilarating.

"I'm sure in my heart that I can run a good five thousand. It may even turn out to be my best event." He ran 13:26.6 for the 3⅛ mile distance in an exciting race in 1978 in Dublin, making up 100 meters on England's Mike McLeod in the last 800 and winning narrowly with a 56-second last lap.

They leave the woods for a paved road that climbs on toward Killakee, running through open terrain with flinty outcroppings. Coghlan laments not being able to see the summits, but there is an eerie splendor to the slopes ascending into mists. Coghlan is asked if in these high and windswept places he experiences a sensation of escape.

"From the crush, you mean? From the people wanting autographs? Yes, I do. But I've come to accept the loss of what little time that takes, simply because there is no sensible alternative." Coghlan is unfailingly patient with even the most aggressive seekers after his touch, his word, a stroke of his pen. "I kind of take pride in the general idea of being noticed," he says, "for it means I have done something well. I try not to let the actual words and people tarnish that idea."

From a ridge, the runners turn and descend toward Bonabreena, finally relaxing, freewheeling. Coghlan runs with the quietest arm action of the world's best runners, and at this six-minutes-per-mile pace he never fully straightens his legs, touching his heels down with the knees still slightly bent. It is a practiced distance runner's stride.

There is no sense of a man with unanswerable speed. The only way to fully appreciate his kick is to be his victim off a final turn. Here, in the hills, he prefers to talk.

Much as Shaw and Joyce and Beckett left Ireland in order to tell about it, Coghlan seems a man able to stand outside his own culture. "I feel I'm half Dubliner, half American, sometimes holding these opposites equally dear. The American part is ambition, I guess. The Irish half has more to do with acceptance." Acceptance, as Coghlan uses it, ought not to be confused with surrender. The harshest acceptance is of the pain of effort.

"I accept defeat as I do success. I can't bring back Montreal, so why brood over it? I've always been sort of a believer that your life is set out for you." Which makes acceptance a more sensible philosophy than raging to change the inevitable, but there seems a catch, namely, the contradiction between a preordained life and freedom of will. "If your life is following a preset plan," Coghlan is asked, "does that absolve you of responsibility for it?"

Coghlan carefully considers this as the runners drop into green paddocks and thicker air, nearing home. "Maybe its ordained that we have responsibility for our actions," he says, trying to dodge the logical incompatibility of the two states, controlled or free, blameless instrument or responsible being. "No, that can't be right."

Finally he says, "What I feel is that we do have choices. We do have control, but in the end we are going to have only one life unfold. In that sense you have to know when to relax and stop worrying about it."

He reaches his front step and hears Suzanne crying, so rushes in to comfort her. "There is always responsibility," he says firmly, holding up the child as irrefutable proof. He nuzzles her into a smile, and in that moment it seems that if one has only one life to aspire to, Eamonn Coghlan's would do quite nicely.

—June 1979

The Golden Mile

That year, Eamonn Coghlan took part in the greatest mile ever run. The race was so compelling that when it was over, it seemed to demand a reconstruction of its parts. As well, it was that rarest of occasions, one which deserved the name its promoters gave it: The Golden Mile.

The streams of talent and preparation and resolve that would converge in, Oslo at twilight on July 17, 1979 arose in improbable springs located across the world. One began in a desert. In 1978 the Arab emirate of Dubai, population 207,000, which rests on a sheik's ransom of oil at the south end of the Persian Gulf, abandoned the idea of hosting a major international track meet in its extreme climate. Instead it donated $400,000 to the International Amateur Athletic Federation to use for coaching clinics. In return the IAAF agreed to stage eight world-class "Golden" events in Dubai's name in selected meets over the next three years.

The first was a hurriedly arranged mile in Tokyo in September 1978. England's Steve Ovett won a tactical race with a 300-meter kick in 3:55.5. Steve Scott of the United States, by then exhausted from a year of almost uninterrupted racing, finished fourth in 4:01.1. It would not be too strong to say that Scott's first thoughts after the race were of revenge. "The IAAF said then that there would be another mile in July, in Oslo," says Scott. "I wanted Ovett again, when I was ready for him. I knew that he only races a few places each year. I figured how could he not show up for this race next season, to defend his title?"

So Scott sat down with Len Miller, his coach at the University of California at Irvine, from which Scott had just been graduated, and planned a training and racing schedule that would have him at a peak in mid-July. Now he would not have to run one or two races every weekend, as a member of a collegiate track team must. It would be the year before the Olympics. "A year to run with the idea of finding out what you can do," said Scott.

In New Zealand that winter, John Walker knew what he could do or, at least, what he had once done. He was the 1976 Olympic 1,500-meter champion and the world-record holder in the mile, having run his historic 3:49.4 in 1975, in Göteborg, Sweden. Walker's fear now was that never again would he approach that time.

Thickly muscled at six feet one and 170 pounds, Walker had seemed to usher in a new age of miling. When he won in Montreal and Cuba's six-foot-two, 185-pound stallion Alberto Juantorena ran the 800 meters there in a world-record 1:43.5, the day of the whippet-slender middle-distance runner, like the U.S.'s Rick Wohlhuter, was judged over. But after the Olympics, Walker's stiff, heavily fibrosed leg muscles began to betray him. For years he had run with inflamed Achilles' tendons, but now he experienced a gripping pain in his calves whenever he ran longer than thirty minutes. The membrane surrounding his calf muscles was growing more rigid, keeping the muscles, which became enlarged with blood under the strain of running, from expanding within their sheaths. Surgery was only partially successful.

Rather than consider retirement, Walker changed his training. If he could only run half an hour at a time, then he would run one hell of a half hour. And he would do it as many as three times a day. In January 1979, after a few months of this work, he decided to test himself at the Muhammad Ali indoor meet in Long Beach, California. After following Paul Cummings' aggressive pace, Walker burst past him on the last lap and set a world indoor 1,500-meter record of 3:37.4. He was enormously relieved, because he had almost unconsciously come to embody the wishes of his three million running-mad countrymen. "There are still pressures from holding the world record," he said. "The mile has become a traditional event, and everyone has some vague knowledge of it. If you broke four minutes were a pretty good runner. But once I got under 3:50, people began oohing and gurgling."

Walker once thought by some rivals to be amusingly transparent in his self-regard, was maturing. "Now that I have the gold medal and the world record, I think I get a richer kind of enjoyment from my running," he said. "In 1975 and 1976 I was striving for perfection. Now I go out to race still with a will to win, but not with the inclination to set records." When an invitation to run a Golden Mile in Oslo was forwarded to Walker, he was quick to accept. "The instincts are the same," he said. "I'll take on anyone, anywhere."

In the winter of 1979 Eamonn Coghlan proved himself the finest indoor miler the world had ever seen. In San Diego in February he shattered the indoor record by 2.3 seconds by running 3:52.6. Scott was second in 3:54.1 and Wisconsin's Steve Lacy third in 3:54.7. Yet during the outdoor season Coghlan planned to explore a new distance, 5,000 meters. "It will serve two purposes," he said, "prove my stamina and to discover how I'll fare against the good five thousand guys. That may even turn out to be my best event." Coghlan and his coach, Gerry Farnan, picked as a goal the winning of the British 5000-meter championship, to be held in London on July 14, 1979, just three days before the Oslo mile. Thus, when contacted about running the latter, he held off.

As the year advanced, the IAAF assigned the organization of the Oslo race to promoters Andy Norman of England and Arne Haukvik of Norway. The international body ordered all its affiliates to make their best milers available should they be invited. West Germany pledged Dr. Thomas Wessinghage, the European-record holder at 3:52.5. Japan would send Takashi Ishii, a high school teacher with a best Of 3:59.7. Australia selected Ken Hall, who had pushed Walker to his 3:49.4 with a 3:55.2.

As Scott had hoped, Ovett accepted his invitation six weeks before the race. Ovett had won the 1977 World Cup 1,500 in 3:34.5 with a prodigious sprint over the last 300 meters and had been unbeaten at a mile or 1,500 since. He was the 1978 European champion in the 1,500, having defeated Coghlan and Wessinghage. Ovett seemed to have the widest range of running abilities ever combined in one man. He had sprinted 200 meters in 21.7 and run a half marathon in 1:05:38. That he had not set a world record in the mile he explained by saying that he raced against men, not clocks. If a record were necessary to win, he was capable of one, as he had shown in 1978 in London, when he had set a world two-mile record of 8:13.51 in beating Henry Rono of Kenya.

A rigorously private man, Ovett had on occasion spoken with a prickly candor. "The British athletics press has this lazy, imperious attitude toward the athletes," he said early in 1979. "We run our guts out on the track, and if we've pleased them enough, we get a demand to attend the press box interview room, like a royal command. But if we don't say what they expect us to say, or we offend their sense of patriotism, we get branded as arrogant." By 1979 Ovett had long been so branded. Unmoved, he carried on with three workouts a day over the rolling Sussex downs near his Brighton home.

Graham Williamson of Glasgow, Scotland, only nineteen, had a best of 3:55.8 and had been third in the first Golden Mile the year before. For seven months Williamson had had a tentative invitation to Oslo, but there had been no confirmation. It appeared that with Ovett and Walker and Scott in the race, the promoters were waiting until the last moment to complete the field. They wanted the fittest runners and, because NBC-TV had bought rights to the race, a few Americans. "All year, I'd been planning to make this race the peak of my year," says Williamson. "I arranged three weeks of training at altitude in Colorado as final preparation." He returned to Scotland twelve days before the race. "My training was going badly when I got home. One afternoon, a week before the race, I was out doing four miles, and everything clicked. That was the day Norman called. "You're in," he said.

Others kept waiting were John Robson of Scotland, and Dave Moorcroft of England, the Commonwealth Games 1,500-meter champion. John Robson wasn't invited until after he'd finished third in the British 1,500 on July 14—three days before the Golden Mile. Moorcroft, who was fighting a hamstring injury and a bad cold, didn't know whether to go to Oslo or not once he had been made welcome. "I wasn't in the correct frame of mind," he says. "I was feeling sorry for myself. Finally I decided to go out to the race with my wife. But even then I was not sure about running."

Steve Lacy and Craig Masback were two Americans who suspected they had been invited to satisfy NBC. Masback had just completed two years at Trinity College, Oxford, where he was a doctoral candidate in political science. In those years, training no more than 40 miles per week, he had cut his mile time from 4:01.8 to 3:54.7. Despite a furious spate of six races in eight days in early July, Masback was still hungry and finagled an invitation a week before the race.

In a mile among equals, the pacesetter rarely wins. Meet promoters, intent on encouraging fast times, make sure to line up a journeyman rabbit for the first half-mile. The Oslo promoters, though, were permitted no mere journeymen, only top-class milers. So they went looking for a runner to sacrifice. "John Robson and I and Williamson were almost told that if we didn't want to be the rabbit we couldn't run," says Masback. Offended, they made no promises. In the Bislett Games in Oslo on July 5, Coghlan won the 3,000 meters in 7:39.1, and that night, after speaking with Haukvik, finally agreed to run the Golden Mile, twelve days later. In the same meet, England's Sebastian Coe destroyed Juantorena's 800-meter world record by a full second with a time of 1:42.4. It was the thirty-second world record set on the Bislett Stadium track.

Understanding less about the 800 meters than the mile, the popular press found the twenty-two-year-old Coe remarkable mostly for his dark-haired good looks and for having a sister, Miranda, who was a dancer in the Lido show in Las Vegas. But followers of middle-distance running saw his 1:42.4 as a quantum leap forward; he had lowered the 800-meter record by more than anyone since Peter Snell of New Zealand, who cut 1.4 seconds from it with his 1:44.3 in 1962. Walker, whom Coghlan had outkicked in the 3,000, was transfixed as he watched the 800. "Coe looked like he could run under 1:40," he said. "He never tied up at all. I think he could run a 3:51 mile right now." Privately, Walker suspected Coe could do far faster.

Coe had just taken his degree in economics from Loughborough University and was trained by his father, Peter Coe, the production director for the cutlery firm of George Butler, Ltd. of Sheffield. After the 800-meter record, Coe traveled north, to Tingvoll, Norway, to honor a commitment he had made earlier, before every English radio and newspaperman was mad to talk to him. "Mind you, it was the best thing I could have done, because I missed all the press appeals," he says. "It was a tiny place, inside a fjord. They had a new surface on the track, all silvery, something from the mines there. And the track itself was undersized. In the 800 I remember being told, 'When you get to the red hut at the corner there, it's two laps more.'" In a spray of soft silver cinders, Coe won in 1:54.8 and then went home to receive his invitation to the Golden Mile.

Coe and his father had considered him primarily an 800-meter runner since he was eighteen. His training had been designed with the aid of Loughborough physiologist George Gandy to give him the springiness and speed of a quarter-miler, but about once a year he ran a mile and showed no fear of even longer distances. He had beaten Coghlan in a four-mile road race, and British Olympic 10,000-meter bronze medalist Brendan Foster went so far as to say 5,000 meters might eventually be Coe's best event.

That he could last out a hard mile Coe proved to himself with an astounding workout a week before the Golden Mile. On a carefully measured stretch of Rivelin Valley Road west of Sheffield, he did six 800-meter runs with 90-second recovery jogs between them. "I don't remember all the times," he says, "but they were 1:52's and 1:53's. The last one was 1:49.5."

On July 13 and 14, most of the principals in the Oslo mile gathered at the British championships at Crystal Palace track, London. Coghlan reached his season's goal in style by winning the 5000 meters with a personal record of 13:23.6. He outkicked such worthies as Mike McLeod of England, Rod Dixon of New Zealand, and world record holder Henry Rono. Coe dropped down to the 400 meters and won his heat in 46.95 The next day he placed second in the final behind Sudan's Kasheef Hassan in 46.87. "I wasn't too pleased with that," he says. Later in the year he would run a 45.5 in anchoring Britain's European Cup 1,600-meter-relay team.

Steve Scott outlasted John Walker in the 800 meters, 1:47.4 to 1:47.6. Ovett toyed with the 1,500-meter field, sprinting from last to first around the final turn and coasting in ahead of Williamson and John Robson. Afterward, during an interview with the BBC, Ovett lauded the strength of British miling, asking, "Why should we have to go over to Norway? The best milers are British. Let the rest of the world come to us."

"After that, he felt he couldn't go to Oslo," says Williamson. Ovett, out on a limb, cut it off by saying he had nothing to prove, that whoever won in Norway would have "a hollow victory" without having beaten him. The rest of the milers, in the main combative men beneath composed exteriors, didn't take such words lightly. As they went to Oslo, they began to conceive of the shape the Golden Mile might take, and there grew among them the unspoken conviction that it would be fast.

The athletes' lodgings in Oslo were to the north of the city, in the Panorama Sommerhotell, beside tranquil Sognsvatn Lake. The 1972 U.S. Olympic track team trained there. The buildings of glass and birch are spare and functional. Sawdust and sand trails run across the forest floor and are used by runners and hikers in summer, cross-country skiers in winter. The city of Oslo spends $30 million a year in support of such facilities as well as over four hundred sport clubs.

"The whole atmosphere of the place, the paths around the lake, the quaint cable car you took down to the town, the way you could sit on the wharf by the fjord and shell shrimp for lunch was relaxing and just distracting enough to be perfect," says Scott, who had run his best 1,500 meters (3:36.0) in Oslo in 1978. "It was fun to bring Kim [Votaw, now his wife] and be able to show her everything. Scott's only worry was over his efforts to join the U.S. team in Moscow the following week for the Spartakiade Games. Despite repeatedly cabling the AAU office in Indianapolis and visiting the Soviet Embassy daily, he had yet to receive a visa.

Coe, who had flown with his father to Oslo from Manchester on July 15, ran through Frogner Park, where he was astounded by the size, number, and unsparing humanity of the Gustav Vigeland sculptures. Later, cruising past the Norwegian women sunbathing topless on Sognsvatn's shore, he slowed, "out of deference." At the hotel he was introduced to many of his opponents for the first time. "They struck me as one of the friendliest collections of people I've met, given what was to come later," he says.

One runner Coe knew and respected was Dixon of New Zealand. They discussed Ovett. "I don't know him at all well," said Coe. "He certainly seems to talk himself into a corner."

"He rather reminds me of the lift operator," said Dixon. "After he's reached the top, he'll have to come down, and then he'll meet all the people he was rude to on the way up." There was a garden party for athletes and press the evening before the race at Haukvik's home on one of the wooded slopes of suburban Oslo. Over ham and strawberries, Haukvik badgered all the lesser names in turn. "He said, in a confiding manner, that this was a race they just couldn't put a rabbit in because the invitations were so scarce," says Masback. "He said, 'So the race is going to be a failure unless you lead.' I reacted violently, and he went to talk to someone else."

Had Haukvik known the thinking of Scott and Wessinghage, he might have relaxed and enjoyed the ham. "Thomas and I went off under the apple trees and made a plan," says Scott. "More than wanting to win at any cost, we wanted to run a fast time. We assumed they'd get someone to lead for two laps. Then I would take the third lap and push it hard, and Thomas would take it going into the last quarter, and we'd both sprint with two hundred to go." Scott was so serious that he told Wessinghage, "If there is no early rabbit I'm going to take the pace out from the start."

The British press, which had been caught flatfooted by Coe's 800-meter record, was out in force. "Why are you here if it's not a special occasion?" a reporter asked Peter Coe at Haukvik's party, because Sebastian's father had not attended the earlier race.

"He can run eight hundreds perfectly well on his own," said Peter, "because he's an eight hundred meter runner. But he's not yet a miler. We've come to learn."

To one side, Masback, in perfect earnest, was predicting a fast race, one that would have eight men under 3:53. An NBC camera crew thought this very funny. Peter Coe didn't crack a smile. "That Masback," he said. "An intelligent man."

Out on the lawn a factory representative with a trunk full of lovely Norwegian sweaters was offering them to the athletes at half price. "I experienced some anxiety," says Masback. "Should I buy one when I knew they gave them as prizes for the first six? Finally Haukvik said if you do a personal record, they're free. So I said at least I'll get *that* and went away to eat all the strawberries I could.

Back in the hotel, Williamson, who had also resisted Haukvik's entreaties to set the pace, sat down with his roommate, Brendan Foster, an astute judge of runners. Before them they had a list of the field. "We got it down to Coe and Scott, really," Williamson says. "For a year I had felt that Coe was capable of a big mile. Coghlan had to be tired from his five thousand. Walker was not at his best and Wessinghage seldom comes off well in a big race. I never expected anything of Masback."

The nineteen-year-old Williamson looked up at the thirty-one-year-old Foster. "What do you think?" he asked.

"I'd bet you third," said Foster.

* * *

The morning was cool and calm with a moist fog over the fjord. One by one the milers rose and stretched and headed out for their easy morning runs. At the far end of the lake Coghlan met Coe, who turned and joined him. Both are men who save their nervous energy for races, so it was not a strained occasion. "Just communing with nature," says Coghlan.

Lacy was communing with himself. For five days, he'd had strep throat and a temperature. This morning it was down to ninety nine degrees. "When I got up I felt runnable," he says. "I managed to do a couple of miles without coughing and hacking. I was hoping that I'd experienced a miraculous recovery. I hadn't, but at least I figured I could run safely."

Australia's Hall passed some time reading a book on English history. Ishii of Japan took a long walk among the evergreens, feeling honored. "I knew I wasn't fast enough to win," he says, "but I was tremendously elated to be given this chance to see how I measured up to the best men in the world." For Ishii, it was like being dropped into an Olympic final, and his assessment of his opponents was fascinating. "I believed Coe would not win because he was specializing in the 800," he says. "Coghlan is basically a long distance racer with great staying power. He is not too strong a sprinter in the home stretch." Had Ishii asserted this to Walker, Wessinghage, Scott, Lacy, John Robson, Moorcroft, or Masback, all of whom had been cut down by Coghlan in the last hundred yards of races, he would have caused a sensation. In fact, Coghlan's potent kick was the reason Peter Coe felt the pace would be swift. "Out of a dozen intelligent men there must be several who don't care to wait around and have Eamonn outsprint them," he said.

Scott and Lacy took the rattling wooden tram from the hotel to the city center and walked again to the Soviet Embassy, where Scott was told his visa still had not come in. (Scott would never make it to Russia. But after the Golden Mile, Masback, staying with an aunt in Paris, would pay his own insistent visits to the Soviet Embassy there. He recalls, "Finally on the fourth day the guy said, 'Are you Edwin Moses?' I said no. 'Do you know Edwin Moses?' I said sure. 'O.K., here is your visa.'" Masback then placed second in the Spartakiade 1,500.)

From the embassy they went to the SAS offices to have Scott's and Kim Votaw's tickets changed to go south. "There were long lines," says Scott. "We waited half an hour, then said screw it and went back to the hotel to have something to eat." Five hours before race time they looked at the menu and settled for spaghetti.

"They only had five things in the restaurant," says Masback. "Fish, hamburger, Wiener schnitzel, fried chicken, and spaghetti. And there were some unclear but heated personal problems among the kitchen staff. Our food was always served by sullen or tear-streaked waitresses."

Coe had relaxed for an hour reading Mao's little red book of quotations, which he had brought from Sheffield. "I found it very funny," he says. "The masses' inexhaustible lust for socialism." Then he and his father had been taken by a photographer to pose on the heights of the Holmenkollen ski jump. They cooperated, climbing hundreds of feet up and down the structure, but felt slightly used. The photograph of Sebastian now in his album shows him standing with a pair of skis and a certain wrinkled-nosed discontent. The picture of his father shows ashen terror. "That must have added seconds to whatever you'll run," he said as they regained level ground.

At midday they lunched and laid the race plan. "We had a slight difference of opinion," Sebastian says. "I thought there might be some stuffing around." But his father assured him it would be fast all the way, and thus the best tactic was not to lead, but to get a good position and stay close to the front. "There was no talk of a world record," says Peter. "It was to be run competitively. The aim was simply to win the race."

Sebastian's concern was for the third lap. "When you figure fifty seven seconds per quarter is six seconds slower than my eight-hundred meter pace," he says, "it wasn't going to feel too hard at first. But those stamina men were going to come on in that third quarter."

Walker had reached Oslo only the day before, having been delayed by leaving his passport in London. He and Williamson had a chat in the hotel lobby. Walker said he was making no excuses, but his Achilles tendon problems had left him short of racing fitness He had a cold and was taking penicillin.

"I didn't feel he should have been talking to me in such a way, says Williamson. "Who was I, anyway? He certainly didn't seem the confident athlete I knew."

The nearer the race, the more time dragged. "It was just an excruciating long day," says Masback, "filled with waiting and vapid conversations. Finally we got on the bus to the stadium early, just to get moving. Walker was wry, unusually funny, unusually relaxed. Coe was so relaxed that he took a nap."

Walker felt the best he could possibly expect of himself was 3:53 or 3:54. He had watched Coe's 800 record run and knew what he had seen. "Unlike what was written so much in 1976," he says, "someone who is big and heavy like me is limited in what he can do, but a light-framed, speedy runner like Coe will not have much trouble carrying his speed over a mile."

Coe and Moorcroft, another Loughborough graduate, took a car to the track with Peter Coe and Miklos Nemeth, the Olympic javelin champion from Hungary. Also in the car was Bela Domokos, a Hungarian photographer who had defected to England in 1956. Domokos began talking to Nemeth about how Hungarian magazines never paid for his pictures. "Gradually Bela began lecturing him," says Coe. "Nemeth's neck grew red as it got beyond a lecture. It wasn't the most relaxing way to collect one's thoughts."

Once at Bislett, which is alongside the large and fragrant Frydenlund brewery near the city center, the Coes were taken onto the field and put up on the awards stand where Peter presented a gold medal to his son for the 800-meter record. The 16,173 fans filling the stands applauded. Coe, graceful in a tan sweat suit, waved in thanks, seemingly calm.

"How do you run a world record?" asks Peter Coe. "You compress all your baser urges into one minute and forty-two seconds of running. Inside, the man is as ruthless as they come."

The warmup area at Bislett is odd, a little flat and dusty space inside the fence at the top of a grassy slope. Coe sat there for a while, keeping an eye on Foster's sweats as he and Dixon dueled in the two-mile, Dixon winning in a fine 8:15.2. "I just soaked up the hum, the general excitement of the crowd," says Coe. "Once I came down to the parking area behind the stand and was nabbed by Charlie Jones of NBC. He asked me about Miranda's legs. He has a thing about her legs. I said 'They're prettier than mine, but not as fast,' and escaped back to the warmup level."

Moorcroft went to the side of the track during his warmup to watch Grete Waitz win the women's 3,000 in 8:31.8, the second fastest ever. "The atmosphere in there was electric," he says. "The track only has six lanes and the banking of the stands is so steep you feel the crowd is on top of you."

Coghlan went to a little park three quarters of a mile away to do his forty minutes of jogging and stretching. Scott, who had sat with the pole vaulters, warmed up inside the stadium, doing increasingly rapid 100-meter strides down the backstretch.

Williamson ran slowly around the outside trying to convince himself that the only reason he didn't feel good was because he was wearing two sweat suits. "When I got out on the track to do strides I felt better," he says. "I stared at Coe's father, wondering what he could be thinking about me." It was a natural thought as the craggy senior Coe is known to seek the iron in a runner. "I want to see what the bastards are made of," he had said in sending Sebastian out to drive the pace in the 1978 European Championship 800.

Now, as he watched his son lace on his spikes, he was feeling what he had denied over strawberries the night before. "I knew something special was happening," he says. "Normally we have little to say to one another right before a race. But I was caught up. I said 'You know, you can win this.'"

"Yes, I know, Dad."

Then they were on the track for introductions. Coghlan, all in green, was doing little twinkle-toed accelerations. Scott got a last hug from Kim. Walker limped slightly and looked glum. Masback and Moorcroft were apprehensive, weary of the long television hype that required the milers to bound one by one to the top of the awards stand and wave. It seemed an unnecessary, almost insulting ceremony in the midst of 16,000 spectators who could neither be more knowledgeable nor more excited. Through it all, Coe appeared assured. "Normally I would have been perturbed," he says. "I hate indecision and delay before races. But I wasn't very nervous at all."

At last they went to the line. As soon as all were still, the gun sounded. Coe, wearing his British racing singlet and purple Louborough shorts, bolted to the front at once to avoid the inevitable pushing within a field of thirteen aggressive men. As it was, he still caught an elbow from Masback as the pack jammed together around the first turn. Entering the backstretch, Lacy, running wide, went smoothly ahead. Knowing his weakened condition wouldn't let him be a contender, he had decided to become the crucial element in a great mile, a respected man setting a hard, even pace. Coe was surprised. "I'd no idea he was going to do that."

As Lacy moved to the inside, Scott and Wessinghage followed him. Coe held fourth. Ishii and Bjorge Rudd, Norway's entrant, fell behind and would not be factors. Of the rest, two men's fates were already sealed. One was Masback. "My plan was to go out near the front and stay there," he says. "That plan lasted about a hundred meters. I got out fine, but one by one everyone marched by and pretty soon I had a perfect view of the race."

The other was Coghlan. "I was not cocky, but too cagey, too careful," he says. "I think I was last in the early running."

At the quarter-mile, Lacy was timed in 57 seconds flat. Scott was a yard behind, thinking here the two of them were again, as so many times during the U.S. indoor season, "doing the work as usual." Wessinghage and Coe were by in about 57.8. Behind them the pack was dangerously tight with seven men working for position. "There was a lot of physical contact," says Moorcroft. "I never got past fifth or sixth. It felt like I was running into a wall all the time." Into the third turn, Coghlan and Walker were ninth and tenth, respectively. Coghlan knew he had to get up. "On the second lap when I thought they would ease, they just kept going." He went wide down the backstretch and passed several men, but made up little on the leaders.

Lacy and Scott hit 800 meters in 1:54.0, with Coe now in third in 1:54.5. Lacy had been perfect with two 57-second laps in a row. Now he stepped off the track, coughing, blood pounding in his head. Scott leaned hard into the turn, keeping the pressure on. Later, both Scott and Coe would give Lacy full credit for making a record possible. Scott also says, "He shouldn't have done it. For one thing, he was sick. His throat infection lingered on and he couldn't train until September. But more than that, he'd broken the indoor world record in February. He is too good a runner to rabbit."

Coe stayed with Scott and daylight opened to the pack. They led by eight yards at 2½ laps, when Coghlan finally took over third from Wessinghage. "I ran as if I had no experience whatsoever," says Coghlan. "I ran three or four little races within the larger one. I made a hell of an effort in the third lap to get to third and once I got there I was exhausted."

Through the third lap, Scott willed himself not to slow. This was how he had destroyed the kick of Villanova's Don Paige in the AAU 1,500 in June. He did not know who was behind him. The crowd was so loud he could hear no footsteps. He had heard no lap times. He didn't care about them. He knew only to run as hard as a man can run.

With 500 meters left, Coe came to Scott's shoulder. Scott, recalling their plan, thought it was Wessinghage. When Coe passed him 30 yards before the three-quarter-mile point, Scott was encouraged, thinking the half-miler had moved too early.

The time at 1,200 meters was 2:52.0. Walker, laboring out of the pack past the seemingly spent Coghlan, heard the split called to Coe and Scott. "Well, it's gone," he thought. "Coming round the turn I actually got into third place," he says, "but I was preoccupied with watching Coe. I was fascinated, if that's the word, knowing he was on his way to breaking my world record."

Coe moved steadily away from Scott. "I was filled with relief that I hadn't been chewed over by the pack in the third lap," he says. "From then on I was just running for the tape." Coe's stride never took on the appearance of being willed. His face showed no strain, only a wide-eyed absorption in his task. He passed 1,500 meters in 3:32.8, a European record. As he neared the tape he looked as if he could run another lap.

Behind Coe, Scott was holding on. Behind Scott, things were happening down the backstretch. Williamson had found the race frustrating for its refusal to develop into a file of efficiently running men. "You could never settle in," he says. "There were always things going on, people coming past. I really only took stock of the race with three hundred to go." He was in fourth. "With Scott and Coe out and away, I was aiming for third. I got by Walker. I cut in on him and he pushed me in the back. Ahead, Scott didn't look that good. I began to think I might get second."

Masback entered the last backstretch in tenth place. "I'd run the whole way back there on the inside with a feeling of resignation, but I sensed we were moving quickly," he says. "I got outside into the express lane with three hundred to go, hoping to pass two or three people before the turn." Masback passed four. "As I went around Coghlan he turned his head and we exchanged glances. I saw despair in his eyes, as if he was saying, 'That should be *me* up there and to make it worse, now *you're* passing me.'"

On the turn, just past 1,500 meters, Masback loomed up behind Williamson, and his reaching stride accidentally caught Williamson's left foot. Two spikes went into the rear of the Scotsman's red Puma and ripped it off his heel.

"One second I was sprinting at Scott, thinking, 'He's not too far away,'" says Williamson. "And the next, 'Christ, what can I do? What can I do?' I kept looking down. I ran a few steps with the back of the shoe tucked under my foot like a carpet slipper. Then I got it off. People began to go by me. My running action was gone." Williamson would finish seventh in 3:53.2. That and his 1,500 meter time Of 3:36.6 were European junior records.

Coghlan was seventh or eighth off the last turn, and still a proud man. He sprinted the last 100 yards faster than anyone else and reached fourth at the finish in 3:52.5, an Irish national record. Masback came in just ahead of him in 3:52.1. As they slowed, Coghlan drew up beside Masback and heard him gasp, "Sorry. You're the best."

John Robson went from seventh to fifth on the last turn. "In the straight I was floating, detached," he says. "I had lots left, and it seemed I was closing on Coghlan and Masback. Through the line Walker was right beside me." John Robson and Walker finished fifth and sixth in 3:52.8 and 3:52.9. At once Walker turned to John Robson and said, "I've lost my record."

Later Coghlan would say, "I'll always remember how Walker took it. Sure, we all say records are made to be broken, but there was something *more* special about that record. It was the first sub-3:50. It was a true landmark, and that night it was forgotten. That's what he lost, and he accepted it instantly."

Scott was not at all inclined to be accepting "It *must* be wrong," he raged, for his time on the electronic phototimer was 3:51.11, one one hundredth of a second slower than Jim Ryun's twelve-year-old U.S. record. To make it worse, Scott had eased several yards before the tape.

As had Coe himself. Yet he had floated across the line in 3:49.0, a world record. "The lesson of the Golden Mile," says Coe's father, "is one that the two finest athletes ignored: Run through the tape."

Coe relaxed through it into pandemonium. "Everyone was shouting, of course, calling a wild variety of times," he says. "My father was the first person I was willing to listen to. He told me I'd done it."

Someone thrust a Union Jack tied to a birch branch into Coe's hands, and he took a jubilant victory lap with a train of photographers behind. "He looked like a combination Pied Piper and Delacroix's 'Liberty Leading the People,'" says Masback.

Coe received a gold trophy worth $13,000, from IAAF President Adriaan Paulen on television during which time NBC's Charlie Jones held his cigarette at the hem of his blazer so it would not appear in the picture—then had it immediately taken back; it is not to be kept.

By the time Coe and his father had satisfied the English press, the stadium was empty. They went in search of a ride to the athletes' reception. "I always thought when someone broke a world record the angel's came down and bore you off to wherever you wanted to go," says Scott. "But there was Coe, walking out confused, just like the rest of us."

Eventually the milers reached the site of the dinner, an Oslo hotel. Coe went to shower in someone's room. Masback stayed in the lobby to make a call home. "In the time I sat there," he says, "Walker got three calls from New Zealand newspapers. He said all the right things. 'Yes, I'm sorry it's gone, but it was a great effort by Coe. I'm only glad to have had a chance to be in the race.' All the right things, but with such an expression of anguish on his face that I had to look away."

As Walker suffered, Coe, damp from the shower, passed lightly by on his way to the reception room. As he entered, the meet's athletes rose in a standing ovation. For the first time what he had done began to sink in, and he was moved.

*   *   *

Runners will say of a successful race, "You wake the next morning and it is gone." It was in recognition of the evanescence of victory that the ancient Olympic Games awarded winners only a perishable olive wreath. Yet the final measure of the Golden Mile consists of whatever its makers carried from it.

Wessinghage, who was eighth in 3:53.2, recalls Coghlan's final kick. "A great gesture," he says. "I wish I had done that." In August he would set the pace for Ovett's attempt at Coe's record in London.

Ovett would barely miss, with 3:49.6. Wessinghage, remembering Coghlan, would hang on to run 3:50.6, the fourth fastest ever. Williamson flew back to Glasgow the next morning. He tried to tell himself he'd been lucky; Masback's spikes might easily have split his Achilles tendon. "But I couldn't help thinking of what I might have done had I not been spiked," he said. "I was so *close*." The flight had to hold for half an hour over Glasgow. "I kept punching the seat in front of me. I was so close."

Scott, Walker, and Masback were back at war the next night, racing over 1,500 meters in Lausanne, Switzerland. "Walker had been discouraged that I had beaten him in Oslo," says Masback. "He went wild to get me back in Lausanne. Which he did, by the chest hairs." Both finished in 3:37.9, behind Scott's 3:37.7.

Coe and his father flew home the morning after the race. "The house was under siege," Sebastian says. "Cars everywhere, cameras, cables. The room was white with light, and there was plastic sheeting over everything." As he walked in, the phone rang and he picked it up. A good Yorkshire accent from the Hallamshire Harriers said, "Hey, if you don't get your forms in for the agricultural show race, you'll not be in."

"I'm home all right," said Coe.

That afternoon he went for a relaxing run, up along the shore of the Howden Reservoir in the Derwent Valley. The land is part of the Peak National Park. Great old rhododendrons and pines come down to a stone wall beside the road.

Coe let his thoughts run free. "I was just glad, blissfully glad to get away from everything," he says. "Right after a race the difficulty is to find your sweat suit and get your shoes changed and give some sort of gentle answer to excited, dumb questions, the most frequent being, 'How do you feel?' when I don't know yet how I feel."

Now gazing out at the moors across the lake, he knew how he felt, and it wasn't historic. "I have other races to run," he thought. "It may be years yet, if ever, before I come to think of the Oslo mile as a landmark."

Then, turning for home, a clearer idea came, one he surely would share with Walker. "These records are only borrowed," he would say, "precious aspects of the sport, temporarily in one's keeping."

—February 1980

A Hard and Supple Man:
Sebastian Coe

By that golden summer's end, Coe had taken into his keeping the 1,500 record as well, running 3:32.1 to become the first man to hold world records for 800 and 1,500 meters and the mile at one time.

In September he slipped quietly into Eugene, Oregon. He came from the morning plane alone in jeans and a gray, untitled sweat shirt. He had spent more than a day in San Francisco trying to get a flight on standby after Pan Am had scheduled him to connect to an airline that was on strike. Coe's consolation had been a suite in a luxury hotel and an evening on the city escorted by Pan Am stewardesses. "You have to take the rough with the rough," he said. He had come to Eugene not to race but to escape, to enjoy a holiday from the sometimes oppressive British newspapers, and to heal a sore calf.

"That arose during a brush with the law," he said while awaiting his luggage. "I was running on the road in a London park. A friend was timing me, keeping pace in her car. The police objected to that and we had an altercation, during which time I cooled off. When I resumed, I strained the calf, so I quit racing for the season."

The road from the Eugene airport passes several lumber and plywood mills, visible within a blue haze of their own making. "That was where Oregon runners worked when I was in school in the sixties," said Coe's host. "When Bill Bowerman was coach, he gave no full scholarships. You had to come out here on weekends, graveyard shift, midnight to eight, and putty patch veneer panels on a conveyor or, if the mill was down, blow sawdust out of the block-long dryers, or clean the glue spreaders with a wire brush and ammonia. Horrible jobs, but we all did them."

"Didn't that cut into your training?" asked Coe.

"I guess it did a little. It must have. But in a way it was worth it, teaching me at an impressionable age about mindless labor. So I might shun it forever."

"Was that Bowerman's object?"

"Looking back, I'm sure it was part of it. At the time, I just thought of him as a modern tyrant, bent on no one getting through life easily if *he* could help it. You'll meet him. He'll want to know what you've been doing in your training."

A gentle run showed Coe the town, the University of Oregon, and Pre's Trail, five miles of soft, cedar-bark-and-wood-waste path beside the Willamette River, named for the late Steve Prefontaine. Coe's six-minute-mile pace gave no hint of his injury; indeed, he occasionally surged away from his guide. "I'm really resting now," he said when caught. "For three weeks after the racing season I may not run at all. I find that I'm not addicted to it."

Coe had taken his degree in economics and economic history from Loughborough University in the spring and would return for graduate study after his vacation. In his days in Eugene he charmed a succession of hosts with shy politeness and a broad range of interests. His intentions were simply to sample the

156

new or attractive things of American life. These included hot-tubbing, *The New Yorker*, as many movies as he could get to (an adept mimic himself, he has seen *Monty Python and the Holy Grail* five times and possesses a copy of the script), root beer, which he described as tasting rather like a visit to the dentist, and, without question, jazz. At a Chuck Mangione concert Coe spoke of helping introduce Dave Brubeck's music to Yorkshire by insisting on it in a film of himself running, and was eager to get to New York later in his trip, to hear Russell Procope, a former Duke Ellington sideman. "My chief regret in life," he said, "is never learning to play an instrument."

Such was the breadth of Coe's interests that, save for a talk at a running clinic, he seldom had need to speak of his sport. The exception was during his visit to Bowerman's aerie on a bluff above the McKenzie River. After lemonade and several of Barbara Bowerman's oatmeal cookies, the party walked through woods to a hillside pasture in which grazed a few small, chunky cattle.

"We're trying to build a herd of Dexter cows," said Bowerman. "It is an Irish breed. They're supposed to be small so they don't eat much, but they still give you a gallon of milk."

Bowerman had sent his minions far and wide in search of this strain of stock. "In Ireland one of my runners was out in the Limerick countryside and saw a field of likely prospects," Bowerman said. "'Are those Dexter cows?' he asked of a stolid Irishman. 'No, I believe those belong to Mr. O'Rourke,'" was the answer.

"Just *like* the Irish," said Coe, laughing, but stopping suddenly, his hand on his hip. "Since last winter," he said, "I've had occasional pain that goes from my back down my left leg."

"It's certainly not a hamstring pull," said Bowerman "or you wouldn't have been able to do what you've done." He pressed Coe against a fir, teaching him an abdominal exercise to align the back and pelvis in a way least offensive to the posterior nerves. Coe walked away from the tree with an elevated gaze.

"Pretty good," said Bowerman. "Not swaybacked at all."

Soon his host had Coe describing his training in detail. "My father is my coach," he said, "and the basic foundations have been consistent, although the headings have meandered a bit as we've experimented. Essentially, it has been one hundred percent quality, not quantity. It is speed endurance, that is, seeing how long you can endure speed. In the winters I very seldom have run more than fifty miles per week, less in the spring."

"No more than that?" said Bowerman. By contrast, John Walker of New Zealand, Coe's precursor as mile record holder, did as much as a hundred miles. Until Coe, recent middle-distance-philosophy has held that speed work alone is destructive of a runner. The athlete's traditional response to interval or speed training is rapid improvement to a point, followed by equally rapid decline. New Zealand Coach Arthur Lydiard's advance in the 1960s was in effect to train his runners for their training, to build up in them such stamina from lengthy mileage that they could withstand and, in fact, benefit from fast track running.

When asked how he managed to stay fresh and strong on so little distance work, Coe said, "My father says that you might not know the accepted lore of athletics, but if you know people and can sense the individual's needs, it can make all the difference." "Hear, hear," said Bowerman. "Yet," Coe continued, "I wouldn't know Why some people can get away with less distance than others. I really haven't a clue."

In Coe's case, part of the reason has to do with the ten to eleven hours every winter week that he spends in the Loughborough gym under the eye of George Gandy, a lecturer in biomechanics and the coordinator of his training program. "It has been described as Coe's commando workout," the runner said. "In the fall, it's the use of everything you can think of in the gymnasium, lifting heavy weights twice a week, working every part of the body. After Christmas, we concentrate on every muscle from knees to sternum, using box-jumping, speed drills, repeatedly mounting a beam, high knee lifts, bounding on grass or a soft-sprung floor. All this was associated two and a half years ago with rapid improvement in my leg speed. It's simple athleticism, really, the coordinated transference of weight and force through the body. Watching different sorts of athletes box-jumping is amusing. Hopping up and down over five or six boxes of different heights, say two to four feet, the vaulters and jumpers are coordinated, the sprinters less so, and the distance runners are just terrible."

It must be that the strength and flexibility Coe brings to the track from such work supports him as well as would the result of interminable slow running. "It was a happy accident that from the first, when I was thirteen, my father felt you ought not to smash a kid on the road, so he kept the distance low. As a junior in 1975, I averaged twenty-eight miles per week and ran successfully—third in the European junior fifteen hundred—against those juniors who were running eighty or ninety miles."

Bowerman listened to all this with an expression of almost beatific gratification, for it confirmed cherished beliefs about the uniqueness of each runner, the need for self-knowledge. "So you've developed a methodology that isn't at all dependent on what others do," he said. "That takes a certain sort of man."

"Well," said Coe, slightly embarrassed, "sometimes the difficult thing is to hold back when things are going well, to remember that what you're doing is, after all, preparation. That's hard when you're in a competitive group."

"How do you avoid racing when you are in training?" asked Bowerman.

"I have always trained alone."

"Tell me about your father," said Bowerman. "He's an engineer?"

"Yes. He's the production director of a cutlery firm."

"Does he talk to you about body mechanics, balances?"

"When I was a child, he always spoke of lines and angles and carrying oneself efficiently. You see, the day I started running was the day he started coaching. After that it was bringing his science to bear, studying everything he could find. He's got rid, he says, of ninety-five percent of what he's learned. The five percent he's kept is very specific. He has no other runners. People ask if he will coach them, and he says, 'I don't know enough about you. I'd have to move in with you.'" Sebastian smiled. "You don't know my father, but that usually ends it."

"I would very much like to know your father," said Bowerman, gravely, sensing that rarest thing for him, a kindred spirit.

"I want you to tell him that he is always welcome here. Always." Before he left

Oregon, Coe was taken fifty miles up the McKenzie River east of Eugene for a run on a trail beside the clear and ringing stream. After no more than three miles, distracted by the scenery, he turned an ankle on a rock, or the root of a vine maple. By the time he had limped back to the car, parked near the river's bank, the foot was swollen and hot. While friends broke out wine, cheese, and fruit, Coe sat on a stone with his foot in the freezing river. Both hosts and guest were vaguely uneasy, but Coe, neither glum nor forcing good spirits, kept the event in perspective, and so soothed the others.

The best of athletes display a gift for control; their success depends upon bending—but not breaking—the body to their will. But in Coe one could sense the uncommon man whose self-possession is so extensive that it lets him comprehend our lives sometimes more easily than we do ourselves.

Perched as naturally upon his mossy rock as an otter, Coe gave as well to musings about the seeming perfection of a partnership between father and coach and runner and son that had so moved Bowerman. How was it sustained? What was the complementary mix of qualities that resulted in a unit of such toughness and grace?

"Does it not seem," Coe was asked, "that if what your father says about coaching is true, that it applies more widely? In trying to fathom another for any reason, for sport or love or accurate writing, must you have to move in with him?"

"I don't know," said Coe. "But if you'd like to try, you're welcome to come to Sheffield for Christmas."

The Coes of Sheffield:

The Coe house on Marlborough Road, near the University of Sheffield, is a hundred-year-old Victorian brick structure of two and a half stories and a cavernous, dismal cellar. Not long before Christmas, a feathery snow was settling upon the strolling carolers as Peter Coe drew his guest from the night, put him beside the gas fire in his warm, cluttered parlor, and gave him a whisky. The elder Coe is a lean, weathered man, comfortable in rumpled, tan corduroy suits. "The clan gathers," he said. "This will be the first time Miranda has been home in two years."

Photographs of his eldest daughter, twenty-one, a dancer and model in Las Vegas and New York were in evidence near a tiny, burdened Christmas tree. Here she danced. Here she simply glowed.

"I cannot express the evil delight it gives me," said Peter Coe, "when I meet my child at a plane or train and glance around at all the jealous, offended men who can hardly credit this vision coming with warm, wet kisses to such a burnt-out case as I."

There were traces of the successful runner about the room, great silver cups and framed racing pictures and a commemorative Wilkinson sword over the mantel, but the photos of Sebastian on display were less than dignified, showing him mugging, wincing goofily. However, in the front hall was an oil portrait of him as a child, a large head atop a thin and passive body. The wide, brown eyes are arresting, their clear, encompassing gaze not benevolent, not precious, but simply open, as if he were saying, what I see is what I get, and I'm not too sure I'm going to be happy about it.

Peter Coe caught the visitor staring at this picture. "Seb at eight," he said.

"Who painted him?" the visitor asked.

"I did."

There was a clumping upon the stairway. "Taking credit again, I hear," said Sebastian, descending. Behind him was his sister Emma, fifteen, tall and lovely with blazing teeth and short dark hair. Wrapped all in black, she was going to see *Dracula*.

"I'm off, too," said Sebastian.

"Where?" asked Emma.

"Where is he always off to?" said Angela Coe, their mother, who had come in from the kitchen.

Emma's brow knitted theatrically. "Now I like that, I do," said Sebastian happily. "No incessant drudge am I."

Emma, in a sunburst of comprehension, said, "Oh, *training*."

"An easy four, Dad," said Sebastian, and was gone

In Sebastian's absence, Peter Coe discussed their plans for the new year and the then undimmed Olympics. "We've had weeks the car couldn't come out of the garage for the snow," he said, "so after the holidays Seb will get out of the English winter to somewhere in southern Europe. Not tropical, mind you, but free of ice and sleet. Just to have continuity."

Peter Coe embodies the assertiveness of the scientific method.

"I'm a superior manager," he said. "I know a good physiotherapist and a good doctor, and I listen to what they say, but they can't know everything, so in the end the coaching is an art, supported by this science. I make the fewest mistakes by being totally empirical. We'll do no training at altitude because we have no experience with it and there's not enough time to get it. Once you introduce another variable like that, you've ruined your experiment."

The direction of the Coe experiment thus far has been to train Sebastian as a sprinter and that done, turn his speed loose over longer and longer distances. "What we do are ranging shots, as I call them, running under and over distance races to bracket the target," said Peter. "In 1978, when Seb was aiming for the eight hundred, we raced at four hundred for speed and fifteen hundred for endurance. Last year the bracket was four hundred and three thousand meters and he got the records for three of the distances in between.

Peter Coe spoke with respect of the other member of his son's training team, Loughborough's Gandy. "George got together with us when Seb was nineteen, and not only has he managed the weights and circuit training, but he's saved Sebastian on occasion. In 1978, not long before the European Championships in Prague, Seb stepped into a hole and turned the same ankle he hurt on your river.

"The hospital put it in a cast. George got him out and to a football physiother-apist, who knew it was wrecked but not broken. With a controlled wrap and constant therapy, he was jogging in ten days and got down to 1:44.3 two weeks before Prague, but ah, that was a disastrous year, that."

The Prague 800 has been dissected as much as any race of that distance ever run. It was the first, and for two years, the only time Coe and Ovett had raced one another. Beforehand, Coe was not feeling well. Originally the plan had been to set a fast pace to test both Ovett and the field and to condition Sebastian, then twenty-one to give everything he had over the full distance. "Well, Dad, do we stick to what we intended?" asked Sebastian before going to the start.

"We've come here to find something out," said Peter dryly. "I want to see what those bastards are made of, and remember this is only a stepping-stone on the way to what we're after."

So Coe opened up from the gun. Down the first backstretch East Germany's Olaf Beyer fought with him for the lead. "It was the first time in my life that someone had done that," said Sebastian later. "I couldn't believe the pace was fast if this guy was there. So I went faster." The time at 400 meters was 49.3, an unsupportable speed. Coe held on until the last straightaway, when Ovett went by. Then Beyer passed them both to win in 1:43.8, the year's fastest time.

"I'll tell you where that pays off," said Peter Coe, sitting by the fire a year and a half later. "On a windy night in Zurich and you're tired and have seven hundred meters left to run and no one to help. Those were the conditions Sebastian faced last August, and the result was the world record in the fifteen hundred meters."

Prague was memorable also for a vignette that confirmed Sebastian in the knowledge of the gulf between casual officials and committed athletes.

Arthur Gold of the British Amateur Athletic Board, who is also president of the European Athletic Association, was the presenter of the medals for the 800 meters. As he draped the bronze about Coe's neck, he said, "Well, Steve, you threw everything at them."

That medal now lies in the bottom drawer of a chest in Peter and Angela Coe's bedroom. A career's awards are all tossed together there, a nest of tangled ribbons and tarnish. "'Our shrine," said Peter, cackling, slamming the drawer shut.

The Saturday before Christmas, Emma and Miranda, tiredly radiant, were in from shopping. Youngest son Nicholas, seventeen, was enjoying a rare moment at home between his two jobs, one with a firm that exports furnace linings, the other in a wine bar. Peter's mother Violet, eighty-two, had come up from London. She gives as good as she gets.

"You can sign on with the Salvation Army soon, Mum," said Peter Coe, "and preach the benefits of giving up strong drink."

"Yes, but I haven't given it up. If you jabbed my arm, it would be Guinness gushing out."

"Ah well, you've lived too long as it is," continued Peter. "This will surely be your last Christmas."

"And a blessed relief it will be," she said, sipping her tea smugly, "to be away from this wretchedness."

*   *   *

After a while Sebastian led the visitor out for a short run and the talk turned to Steve Ovett, the mysterious rival from Brighton. Ovett had not run the Oslo Golden Mile in which Coe set his record, but later in the season, besides his 3:49.6 mile, ran the 1,500 in 3:32.2. In fact the phototimer read 3:32.11, a bare one hundredth away from tying Coe's record. "The amusing thing," said Coe, "is that Steve has always said, 'World records don't mean much. Racing is about people and not clocks,' and that's laudable. But even though the races in London and

Brussels were so clearly organized for records, and he missed by so little, he still said only that he was perfectly happy with the times. He would not say he was going for the record."

Thus there seems an urge for consistency in both these men: Coe, so specifically trained for the purpose of giving everything; Ovett, firm in his intent of being the complete racer. It seems a match that will bring out the best in both of them.

Yet Coe and Ovett don't need each other. They are not defined against each other except in the English popular mind, which measures the gracious Coe against the private, brusque Ovett. Both have superbly supportive families. Both are determinedly pressing back the limits of the mile. Each would continue in the other's absence. But it is their fate to carry on the recurring pattern of great milers happening in pairs. They are the Gundar Hägg/Arne Andersson, Roger Bannister/John Landy, Jim Ryun/Kip Keino, John Walker/Filbert Bayi combination for the early eighties, although it seems that Steve Scott is almost ready to make it hot for both of them.

In the morning, the day before Christmas, Sebastian awoke with a sore throat. "He gets his length of limb and his athletic strength and coordination from me," said Peter after sending him back to bed. "His susceptibility to respiratory infection comes from his mother."

Peter and Angela decided to take their guest to see the historic city of York.

"Mum, now drink anything you like from the bar while we're gone," said Peter.

On the road, Peter mentioned that he had been sunk in the North Atlantic during the war. "Four of our six boats were blown apart. I was picked up by a seaplane." Later he was a prisoner of war, it taking three escapes to get home. "And for what?" he said. "My family is crumbling around me. Angela is reading Updike and Emma has introduced a viper in our midst known as Fleetwood Mac." The visitor marveled again at Sebastian's naturalness in all sorts of situations, his nervelessness in racing. "Roger Bannister was struck by that, too," said Angela. Indeed, 1956 Olympic steeplechase champion Chris Brasher has written of Coe, "Never have I been so refreshed by the sanity of a man. . . I love him for what he has done to destroy the myth and legends of modern sport."

"But he hasn't always been thus," said Peter Coe. "As a child he had all the hallmarks of the nervous type: thin, with eczema, and he wrote drivel for exams at eleven or twelve. He was a bundle of nerves in his early races. But having gotten him to recognize the problem, he took over. At sixteen, after he had won the national youths fifteen hundred, he almost gave up running to work for exams."

"But we pointed out that running was good for academics," said Angela, "so he wrote out timetables for his holidays—so many hours on geography and so on—and he kept to them. It's that tremendous discipline of his that we respect."

York Minster cathedral was begun in 1220 A.D. Inside, Angela Coe led the visitors to the Five Sisters, tall, densely worked, sea-green stained-glass windows. The vaulted arches above were white, with right gold carvings. "It's a very warm cathedral," said Angela. Then, more crisply, "I can almost be religious here." Peter, for his part, pointed out that the heads of many statues had been missing since the time of Oliver Cromwell, whose conviction it was that effigies were idolatrous.

As he strolled about the cathedral, Peter's thoughts turned again his son.

"Sebastian is success-oriented and not just at sport," he said. "The better he ran, the better he wanted to do academically. He's not an intellectual [for Peter it seemed there have been no reputable intellectuals since Wittgenstein] but then, who wants an ineffectual splitter of hairs, unable to act with decision? At times he's had an antagonistic faculty at Loughborough. His department chairman actually said something like, 'A gold medal would be a small help, I suppose. It's been difficult for Britain since the failure of the linen industry in Northern Ireland.' His exams last year were the final pressure. The world record in the eight hundred was the tremendous relief of having it done."

Outside, the Coes walked the ancient wall around the old city in golden, year-end light, stopping to watch a man carrying a Christmas tree and a bottle of whisky along the cathedral path under a softly diffused Turner sky.

When they reached home, they inquired how Grandmum had fared all alone on Christmas Eve. "It was lovely," she said. "I put off the telly and sat in the blissful peace and watched the sparrows attack the frail, wild birds."

Christmas morning presented a cold, rimed land. The Coes visited neighbors and friends, Sebastian saying at each stop, "Mum put the turkey in at ten last night. It ought to have at least died by now."

At the home of brothers Ian and Dr. Bob Hague, longtime friends of Seb's, Peter delivered his theory of successful womanizing. "You don't have to do anything but *enjoy* them," he said, bending near Bob's beautiful friend Diane. "They're sensitive to that."

Then home to dinner at a table graced by a worked-iron candelabrum Sebastian made when he was twelve. The children heaped lyric abuse upon Angela's frail, limp decorations, to which she replied, "It's yeti droppings for you this year."

Emma and Sebastian told a lengthy story about how Peter had once carefully listed his virtues as a father, how he'd promised to see to all their needs, concluding with, "Of course, if it's *fun* you want, I can't help you."

Later, over Christmas cake in the parlor, Sebastian was asked about his feeling for the Olympics. "I think because of the two-weeks-every-four-years nature of the thing, with TV fighting for audience figures and the press needing to sell papers, it creates an unnatural clamor. That puts undue pressure on athletes to be perfect on a given day, when simple odds dictate that only a few will be at their best. Today I have a cold, for example. So there is pressure and danger and oversimplification, and that's not what sport is or should be about."

Yet the Olympics are the best means we have of bringing together the Coes, the Ovetts, the Scotts.

"Yes, and I've got a lot of friends in the press who have a valuable job to do. The people I draw the line at are the feature writers, the new-angle people with little concern for the sport."

At the press conference Coe gave after returning from his orld record 800 meters, Monty Fresco of the London *Daily Mirror* said, "One more photo, Seb. Let's have this lady standing here with you," and there was a girl in a bikini.

"No way," said Coe.

"What's the matter with you, girl trouble or something?"

"Turn it in," said Coe, in Cockney, and walked out.

Thus he struggles to be accurately perceived. No amount of self possession can make up for the mistakes and gaucheries of others.

"How have you become so free of anxiety before competition?" Sebastian was asked.

"In having to be awakened before the Oslo race, I guess I gave the appearance of calm, but I get nervous. The question is, how does one keep it from eating you away. I don't know. I can't say I consciously mastered it. It's just something that evolved, being less and less nervous." Sebastian glanced at his family. "Feeling I'd be well and truly supported in my efforts had to be a part of it."

Peter Coe looked around the room., his eyes at last coming to rest on his mother. "Clean these dishes, will you, Mum, and then get back to the cellar."

That evening Peter Coe and the visitor walked the frosty streets. "Perhaps I had best explain," said Peter, "that my father was not a happy man, but dour. One might even say bitter. In reaction, my mother and I developed a certain humor, involving a good deal of fantasy, which I'm afraid my father never understood."

So it took the influences of at least three generations to bring this family to the bloom it now enjoys. Peter, the scientific manager, was made by his background inordinately sensitive to the stages of his own children's needs. Capable of discipline and pride of authority, but also capable of setting them free when the basic lessons had been learned, he had sent Miranda to dance in Las Vegas at nineteen, Nick to his labors at seventeen, and Sebastian to run, binding them only with the strands of his advice. His grumbling about constant decay now seemed a misanthropy born of the highest hopes infusing him in a wish that people be better than they are. That wish lives uneasily with the cold, empirical observation that they will stay exactly the same.

Two days later Sebastian and guest did a 14.4-mile training run up the Derwent Valley, west of Sheffield in the Peak National Park. As is his custom, Peter Coe drove behind to warn the odd motorist of the runners, to watch and think. It was a hard effort, a 5:30 pace in wet track suits and slickers. The wind and rain howled out of the Pennines, stopping the men cold in places, blowing white water back up from the spillways into the lakes. "Silly to complain of conditions on a track, isn't it?" said Sebastian.

During the last six miles the guest fell behind. Soon the car came even with him. Peter rolled down the window. "I don't know what you're listening to out there," he said warmer and dryer than any soul had a right to be, "but I've got Schubert in here."

This singular training, with the man out front running hard, and the man in back musing, listening to music, has the effect of making every session a clearly evaluated piece of work, with a point to it. Hard, concentrated running is what Herb Elliott of Australia did, and Filbert Bayi in Tanzania, but they did it alone. They didn't have the presence of the protective, perfectly tough mind in the following car.

"I'm harder this year than last," said Sebastian afterward, wearily. Peter put a fatherly hand on his knee. "Clear to see," he said. "The last two miles seemed endless." Sebastian sat pale and drained during the ride home. Even Ravel didn't revive him.

That evening he and Emma went to see *Manhattan*, where Sebastian was stricken with Mariel Hemingway and impressed with Emma's laughter at the most risqué dialogue. Driving home, he turned on the radio, identifying a Brahms piece after three measures. On another station the BBC was airing a program on great moments in British sport. Announcers shrieked over Red Rum taking the Grand National again and again, James Hunt winning the world driving championship, and then Sebastian, sprinting toward the line in Oslo. Taken off guard, he reached out and shut it off and then, at Emma's wailed appeal, put it back on.

". . . so flowing,'" sang the announcer, "so balanced, so graceful. . ."

"As he smashes into the gate," said Sebastian, parking.

The Olympic Dilemma:

As planned, Coe began 1980 by spending nearly four months in Italy. His training went well. "He'll be stronger and faster in all distances," said Peter after one of his frequent visits. But, during those months President Carter began the movement to boycott, the Moscow Olympics and was supported strongly by Britain's Prime Minister, Margaret Thatcher.

Curious about Coe's thoughts, the visitor arranged to meet him in mid-March in San Vittore Olona, Italy, at a strange cross-country race called, innocuously enough, the Cinque Mulini (five mills). The route required the runners to scramble across plowed fields, through barnyards, flour mills, up and down steps, past barking dogs, through dark rooms.

"It's not dangerous, it's fun, said Norway's Grete Waitz, who would win the women's race easily. Coe's impression differed slightly.

"There's been a horrible mistake," he said. "I was told it was flat, fast, and grass." He planned to run with one thing in mind, his safety.

Four hours before the race, over an omelette and a bowl of minestrone, Sebastian and his father poked through the disorder threatening the Games. "The Olympics are a dinosaur running out of cities," said Sebastian. "And they will be seriously devalued if American athletes don't compete. But the damage done by the boycott may be greater than anyone suspects. It may put all international sport at risk. I say that out of concern that international sports authorities may come apart on this issue, and out of a wish for consistency. It has been expedient for our governments to use athletes."

". . .the most vulnerable and nonarticulate segment of the community," said Peter.

". . .in this case. But in 1978 in South America, World Cup soccer matches were played in stadiums that a certain government had been using as internment camps for political prisoners. I'm not saying that's right. I'm not defending Argentina or Russia. I'm simply asking for consistency. If we have that, it follows that if you use the politics of a nation to judge whether or not you compete with that nation, you might as well say international sport is finished. It's like assassination, isn't it? The initial appeal—some prickly thorn out of the way. But then it gets out of control . . . and no one is safe."

Coe carefully outlined the difficult situation British athletes found themselves in. Their government has asked them to boycott, but their Olympic Association has voted to go.

"Unless somebody orders me not to go, I am going to the Games," he said. "But since it is a personal decision, what must not happen is eternal postmortems. All the individual reasons must be respected. You can't have people asking, 'Well, I stayed home; why did you go?'"

"In no way," put in Peter, "does going to Russia indicate support for Brezhnev or that country's behavior. To be called unpatriotic in no way makes it so, just saying it. If you do, you don't understand athletes."

"There the question seems to turn," said Sebastian. "It is a clash of two worlds. Governments, politicians are ruled by expediency. Athletes live in a world of natural law."

"When Olaf Beyer crossed that finish line in Prague," said Peter, "his lungs torn asunder, he was not thinking of the greater glory of the East German government. And if he's asked about Coe, he's going to say, 'An extremely courageous man who did a thing that created one of the great races ever.' He's not going to say, 'A lackey, of the collapsing capitalist system . . .'"

". . . who, like it, has the innate capacity for self-destruction," said Sebastian, grinning.

The men's field began the Cinque Mulini 9.5 kilometers on a sports ground beneath Lombardy poplars, running through brassy music, cheers, and mud Coe ran carefully in the pack, his power useless in the squishy ground. (Later he said, "Halfway through I wanted to stop and go to the director and say, 'You must be bloody well joking.'") Leon Schots of Belgium won. With a couple of hundred yards to go, Coe was twenty-third, but kicked spectacularly, throwing up a rooster tail of mud like a motorcycle, and finished twenty-first.

He patiently signed autographs for a while, but the afternoon was chilly. Just as he felt it was time to begin jogging back to the hotel, a tardy Italian reporter arrived with a wish to talk.

"Well," said Peter, "he's off round the . . ."

"The bend," said Sebastian, and he was gone.

The Moscow 800:

Nikolai Kirov had one chance and he knew it. The jostling pack of nervous Olympic 800-meter finalists had passed 400 meters in a disappointingly slow 54.5 seconds. Around the first turn of the last lap, Kirov, a short man, ran outside the elbows of the leaders, Agberto Guimares of Brazil and David Warren of Great Britain. He knew that Warren's more celebrated compatriots, Coe and Ovett were close behind him, and if he waited until the homestretch to kick they would outsprint him. He also knew that if he kicked on the backstretch with 250 meters to go, he would probably die in the last 50 meters. These were the Moscow Olympics. Kirov is a Soviet citizen. He kicked on the backstretch.

Kirov flew ahead at a point just beneath the windblown Olympic flame, and as he built his lead to two meters and then three, those in the crowd rooting for the U.S.S.R., perhaps eighty thousand of the one hundred thousand filling the great bowl of Lenin Stadium, emitted a deep-throated roar, a sound subtly different from mass expressions of delight and encouragement in Western stadiums. There seemed a hunger in it, a more visceral need, because during the first three days of track and field competition in these boycott-thinned Olympics, the Soviets' men's team and that of East Germany had not conducted their expected dual meet for the majority of the medals. Instead, a remarkable British team, perhaps the United Kingdom's strongest in Olympic history, had stood out as an island of eccentric individualism in a stolid, Eastern-bloc sea.

Allan Wells of Scotland had won the 100 meters. Daley Thompson, the son of a Nigerian mother and Scottish father, won the decathlon. And now, as Kirov bolted down the backstretch, Ovett worked his way out of a box and charged after him. Coe, whose habit it is to run wide and thus preserve his tactical freedom, was in tenth. It was his plan, as the world-record holder and the fastest quarter-miler in the field, to simply cover any moves made by the others and win in the stretch. Already, near the end of the first lap, he'd had a golden opportunity. Ovett had been sealed tightly against the rail. If Coe had begun a sustained drive then, Ovett couldn't have escaped to follow. But Coe stayed where he was. And finally Ovett pushed his way free.

Now, as the last turn approached, Ovett closed on Kirov. The pack began to string out. Still, Coe stayed where he was. Here the race hung in balance.

Coe had attempted to prepare for his races by tuning out the cacophony dinning upon the British athletes. But try as he might, he couldn't escape the fact that the Games were unique in being Russian. From the thousands of security men stationed about the city—unnerving in how they stood rock-still in the woods of the Olympic Park, their heads hidden by low branches—to the way Tass altered an old interview of Coe's to fit the Soviet position, to the continual thanks the British athletes and officials received from the Soviets for coming to the Games and thereby, the Soviets felt, legitimizing them, Coe was assailed by politics. And the assault was joined by his own nation's press, which seemed determined for a while to match Soviet propaganda blow for blow. Reporters complained that positive remarks about anything Russian were being cut from their stories. "The question," said a sour Peter Coe, "is not whether sport and politics can be separated, but whether sport and tabloid journalism can ever mix."

Sipping tea in the Olympic Village courtyard, being eaten alive by the mosquitoes that abound there, Sebastian had ruminated on how long the grudges caused by the boycott will last. At the suggestion that the Games in Los Angeles might return the Olympic movement to better times, he looked up, startled, "You really think they'll be held?" he asked.

As he moved easily through his quarterfinal and semifinal heats, winning both, he was lifted by a letter from his sister Emma. "Oh, do get some gold," she wrote, "it suits you so."

But gold is seized, and as the 800-meter finalists came out of the last turn, Ovett, the daunting, remote Ovett who, said one observer, seems to freeze his opponents with the force of his will, was out front and pulling away.

Coe was in fourth. He had ten meters to make up. He had waited too long. He ran down Guimares, and then the dying gambler Kirov, but he lost by half a second. More than that, he hadn't gained on the flying Ovett in the last half of the stretch. Ovett finished in 1:45.4, having run his last lap near 50 seconds flat. He darted around a restraining guard to have a word with his mother, Gay, and then stood on the victory stand aglow as the Olympic flag was raised in place of the Union

Jack. The last time British athletes won as many as three gold medals in Olympic track was in 1964. Now they had three within 24 hours, and good prospects remaining in the 200 and 1,500. A group of British fans deliriously sang "God Save the Queen" and waved Union Jacks, and Soviet television held its cameras on their celebration throughout.

Ovett declined to meet with the press, as is his custom, but he was overheard to say of Coe, "I hope no one writes of him as a failure." Coe dutifully allowed himself to be led before the assembled inquisitors. He seemed shrunken, for he needed no one to tell him his mistake. "I threw it away in the last lap," he said. "I simply didn't respond when the break was made at the front."

Peter Coe sat in the press bar, silent among his champagne-drinking country-men. A silver medal moved him not a whit. "All that is left," he said, fastening on the only possible redemption, "is to win that bloody 1,500."

The Moscow 1,500:

The nine finalists were led single file slowly, formally, from the funnel where they had left their sweat suits, to the start. Ovett walked pigeon-toed; he is a picture of fluid strength only in flight.

Coe, who shared the 1,500-meter world record (3:32.1) with Ovett but had never raced him at the distance until this moment, walked calmly to his place in Lane 6, then trotted a little circle behind the other finalists. He was the last to be steady on the line. Then the gun set them running.

Slowly. Coe went carefully to the head of the pack, but didn't cut to the inside. East Germany's Jürgen Straub moved up along the rail, and the two of them led through the first lap in 61.6. Ovett ran on the outside in sixth, a meter or two behind. Their faces, and those of he rest of the finalists, showed alertness but no irritation at the gentle pace. They had expected nothing more. In the 1976 Olympic 1,500 the first lap had been a sluggish 62.5; in 1972 it had been 61.4. Here in Moscow, with Tanzania's front-running Filbert Bayi having chosen the steeplechase (in which he had finished second to Poland's Bronislaw Malinowski) over the 1,500, no miler felt that leading would help his cause one bit.

So they waited, and slowed even more. Some grew nervous, telling themselves to stay balanced, to smooth out. Coe would later acknowledge that there was more pressure on him than in any other race of his life, but his sensation in this early stage was of clear intent. "Losing the eight hundred was a terrible disappointment," he said. "If I hadn't had the fifteen hundred coming up, I'd have been tortured with recriminations. But the fifteen hundred was there. "There was no choice. I *had* to make myself ready for it."

Both men had sailed through the preliminaries, Ovett winning his first-round heat in 3:36.8, appearing to do so as easily as that time—equal to a 3:54 mile—has ever been run, because as he coasted stop he happily drew the letters I L Y in, the air for the T.V. cameras, a tender message for his girl friend, Rachel Waller, in Maidstone. Coe's semifinal went smoothly until the last turn, where he permitted himself to be boxed by a rush of men. He had to drop to fifth and sprint around them, which he did impressively to win in 3:39 but it was a scare. "A blinding error," he said. "If that happens in the final it will be a disaster."

The incident provided more ammunition for those who believe Coe too nice a guy to win. Much of the British press, while lauding Coe's gentlemanly qualities, felt him hindered by them. "Coe is the man you'd want to dinner or your daughter to marry," said one reporter. "Ovett is the man you want on your side in a fight."

"That sentiment was hardly to the taste of Peter Coe." "What has happened to our world when you can't be tough *and* nice?" he asked acidly. "That logic is a slander on all champions. Are Nicklaus and Watson somehow not decent blokes because they make crucial putts under pressure?"

If Ovett had an advantage it was not in character but in experience. Since May 1977 he had won forty-five straight 1,500-meter or mile races, including a World Cup and European Championship, almost all with an overpowering finish over the final 200 to 250 meters. Coe in that time had concentrated on the 800. The Olympic final was only his eighth race at 1,500 meters (or one mile) in four years.

Yet, though Ovett was quoted in the London *Daily Express* as saying the 800 win made him feel capable of breaking the 1,500 record by as much as four seconds, Coe and his father put together a plan similar to that which they had tried in the 800. "Looking at the video of the eight," said Sebastian, "the *only* thing that was O.K. was my finish."

The problem was in securing a good place to kick from. "We received a marvelous cable from England," said Peter. "It read: GET YOUR FINGER OUT, COE. I'VE GOT MONEY ON YOU, and was signed by a Mrs. Mullory, whoever she is. Well, the plan was Mrs. Mullory's instructions put plain: stay out of trouble and sprint home from the turn."

As the finalists neared 800 meters, Straub was on the pole, with Coe on his shoulder. Ovett moved to Coe's shoulder, forming a wing of poised athletes. Peter Coe was pleased. "Seb was up, in a controlling position. I felt a fair race was on."

And then, a wondrous gift. As the field passed 800 in a restrained 2:04.9, Straub accelerated. Coe ducked in behind him and Ovett kept a close third as the bunched pack suddenly became a single line of men working very hard. "When Jürgen nailed his sail to the mast with seven hundred to go, it let me do what I do best," said Coe. "I found a rhythm, a lane of my own.

They had run the previous 300 meters in 47 seconds. Straub led through the next in 40. In the stands, Peter Coe was ecstatic. "No one in the world can sustain that speed as Seb can. And to have Straub apply it for him. . . The 1,200-meter time was 2:59.1.

Straub had run the next to last lap in 54.2. "It didn't look that fast because Seb and Steve are the supreme stylists," said the elder Coe.

With 300 to run, knowing eyes turned to Ovett. When would he kick? Two-fifty passed . . . 200, but there were no moves, only Straub's ever-increasing pressure. "The pace was such that it took the sting out of all of us," said Sebastian later.

In the last turn Straub faltered slightly. Coe went wide and passed and as the three leaders swept into the stretch, Ovett was right where he wanted to be, off Coe's shoulder. For an instant there was a predator's gleam in his eye as he called upon his kick. Ovett came even with Straub. And there he stayed as Coe sprinted beautifully ahead. As he passed the victory stand with 50 meters to go, it was clear Coe would win. Ovett strained in desperation, lost his form and was third behind the ferocious Straub.

Coe's last 800 was 1:49.2, far more impressive than his final time 3:38.4, but he cared about none of that. As he crossed the line he showed a joy these Games had not yet seen. Coe went to his knees in exaggerated gesture of thanksgiving, touching his forehead to the track. Then he was up on a victory lap, dodging a guard who was there to prevent such frivolity, his face as open as a child's in its array of emotions. Clearly, Coe's earlier calm had shielded tremendous strain. "I was surprised by the strength of my reaction," he would say a day later. "When I watched that display on the replay it was a bit embarrassing. But it was such a bloody marvelous relief."

Ovett smiled and waved during the medal ceremony, but afterward in the tunnel, appeared grim. "I was so high after the eight hundred that I couldn't get up again," he said. Later, explaining his practice of shunning the British press, he said, "They'll never leave me alone no matter what I do. They're like a wolf pack attacking."

The final day of track and field seemed to offer the most vivid images of the Games, and for an American the most wistful. Here was East Germany's defending champion Waldemar Cierpinski in the marathon, taking the lead with four miles to go in the caramel-sweet atmosphere near the Red October Confectionery Factory and striding home so strongly that he was without question a deserving winner. Yet how could one not miss Bill Rodgers or Tony Sandoval?

Here was Tatyana Kazankina of the U.S.S.R. also a 1976 champion running her last 800 meters in 1:59 to win the 1,500 in 3:56.6.1. What might Mary Decker have done against her?

No one could have beaten Miruts Yifter of Ethiopia. The 5-foot-3½-inch, 115-pound father of six added the 5,000-meter gold to the one he had taken in the 10,000. Tanzania's Suleiman Nyambui was close, 13:21.6 to Yifter's winning 13:21.0, but once Yifter was ahead with 300 to go he was in control. Ireland's Eamonn Coghlan gave it all he had, but for a second straight Games did no better than fourth. "I must be near some record for disappointment," he said. But then he spoke of races to come in future weeks, compelling miles against Bayi and Coe and Ovett and Steve Scott, and one knew he was unbroken.

As the athletes flowed out of Lenin Stadium on that last long twilight, past leaping Ethiopian tribal dancers, to the Village where Eastern Europeans were greedily filling sacks with precious fruit to take home, where the British celebration ended with Sebastian Coe covered head to foot in talcum powder, the mood seemed a reflection of Coe's own dominant emotion at his golden moment—that of sublime relief.

"It is intoxicating just having it over," said Peter Coe. "I don't even plan on seeing the grand Russian pomp of the closing ceremonies. No, the last thing I want to remember about these Games is that picture of elation as Seb crossed the line, a man who had borne up and gone out and done exactly what he had set himself. You can hang the rest."

—August 1980

Concentrate on the Chrysanthemums

We came to the Island of Kyushu at twilight, gliding above black offshore rocks, lumpy hills, refineries. It was a jarring landing. The road from the airport was lined with palms in dubious health. Leafless persimmon trees still bore their orange fruit. In hundreds of tiny drained rice fields, stacks of straw shook in the cold wind.

As our taxi approached the city we saw bundled peasant women tending smoky fires on street corners.

"I'm excited," said Frank Shorter. "Partly at being in a strange country, but it's more than that." Frank is given to analyses of his mental states.

"This is the first time I've started a trip knowing I couldn't be any better prepared," he said. "I've done more long runs than ever, I'm effective over shorter distances [he had won the national AAU cross-country championship in San Diego the day before], and my weight is right. I'm not torn down by too much racing like I was last summer.

He paused a moment, flinching as the cab cut off a cement truck. "Of course, it's frightening to feel like this. I've followed the program perfectly. If I run lousy, there's something wrong with the program."

This was November 1971, and Frank and I were in, Fukuoka, Japan, to test our programs in what amounts to the world marathon championship. Since 1966 the Japanese have invited the cream of the year's marathoners to have at it over a flat course in traditionally cool, fast weather. Derek Clayton of Australia became the first man run the 26 miles, 385 Yards under two hours and ten minutes (2:09:36.4) in 1967 in Fukuoka. The slowest winning time since was 2:11:12.8 by Jerome Drayton of Canada in the rain in 1969. Six of the fastest marathoners of all time have run their best races through the streets of Fukuoka, although Clayton improved his world best—there is no world record in the marathon because of varying terrain—to 2:08:33.6 in Belgium in 1969.

I had been invited on the strength of finishing second in 1970 with 2:11:35.8 and for winning the 1971 national AAU marathon championship. Frank had been second in our nationals with 2:17:44.6 in his first marathon and had won both the 10,000 meters and the marathon in the Pan-American Games.

At the hotel we met Eiichi Shibuya, the official in charge of our arrangements, and handed over two bottles of Johnnie Walker. He bowed. We bowed. His smile was reminiscent of Teddy Roosevelt's while standing over the lion.

"Mr. Kenneth Moore [my name was pronounced, as, it was all week, "Moo-ah"] remembers the Japanese custom of high import taxes on our favorite whisky."

While our steaks slowly incinerated upon their heated iron platters, we met the runners from Australia and New Zealand. John Farrington, twenty-nine, an administrative officer at Sydney's Macquarie University and fifth here last year, shook hands and looked dourly out the window.

"Look at those flags," he said, "Standing straight out from the poles. Bloody

171

awful conditions.

Jack Foster, thirty-nine, a clerk in Rotorua, New Zealand, sought to calm Farmington. "We've got five more days, John. It must stop."

Foster was fourth last year. His large eyes and wrinkled forehead give him an appearance of shyness and uncertainty. In September he had run eighty laps on a track in 1:39:14.4, the world record for twenty miles.

Jack introduced two of his New Zealand teammates, John Robinson and Terry Manners, both thirty-two.

"Not as fancy a field as it might be," said Jack. "Clayton says he's not racing again until Munich. Too much chance of injury. Ron Hill [of England, the only other man ever to crack 2:10] is only doing cross-country this winter. Bill Adcocks [also of England, winner, at Fukuoka in 1968 with 2:10:47.8 is injured. Karel Lismont of Belgium [the European champion] didn't answer his invitation, and the Japanese are sworn never to invite Drayton again."

"Why not?"

"Last year, after agreeing to run, he wired that he was injured. And in '69, when he won, he left his trophy. Apparently, the Japanese felt they lost face."

"Things are beginning to fall into place for me," said Frank. "Politics and face and duty-free Scotch."

"Well, it never hurts to make oneself welcome," I said. "Certainly not," said Jack.

"In any case," said Robinson "there will be a few men out there Sunday who can run a bit."

Akio Usami, Japan's defending champion, and national record holder (2:10:37.8), was at another hotel. A graduate student at Tokyo's Nihon University, he had won marathons in Athens in April and at Munich in September.

Two Finns, two Russians, a West German, and another New Zealander were expected.

"They invited four Kiwis?" I said.

"Oh, no," said Robinson. "They only paid for Jack. Terry and I had to put down fourteen hundred dollars apiece air fare and expenses, to race here."

"My God," said Frank. "Why?"

When Robinson spoke, all the blue showed in his eyes. "New Zealand can afford to send only eighty competitors to the Munich Olympics. How many will the U.S. send?"

"About four hundred and fifty."

"There. Our athletes are selected on the basis of their world rankings, which is the only way to choose between a swimmer and a runner, for example. We marathoners have to go under 2:16 simply to considered. That time will put a man in the top twenty in the world unless a dozen do it here [in 1970 tenth place at Fukuoka was 2:16].

"We can't hope to produce those times in New Zealand because all our courses run over mountains. But if we're any kind, of runners we ought to do it here."

"So you paid that kind of money to try," said Frank. "What do for a living?"

"I'm a phys ed teacher. Terry is a house painter." Later, as Frank and I walked to our rooms, he said, "I couldn't do that. Not unless I was positive I'd make it." He thought a moment. "Maybe he's ready."

* * *

We tried to run twice a day. I went out before breakfast. Nearby was a park and shrine. Crossing the gentle curve of a bridge I could look east and see canals reflecting red sunrise, silhouetting other bridges. A blue-roofed pagoda rose out of twisted, rope-wound pines. A bronze statue of an ancient Buddhist priest sixty feet high sheltered pigeons. Returning, the growing light revealed the foulness of the canals, shallow slime over broken glass and ordure.

Afternoons we were driven to more distant Ohori Park. A lake was spanned by a series of islands connected by more bridges. Willows grew over a cinder path. We ran with schoolboys, soccer teams and karate groups. We were photographed incessantly and on following days our pictures were brought back to be autographed.

Frank, at five feet ten inches and 130 pounds, looks fragile (Marty Liquori has called him "a vertical hyphen") yet he always braved the traffic and ran back to the hotel. Shibuya-san, an occasional jogger himself, was impressed.

"Mr. Shorter has much energy."

"Yes."

"Why do you think it is so?"

"He credits it to his drinking."

"He drinks?"

"Oh, yes. Lots of beer and gin-and-tonic."

"I drink wine. And beer and gin. But no tonic."

"So close, and yet so far."

We had no commitments, yet we were always occupied. Perhaps we are slow, or have lengthy attention spans. We certainly lingered over our meals, in conversation or, in Frank's case, in attempting to eat.

"I'm really up for this race," he said early in the week. "I have no appetite at all." For lunch he usually could get down a chocolate sundae and a gin-and-coke.

I asked if he had any objection to my publicizing his fondness for gin.

"Well, it's me," he said. "I sip it to relax and I've always done it. But if I bombed out in the race, a lot of red-necks would say 'see how the lush drank himself out of contention.' It wouldn't be true, but I'd hate to give them the ammunition."

Later in the day the Russians arrived and passed out little bottles of vodka.

The previous year the Russians had been archetypal proletarians. One, Yuri Volkov, who finished eighth with a Soviet record 2:14:28, is a metalworker and has a scar, of unstated origin, from jaw to hairline. He made noise when he ran, stamping on the pavement as if killing spiders. We all nodded knowingly the morning after the race when he could not walk, so damaged was one Achilles' tendon. This year's Russians were smooth. Both were twenty-eight, phys ed students and, on five words of English, urbane. Their names: Vassily Shalomilov and Yuri Maurin.

They had brought a manager, a robust, gray-haired man who burst, when least expected, into songs about Volga boatmen. He spoke no English and continually pressed us for autographs. If you happened to have a ballpoint pen in hand, it wound up in his. He did know one English word: "souvenir."

In his room, Frank discussed his feelings toward Russians.

"It is a culturally indoctrinated suspicion. I find myself wondering, 'What are they *really* thinking?' It's hard to articulate, harder to explain. I have to fight it."

I said, "I lost that in Leningrad." Frank and I had run there in the U.S. vs. U.S.S.R. meet the year before.

"Yeah," Frank said. "When Mikityenko gave us those little wood carvings from his children."

*   *   *

Between meals and workouts we were entertained by the press. The marathon was sponsored by the *Asahi Shimbun* newspaper chain, whose Fukuoka offices took up the first seven floors of the hotel building. Our pictures appeared daily and some of the interviews attained a depth seldom reached in this country. Having run second the year before, I drew a lot of fire. When my undergraduate major was exposed, I was pegged "the philosopher-marathoner" and asked such questions as "What is there about you which longs for the suffering of the race?" or "In what way is your soul satisfied by the marathon?"

It was a heady atmosphere and I succumbed. "After every experience," I said, "it's natural to reflect that you might have done better. Only after a marathon can I say I have given everything."

Farmington added, "Marathoning is like cutting yourself unexpectedly. You dip into the pain so gradually that the damage is done before you're aware of it. Unfortunately, when awareness comes, it's excruciating."

"That's why you have to forget your last marathon before you can run another," said Frank. "Your mind can't know what's coming." We were distracted from these musings by the arrival of the Finns. Seppo Nikkari, twenty-three, and Pentti Rummakko, twenty-eight, spoke nothing but Finnish. The Japanese were unable to unearth an interpreter. Nikkari, tall and gawky, with a feathery, blond mustache, did not seem perturbed. Disdaining the dinner menu he barged into the kitchen and pointed at what he wanted. When people in front of him did not make way fast enough when the elevator reached his floor, he cheerfully propelled them into the wall.

"He does not seem to have perfectly adapted to civilization," said Farmington.

Rummakko was slender and silent, with eyes in great dark hollows and gaps between his teeth. Fourth in the 1970 Boston Marathon with 2:14:59, he has raced internationally for years.

"It's unnerving," said Robinson. "You get the idea these fellows don't live for anything but running."

Nikkari seemed to develop an affection for Farmington, jumping in his taxi to the park, pounding on his back at unpredictable intervals, when they ran.

"I don't really *detest* the bloody ox, you know," said John. "I mean I haven't struck him between his blinking eyes. I will however, take pleasure in thrashing him by a few minutes."

Shorter discerned a plan. "The kid's got Farrington's number," he said. "You have to put so much effort into this race that you can't afford to dislike your opponents. It's a waste of energy."

One afternoon the phone woke me from a nap.

"This is cork."

"Who? From Ireland?"

"No. Cork, on ninth froor robby."

Tentatively: "Clerk?"

"Hai. You are Mr. Moo-ah?"

"Yes."

"You have visitor. Prease come down."

It was the man from the Tiger sports-shoe company. Mr. Yoshihiko Hikita provided us all with leather bags stuffed with his company's racing and training shoes. Not more than twenty-five and rigid in his black blazer, Hikita-san seemed awed by us.

"Just say 'This shoe rubs a bit,'" Farmington whispered to us, "and in two minutes he's back with another pair. Meanwhile, you've tucked away the first. That goes on and on.' I brought practically no luggage."

"A bloke could get really spoiled over here," said Robinson, clutching half a dozen shoe bags to his chest. By the end of the week he had filled a packing case with shoes, track suits, and camera equipment.

Hikita-san was proud of his new "Ohbori" model, named, roughly, for the park where we trained. He had sent a pair to Foster and me earlier and we had promised to race in them. Foster pointed out the shoe's ventilation.

"People at home asked me what all the little holes were for. I told them that's for the blood to run out."

Frank tried on a pair.

"Mr. Frank Shorter," said Hikita, "in your real opinion these are best shoes?"

"Yeah, they're great. But a little too wide."

"Ah so. But it is not possible to make narrower so soon before the race."

"I think they'll do."

That afternoon Frank ran a hard hour through the park in his regular, non-Tiger training shoes. After dinner Hikita-san was waiting for us in the lobby. He gave Frank a searching look.

"Why," he asked in a low voice "did you wear Adidas shoes today?"

Frank gently reassured him that he would race in Tigers. He had simply preferred not to run ten miles in brand new shoes. He mentioned again that his feet were very narrow.

Hikita withdrew and returned shortly with pieces of string and rice paper. He carefully traced the outline of Frank's foot and measured its circumference at the ball and around the arch, marking the string with red ink. Then he retreated, saying "We will try."

Frank, his bare foot propped on a coffee table, said softly, "I wish I hadn't worn Adidas today."

"Why? I've seen you play Adidas against Puma without mercy."

"They didn't take it like that man."

*   *   *

Runners are usually perpetual convalescents, leading a life of rich, vigorous afternoons, nodding evenings, and stiff, groggy mornings. Easing training before a race sometimes humanizes us, but we are incomplete tourists. Our sense of mission makes us unwilling to tire ourselves in search of culture or Christmas presents.

One morning Shibuya-san told us we were scheduled to go to a Shinto shrine to be purified for the race.

"It makes no difference whether or not we are believers?" inquired Frank.

"No difference. It is automatic."

"That sort of thinking might have saved us a few million in crusaders, heretics, and Northern Irish," Frank said.

We were greeted by a tiny, energetic man in beige and dark brown robes. Nobusada Nishitakasuji explained in rapid, precise English that his family had served as priests at Dazaifu Shrine for thirty-eight generations.

Detecting an accent, Frank asked if he had ever been in the United States.

"Harvard Divinity School," he said.

He led us through high stone gates and gilded arches to an inner courtyard. Under a sacred plum tree we were given a sip of ceremonial sake from a three-tiered golden bowl. Small printed fortunes were selected for us according to the animal of the year of our birth.

Shibuya-san translated my fortune.

"If you desire something a long time, you will get it. Beware of serious illness. Don't sell your house.

The priest excused himself and hurried off.

"Where is he going?" asked Frank.

"I believe he has a Rotary meeting," said Shibuya.

*   *   *

I had not been feeling well. The combination of the San Diego race, in which I finished sixth, the long flight, and the seven-hour time change had subdued me. Three days before the race I awoke feeling honestly sick. At breakfast Farmington said, "I tell everyone they're coming apart at the seams, but you really do look pale."

I reported to Shibuya, who took me to a clinic. My temperature was 101 degrees, the diagnosis, virus. I received a shot of antibiotic, some orange pills, and signed half a dozen autographs for a row of giggling nurses.

I was ordered to my room. Shibuya looked in every couple of hours. I got him to sit on the bed and talk about the Japanese attachment to the marathon.

"We made marathon important because it is one event in which a man needs not to be tall to be great," he said. "In marathon and gymnastics we can do well against the world."

"There is great pressure upon runners to do well?"

"Yes," he said. "Sometimes there is too much."

"Will you tell me about Kokichi Tsuburaya?"

He sighed. "Yes. there were many pressures on Tsuburaya. He came from a small town in the north, Sukagawa City in Fukushima Prefecture. There is only a cigarette factory there. The city had nothing to be proud of except Tsuburaya. There were signs on the buildings that said TSUBURAYA IS OUR PRIDE. When he won the bronze medal in the Tokyo Olympics, there was a great celebration. Everyone said, 'In Mexico the gold.'

"Tsuburaya was in the Japan Self-Defense Forces. He was in the 'department of training,' a leader with responsibilities. In our tradition, the leader is always the best. The JSDF is very strict and insists on training hard, hard, hard. There is no limit. My own sister trained with other women to challenge U.S. guns with bamboo poles.

This tradition has been carried on by the JSDF and influenced Tsuburaya. He trained so hard that he injured his Achilles' tendon. His commanders wanted the honor he would win, so he was not permitted to rest. For a year he ran poorly.

"In 1967 he committed suicide by slashing his wrists. He left a simple note to his mother. It said, 'I can't run any farther.'"

I asked how his death affected the Japanese.

"We were sorry."

"Were people sympathetic or did they think he was crazy?"

"He was not insane. We could understand. We were just sorry he had no friend or leader who could guide him. He had a heavy burden. We criticized his JSDF captain. We said 'Why didn't you help Tsuburaya?' He said only, 'We never let up.'"

* * *

When Shibuya had gone, I slept. In a dream I found myself at the start of the Olympic 5000-meter final. I had trained in secret for years, preparing for this single race. I tore through the first mile in four minutes even, pulling to a huge lead. In the second mile, in spite the pain, I surged harder, responding to the astounded, howling crowd, and ran it in 3:58. Over the last few laps, when I should have dropped I began to sprint, lapping the earth's best runners, lowering the three-mile world record by a minute. In the stretch, amid the torture of the effort and the screams of the multitude, I delivered the limit of my energy and all my body's chemical bonds burst. Only a wisp of vapor crossed the finish line, leaving my nylon shirt folded across the tape.

When I awoke, my fever was gone.

* * *

We had developed a cocoa ritual. Before bed the English-speaking runners gathered in a coffee shop off the lobby to choke down a few more carbohydrates. (The traditional, prerace steak has been discredited. Recent marathon records have been set on cream puffs and pecan pie.)

Feeling recovered, I put in an appearance. Farmington was at the window.

"I hope there are a lot of little Japanese down on their knees somewhere, praying for the weather," he said.

"Surely you don't have to worry about a fast time?" John was the year's second-fastest runner with 2:12:14.

"It would help my chances for Olympic selection. Our committee has decided to send only twelve men to Munich in track and field. There are twenty-one events. Once they are selected no one else can go."

"What if a runner was the best you had in an event, but wasn't selected and offered to pay his own way?"

"The committee would say no. It wouldn't be fair to the other unselected athletes who couldn't afford it."

"What if *everybody* could afford it?"

"They would still say no. It's tough to make the Australian team. It's always been that way."

"Do you think it should stay that way?"

"I will if I make it."

This created a silence. Finally Robinson spoke: "I say, had a peek in at the massage parlor next door? Fabulous!"

*   *   *

In the morning I jogged a few miles. Outside the hotel I found Robinson changing shoes. He ran a hundred yards down an alley, returned, sat down and began changing shoes again.

"Foot problems?"

"'Oh, no. It's just that to get these back into New Zealand without paying twice their value in duty, they have to be used."

Upstairs, I met Hikita-san coming from Frank's room. I looked in. Frank looked ludicrous in a flowing *yukata* and Ohbori shoes. He seemed dazed.

"They're perfect," he said.

"New shoes?"

"Yes. Somehow they made a narrower pair. But he tried to take my Adidas. He said, "Since you have no further use for these and tried to slip them into his bag. Don't they trust me?"

"When they know you better, Frank."

Usami came to the hotel to be photographed with his foreign challengers. We were made to sit in a row and hold up our bare feet for the camera.

Farrington felt Usami's rock-hard thigh.

"Your legs feel very, very tired," Farrington said.

Usami seemed about to explode with suppressed glee.

"Yes," he giggled. "Very tired."

"Well they ought to be," said Farmington. "You ran fifty kilometers before breakfast."

Usami laughed, throwing his head back. "Yes, yes. Exhausted."

*   *   *

I had regained my will to live, but the will to run is a more delicate flower. In hopes of nourishing it, I bought a bottle of Japanese champagne with dinner. It was sweet, but without the fruity quality of good sweet wines.

"Alcoholic cream soda said Frank.

"It's better than their red wine," put in Farmington. "That tastes like kerosene."

Soon we were telling stories. I talked about red-necks and bleeding feet in the Olympic marathon ("Gawd damn you, git awn up there where a American ought to be!").

Jeff Julian, the fourth New Zealander and a banker, told a Ron Hill story.

"Ron went to the Munich pre-olympic marathon in September," said Julian, "but he didn't enter. He simply ran over the course the morning of the race. Then, after Usami won, Hill came up and told him—I imagine a finger wagging—'You second next year in Olympics. *Second. Me first.'"*

Robinson and I frowned. "Ronnie should know better," I said, "Winning is never so sweet that losing can't be sourer, if you get your hopes up like that."

"Right," said Robinson. "I was just thinking it's nice they give ten trophies here. I'll be perfectly happy to take home any of those at all."

The day before the race we tried out our endurance in the opening ceremonies. In a ballroom before banks of flowers and the flags of the represented nations, we heard from the mayor of Fukuoka, the Japanese minister of education, the president of the Japanese Amateur Athletic Federation and the president of Asahi Shimbun. Frank was edgy.

"I have the feeling I got here a day early," he whispered. "I'm ready right now. My stomach is starting to churn."

"Relax. We'll have a drink afterward."

"You know, the winner of this race, really will be the favorite in Munich."

"Concentrate on the chrysanthemums and lilies, Frank. Think of the care some tiny, *patient* gardener . . ."

"We can do it, you know. I really feel it."

"Think how he watered and pruned and fertilized, creating blossoms that invite quiet contemplation."

"Those Russians look fit enough. I wonder if they're as nervous . . ."

"Pretend you're that patient gardener, taking pleasure and fulfillment from simply watching . . ."

"When I think of the start, all those frantic Japanese, ready to die. . . . The way they're going to drive us . . ."

"Frank. That way lies madness.

"You're right. What were you saying about flowers?"

*   *   *

Race day dawned crystalline and calm. Then at breakfast, in full view of Farrington, clouds scudded up from the southwest and it rained. Frank and I sat by ourselves.

"I don't feel like I have to win this, you know?" said Frank. "I want to, but I'm calm."

We were bused to the stadium, where we would start and finish, and were put in a bare, unheated room under the stands. We slathered Vaseline in our shoes and wherever skin rubs against skin. Remembering the Pan-American marathon in Cali, where he had to seek relief in a cane field, Frank went out to find a toilet.

"It's banjo, isn't it?"

"*Benjō.*"

"Yes. Would be embarrassing to get that mixed up."

Farmington was peering at an infinitesimal blister on Robinson's heel and saying, "Now *that's* going to be trouble. . . ." when we came under attack. Fireworks exploded somewhere and a crowd of crazed, clucking officials swept us out onto the field.

We jogged a mile to warm up. The Japanese runners were grim except for Usami, who smiled at friends in the crowd. The rain had stopped but not the wind. We were assembled on the line.

The starter's gun refused to discharge. We were reassembled and, finally, set off. More skyrockets detonated overhead. Usami jumped for the early lead. He did not get it. Farrington darted out of the inside lane and stayed in front until we were out of the stadium. Foster and Shalomilov kept close. Frank and I were fifth and sixth until Nikkari elbowed through.

Once on the road, the wind was behind us. The route followed the westward curve of the coastline out onto a flat, sandy peninsula. We were to return over the same road. Usami took the lead and his pace immediately split the field. Farmington and Foster stayed with him. Frank, Nikkari, and I surrendered 30 yards.

"What do you think?" I asked "It's under 4:50-mile pace."

"World-record pace."

"We can't let them get more than eighty yards."

By two miles we caught them. At 10,000 meters, reached in 29:47, the six of us were together, 100 yards in front

The crowd was immense, six and eight deep, mile after mile, and it roared at us with sustained fury. It possessed thousands of paper Japanese flags and slashed and beat the air with them in a frenzy of exorcism. The evil spirits surrounding Usami were given, at the very least, headaches

Moving with us was an entourage of official buses and police motorcycles. The camera truck vented oily, black exhaust. When it came too near we would shout and wave it away. Frank, saving his breath, merely spit on it.

A little butterfly of a Japanese kept fluttering up to us and falling back. At eight miles I dropped back with him, in crisis. The symptoms of midweek had returned, weakness and swimming nausea. I deluded myself. World-record pace would kill them all. It was infinitely more wise to run economically, give them their too costly lead, and take it back when it counted.

Robinson and Rummakko passed me.

Manners passed me. In spite of slowing, I felt no better. I was cooked.

The course turned gradually into the wind. Frank took refuge behind Foster and Nikkari. Farmington ran at his side. They had left all settlement and now ran between white sand dunes and low pines. The crowd vanished and they could hear each other's breathing. The pace slowed.

Farmington watched Nikkari's ungainly shuffle, and said, as if insulted, "The bloke's got no bloody calves."

Frank said, "Boy when we go around that turn, all hell is going to break loose."

Farmington shot him a look of panic.

Usami had taken them through the last 5,000 meters in 16:21.

Frank led the next in 15:11. Several hundred yards after turning for home, he met me laboring among the stragglers.

"Put it to them I said, needlessly. There was blood in his eye and he was running with a light driving precision.

With nine miles to go Frank had gained 200 yards on Usami and Foster, who were running together. The crowd changed in tone. Applause for Frank was warm, but the resounding encouragement behind him was of a different order. He used it to gauge his lead.

"The race is always between twenty and twenty-six miles," he said later. "My only doubt was that my mind was ready to put my body through that. When I got into it, I still didn't know. There was the pain, and there was a peculiar frustration. I can run a four-minute mile. It was agonizing for a runner like me to not be able to do anything but crawl."

They ran the last three miles into the teeth of the wind. The gritty, powerful Usami shook off Foster and drove on after Frank.

"It was the hardest I've ever run," said Frank. "Even in the heat of Cali, I felt better. Here, I was so helpless."

He won by 32 seconds in 2:12:50.4

"I finished and a great feeling of thankfulness swept through me. There was no sense of conquest, none of this baloney about *vanquishing* anybody."

Across the line, he waved away blankets and fought off officials and reporters to stand at the finish and embrace Usami.

"My only thought was, Here we are, goddamn it! We made it!' This man had suffered as much as I had. We all had."

He stood there and shook hands with every finisher until I came in. I was the twenty-eighth person he shook hands with.

*   *   *

In the last hour, I crept. The kilometer times were gibberish, so different were they from what we had expected. I thought about quitting. Ambulances waited every three miles. I remembered being taken from the Pan-American marathon with heat exhaustion. "I never quit!" I shouted aloud. "Never! Never! Never!"

I repeated this every 500 yards to the end.

More Japanese passed. My hip stiffened. The West German, Manfred Steffny, a pale, delicate runner who had arrived only two days before, passed. He asked me what was wrong.

"Fever, sick, blisters, don't give a damn . . ."

He left me spouting afflictions. I was the last of the foreigners. People called "Moo-ah, Moo-ah," held their children by the shoulders, and pointed them at me. I imagined them saying, "See, even the silver-medal winner of last year can be reduced to a stumbling, tortured wreck." I was a wheezing moral.

In some places the crowd had departed. Paper flags drifted across the street like candy-stripe leaves. A few children waved sticks from which the paper had been torn.

I watched the hills, the pines rising out of courtyards, trying to mask with images the meaningless pain.

Entering the stadium, I caught a wobbling Japanese. He spurted. I kept close and jumped him in the stretch. Frank was there. "Are you all right?" he asked.

"Yeah, I never give up."

Foster was third, Nikkari fourth. Manners fifth, Farmington sixth ("The bloody gales. I couldn't move after twenty miles"), Rummakko seventh. The times, because of the wind, were slow. Of the New Zealanders, only Foster cracked 2:16.

The award ceremony was tedious. Frank put up with it somewhat better than I, accepting four trophies and two medals. The top ten finishers mounted pedestals. Squarely on No. 10 beamed John Robinson.

* * *

In the late afternoon, after hot baths, we were escorted to a buffet for congratulations from dignitaries. Oysters cascaded from a Fujiyama carved in ice. The Olympic torch, fashioned out of butter, rose above a track of pâté, upon which raced stuffed lobsters. Frank was brought a beer by a pretty girl in a kimono. "She is the most expensive bar hostess in all Fukuoka," said Shibuya-san.

"Why?" asked Frank. The girl fled.

We met Colonel Leonard Fisher, commander of the U. S. Air Force units in the area.

"Frank, my boy," he said, "youse ran a great race. We almost got out of the car to cheer."

After dark we were taken across the street to the Fukuoka Famous Strip Show. The Soviet manager sat in front of us. When it was over, he turned, pondered for a long, effortful moment and said, "O.K., yeah?"

"My God," said Frank, "I thought he was going to say 'souvenir.'" We wound up at a dim French restaurant. The Russians demanded vodka, inspected the label, and decided, scornfully, "nyet." Shalomilov then stood and triumphantly drew a huge bottle from beneath his coat.

"Real vodka!" he shouted.

The New Zealanders fell to screaming Maori war chants. Shibuya sang a Spanish ballad in a steady tenor. The Russians crooned Caspian work songs, and one of the Finns (Nikkari since Rummakko refused to open his mouth) produced something characteristically unintelligible.

Robinson soon announced, "That vodka's great stuff. My blisters have gone away already."

Frank and I under overpowering, duress, sang "Show Me the Way to Go Home" and went home. We fell asleep in the taxi. I remember the last thing he said: "I get like this after every marathon, so damn tired."

—May, 1972

The Great Hawaiian Footrace

As we assembled beside the beach on our first morning, sipping tea and daubing sunscreen on our shoulders and faces, we happened to catch sight of a pod of finback whales offshore. Through the hotel's telescopes we watched them, submarines of solid flesh, barnacled and dark, blasting their vaporous breath into the warm Pacific air.

"Good omen," said Dr. Jack Scaff, one of the originators of our approaching venture. "Of course we're only ready to accept good omens. If Madam Pele had engulfed the hotel in fire and lava, *that* would have been a good omen, meaning we must forsake the things of civilization and take ourselves to the wilderness."

The thirty-six of us formed our own little pod on the hotel's front drive. A small gun was fired. We began to run. The Great Hawaiian Footrace, whose 500,000 meters (312 miles) would take us two and a half times around the island of Oahu, had commenced.

We joined the main road along Oahu's north shore and headed west beside pastures so thick the grass swept horses' bellies. Our task lay before us with deceptive simplicity. Three light blue vans carried our households, and gave us directions and water as we ran. When we reached Mokuleia Beach Park, eighteen miles distant, our times would be recorded and we would put up a brightly colored tent village, there to enjoy food, inexhaustible beverages, and each other's company until the next morning when we would break camp, load it into the vans, and set off afresh. After eighteen days of running—and two to recharge in Honolulu—we would finish, having stayed in fifteen different beach parks. We had only three rules: no sunburn, no littering, and always check in and out of camp, "So we won't call out the sea rescue teams and then find you in some bar," said Scaff.

Conceived by Scaff and Dr. Tom Bassler as fanciful impossibility, then actually organized by Donna Scaff, Jack's patient and winning wife, as a rigorous running holiday, the experience would only be given its final character by the land and people we met. And by us.

The race had been advertised only once, a year earlier in *Runners World* magazine, and as it demanded three weeks and a six-hundred dollar entry fee (to cover our catered meals and five nights in hotels and assorted extras), it seemed that whoever signed up had to enjoy some financial ease or represent the leading edge of the running craze. As it turned out, mania was more nearly our common denominator than money, but our flamboyance assumed wonderfully diverse forms.

"There is no one more competitive than I am," said lean Ed Shaffer of Walterboro, South Carolina, who had piloted 747's for Pan Am until a few months earlier when he had reached the mandatory retirement age of sixty. He had departed grudgingly, believing that a man who could run a 3:11 marathon, as he did this year in New Orleans, wasn't going to slump over in the cockpit. Shaffer used to race cars on the European circuit, but found success there had more to do with machinery than merit. "Running is far more competitive," he said. "You go to the line here, you go with body and soul." Shaffer's other calling seemed the siren's song. He'd been married seven times, to five women, and wasn't about to retire from that. "It's unnatural for a man to live alone," he said as he watched a lovely Pan Am stewardess put up his tent. "I get married for the honeymoons and the dinners."

More solitary was Leon Henderson, thirty-two, of Eugene, Oregon. In the early sixties, Henderson and I had been high school milers, teammates, and competitors, he showing the greater promise. But after he graduated he spent a year in New Zealand where he was won to the joys of fell, or mountain, running. Our ways parted, mine becoming the rather densely peopled one of track and marathon racing, his the more personal of running over every summit he could see. Now, in this long race, our paths at last converged. A stocky man of enormous strength, with clear, visionary eyes and a thick, blond beard, Henderson had worked most often as a ranch foreman, although there had been a disastrous five weeks in the employ of a Los Angeles photographer, shooting stills of 'The Gong Show.' He had departed when its gratuitous cruelty drove him back to his beloved Oregon mountains and big trees. On first hearing of the Great Hawaiian Footrace, a shock of recognition had hit him. "I somehow knew this was the event for me," he said, echoing the sentiments of much of the field. "I look at it as a matter of survival."

He had trained by running across the wild expanses of the Kahua Ranch on the Island of Hawaii. Because of his proven ability to run back-to-back thirty-mile days, he seemed a good bet to win.

Henderson's temperament is kindly, among friends, but he can exhibit a certain pleasure in keeping his auditors off balance, as when he spoke of the new sport he invented: disorienteering. "If you follow the trail, you're disqualified. If you go where anyone else goes, you're disqualified, as you are if you find one of the checkpoints on purpose. The only way to win is to get completely, uncaringly lost."

Duly consternated at such talk was Harvey Shultz of Clawson, Michigan. A grizzled machinist with the rock-hard torso of a boxer, Shultz at forty-four had run for less than two years. He belonged to the "adventure" category of entrants who were entitled, when intrigued by a sugar mill or a flea market, to turn off their digital watches while they explored and restart them when they pressed on, us keeping their own elapsed time.

After seven miles of our first day's run, we gulped a cool drink from the hose of the Church of Saints Peter and Paul overlooking tranquil Waimea Bay. The pink church tower shaded us and from within—it being Sunday—we heard the sweet strains of hymns. For Harvey Shultz this temptation proved irresistible. After drinking, he pounded on the church door, asking admission.

"But you need a shirt," whispered the usher, staring at Shultz's total attire, soaked yellow shorts with red hibiscus flowers on them.

"Well, I'm *running*, man," he said. "My things are miles from here."

Charity prevailed and Shultz was given a shirt. At least it used to be a shirt. Now its buttons were gone, along with its sleeves. It was a little cape, actually, but it served, and Shultz sat through the remains of the mass, beatifically sweating. When he came out, the rector insisted he take the thing with him.

By this time the rest of us had run through the sleepy little town Haleiwa and on through steamy sugar cane fields, the heat rising from the road, to our finish at

Mokuleia Beach Park. As we crouched around the welcoming blue van at the side of the road, munching cut pineapple and drinking juice and Primo, the Hawaiian beer, we looked up and saw an apparition. It was a brawny man, with bloodstreaked legs and a tattered little cape stuck to his shoulders. His toes were torn and muddy, his body covered with bits of straw and weed. "Must have taken a wrong turn," he said in a weary tone that suggested this sort of thing happened often. "I went over a chain barring the road and passed a lot of signs that said, 'Private—No Trespassing.' I kept a comin'. When I thought I ought to be almost here, I came to a stream, swam that, then there were more signs, but I kept a comin'. As I got tired I just remembered Dr. Scaff's advice: 'Keep The Ocean To Your Right.'"

After our tents had been erected on a lawn covered with the tiny sharp lumps of ironwood cones, Scaff looked out over the eastern bay, breathing in the view of the green land we had crossed. "It's like the outer islands, isn't it?" he said, pointing out the minute pink tower of Harvey Shultz's church, nearly lost in the distance.

"Harvey has been on insulin since he was five," he said suddenly "At forty-four, he's lived much longer than almost any other juvenile diabetic." He confessed admiration for the man's brute strength. "If he seems aggressive or eccentric, I believe it's because he's living every day as it were his last."

We were splendidly cared for. Gil and Tippy Dias, a middle-aged couple, were children of the sea, she from Tonga, he from Hawaii. They saw to our feeding. Every evening Gil gathered a few good swimmers and tugged a hundred feet of delicate gill net into position outside the surf or reef. At dawn he brought in the fish, which would be broiled and served with our dinner. He seemed to know every current in every bay, the habits of every species. "The mullet are like a flock of sheep," he said. "If one jumps over the net, they all will.

Running with us on selected days was Lieutenant Dave Benson, the chief of the Honolulu Police Department Traffic Division. Undeniably athletic, he was nonetheless larger than the usual habitué of long-distance running, his weight dropping from 245 pounds to 238 on the first day. Congenial and exuberant, he conveyed to us a sense of easy security. Recounting some of the troubles between local Hawaiians and incautious tourists, he made them seem distant stories, quaint, with little bearing on our idyllic and noninvasive passage.

A dozen of us were subjects in a medical study being conducted by Dr. Rudy Dressendorfer of the University of California at Davis, and Charles Wade of Tripler Army Hospital. Blood and urine would be taken at dawn on eight selected mornings to see through our enzyme and hormone response whether this 130 miles per week of hot weather running was strengthening us or eating us away. Assisting was University of Hawaii zoology student and cross-country runner Becky Russell— blonde and tan—whom Henderson immediately dubbed the Race Bunny. It was a role she accepted, she said archly, "Only to prove that an ardent feminist can have a sense of humor," but she had a certain knack. "Do you mean," she said with a pout as we milled around before the start, "that this is the last day I get any of you guys fresh?"

It was. Our daily routine quickly developed into one of rising at dawn, pressing resolutely through our two to five hours of running while the day was still relatively cool, and then resting. If there was a luxury in what we did, we took it here, in the many stages of recovery. Immediately upon finishing we sat and lay in postures as far removed from running form as possible and soaked up liquids. Scaff had to keep upping the order for Primo until it leveled off at fifteen cases a day, or an average of ten beers apiece. Russ Melanson, a fireman, while filling out his record for the doctors of what he ate and drank, said, "I get to eighteen Primos and after that I write, 'I forget.'"

Once rehydrated, we passed into a stage of ravenous hunger, consuming sandwiches and fruit and juice and soft drinks until the day's one large meal in early evening, delivered to us from Honolulu. The first night at Mokuleia we ate through dinner, through the next day's breakfast through the next day's lunch. "There's nothing to eat until the next truck," said Schaff, who estimated we each were burning five thousand calories a day. "And, uh, there's one other thing. Tomorrow there's no road."

You can't drive around Kaena Point, the dry and desolate northwest protrusion of Oahu. So after we had run three miles on our second day, the vans gave us one last drink and turned away for the fifty-mile drive down the flat center of the island and back up the west coast. We had to take care of ourselves for six miles of we knew not what, and as much longer as it took the vans to find us on the other side. We were to finish at Waianae Regional Park, eighteen miles away.

Cautiously, we ran in little groups, scouting the rutted sandy track, dodging crumbling lava outcroppings, holes as big as bathtubs, as big as swimming pools. As we passed the point's lighthouse, we mounted a rise and were struck with the whole Waianae side of the island, its steep green valleys running back between dark, sere cliffs. Waves burst up at us from the rocks below. "Now this is *country*," said Henderson with dismaying vigor. "A man could make a hard race of it the next two times through here."

When we regained paved road, Henderson trod on it with distaste, but Jeff Jones, thirty-three, a math teacher from Westport, New York, shot ahead. He had hidden his competitive intentions well, having said to Henderson the day before, "Please don't ever change your shorts. When those black shorts cross the road, I cross the road. I plan to focus on them in my trance for three hundred miles."

Henderson and I, knowing we had a hot twenty-three miles the following day, let him go and tried for that elusive rhythm where every running muscle is working just as hard as all the others, so you wear out evenly. We cruised into Waianae town forty-eight seconds behind Jones. Right behind us were John McCormack, a twenty-nine-year-old fireman from Brooklyn, and Doug Peck, a cross-country skier and ultramarathoner from South Lake Tahoe, California. Things were sorting themselves out in the competitive division.

We sat on a log and drew on our Primo and reflected upon where to put our tents. "Looks shady under that thorn tree," said Henderson. As he pointed, cars screeched into the parking lot behind us, their doors slamming before they stopped. There was a high school across the highway and it seemed to be emptying. Kids were running all around us, shouting, trembling in the cold grip of adrenaline. They gathered under the same *kiawe* tree Henderson had thought attractive. Two brown young men stripped to the waist, and purposefully set about trying to kill each other, the sound of their punches carrying with disturbing solidity. There must have been rules, because whenever one choked or kneed the other, the crowd rushed in and separated them. As their faces and chests ran wetly scarlet, and still the blows landed, we sat there, cavalier and defenseless, unable to imagine getting up the energy or the hate to work such destruction on another. Then, suddenly, some sort of arbitrary conclusion was reached and the crowd broke and flowed around us, going back to school, taking no notice of weary t0ransients.

All was peace again so quickly we wondered whether we had not had a communal dream. "On second thought," said Henderson, "I think I'll set my tent over here in the sun."

Then we heard Shultz. "Hey does the laundry take out burrs?" he shouted.

We turned. He was again covered with crusts of mud and scab. "Harvey, look at yourself."

"I know," he said, "I even got blood on my cape."

He had climbed the cliffs back at Kaena Point, thinking that because telephone wires were up there, a road might be. "I climbed ledge after ledge and it got awfully hard, so I looked down and I said, oh no . . . the path's down there." His crashing descent had been at the expense of his legs.

"Your shins look like something dead on the road," said Scaff. "I hate the sight of blood."

"Harvey is an accumulation of everything that has ever gone wrong with a runner," said Henderson, who only then noticed his glasses. The lenses were partially blacked out in a honeycomb pattern, making the world appear to Harvey as through the front of an old radio. "What on earth do you wear those for?" he asked, thinking the answer must have to do with keeping light from diabetes weakened eyes.

"Only cost twenty dollars," said Harvey. "Regular glasses are twice as much. But you're right about what a mess I am. Look at this blister on my heel."

Henderson asked if he had any moleskin with him.

Harvey glanced at the lawn to his right and to his left. "I haven't seen a mole," he said, with innocent desperation, as though he might be expected to catch one, "in the longest time."

During lulls in a four-hour lunch of Portuguese sweet bread, honey, Primo, roast beef, cheese, Manoa lettuce, oranges, and more Primo, we swam in a little bay, signed a petition against a deepwater harbor for oil tankers at nearby Barber's Point, and showered in the park lawn sprinklers. And talked. Ed Shaffer talked of his days as a copilot when he tried to drive his pilots crazy. "If one wanted to land good and quick, I'd circle. If he wanted to circle, I'd take her down right now." We figured Ed had saved Pan Am thousands it never had to pay when his spooked pilots retired early.

We heard the tale of three high school kids from Ramona, California. Bruce Breon, Ralph Mittman, and Larry Hargis had somehow talked their teachers into cutting them loose for three weeks in April and May on the promise that they'd write extensive reports on their experience. They'd dived for golf balls in Southern California water hazards and sold them back to pro shops to raise their fare.

They'd solved one conflict by quitting the Ramona track team so they could run here. "Cross-country is what I love," said Mittman. "But I've never seen anyone do it like Harvey."

"That's not cross-country," said Henderson. "That's rock surfing. Hey, Harvey, rock's up!"

At 5:50 A.M. of the third day, Henderson tossed back the mosquito netting and looked at the sky.

"Oh my God," he whispered. The air was crystalline and still. A sliver of moon glowed brightly in the warm dawn. "Not a cloud."

We were running by seven, easing into the idea of twenty-three miles, when Dave Erb, twenty-eight, a Colorado Springs builder, who had been laying off the pace the first two days, moved strongly ahead. In ragged single file we ran down the west coast of Oahu, the first twelve miles along the Farmington Highway, a four-lane glut of buses and trucks and menacing boxy vans with darkly tinted windshields. The vehicles blasted by our elbows with what seemed blind indifference, each tightening our nerves one increment more.

Then we left the main road and followed an old highway eight miles through cane fields. In sections the cane was being burned before cutting. Rats and mongooses ran before the fire. Huge trucks bore unruly loads of charred cane. Through the smoke and floating ash we got our first look at the tiny profile of Diamond Head, far off to the southeast, proof that we were making progress.

As Erb, Jones, Henderson, and I formed a little group, we hit freeways, used car lots, and taverns along Kamehameha Highway. Flimsy suburban roofs terraced the slopes of Pearl City above us. After twenty-two miles, when I yearned to be done, Jeff Jones seemed to come to himself. "How far are we going today?" he asked, apparently just having thought of it. Henderson stared at him.

We finished the leg at Neil Blaisdell Park on the shore of Pearl Harbor. Jones said that he had never broken an hour for ten miles, not possessing the speed to sustain a six-minute-mile pace. Yet he had been averaging sevens for the fifty-eight miles we had covered in the first three days. "He must be a natural ultramarathoner," said Henderson later. "He's got that one pace and can go forever. We're lucky we're not doing forty miles a day. I don't think he'd notice."

Harvey Shultz, by now our celebrity, ran superbly, finishing well up. For once he had kept to the course. "Remember those streams we crossed just past the cane?" he said. "I got up on the bridge railing, ready to jump down into the cool water, when I thought to take my glasses off, and my God, it was forty feet down there." When Harvey revealed that he carried no health insurance, Doug Peck said, "That explains why you're so careful."

With the longer run, fatigue lingered. Camp faded in and out in brief tableaux: Dr. Ben Kuchar and his wife Shirley of Palos Verdes, California, he sixty and she much younger, showering in the park's cold water hose while faintly disapproving schoolgirls watched; Henderson hectoring Peck and his friend, Sally Beugan, who was winning the women's division, about their careful vegetarianism, saying, "You'll admit, won't you, that a cow is just a conspiracy of some vegetables against other vegetables? Here, have some mullet. It's the corn of the sea." And Ed Shaffer, holding forth on racing needs, saying, "Now you can't run a race without support, and by that I mean *female* support, so in the last miles you can imagine the finish, how you'll get a cool drink and a relaxing foot massage and a tender caress, and someone asking in a soft southern voice, 'Is there anything else you need?'" Ed's laugh, as we drifted to sleep, was lecherous and wild, absolutely untrammeled.

In the night, Jack and Donna Scaff awoke to the hissing of an aquatic watering system. Sleepily, they went through camp dropping cases of soft drinks on sprinkler heads. "Lucky no one put his tent over one," said Schaff in the morning.

To compensate for the long trek of the day before, we had to run but thirteen miles along construction-rife Nimitz Highway into Waikiki. Doug Peck won the leg, followed by John McCormack, whose relaxed, high-kicking stride appeared stronger every day. The finish was at our hotel on a back street. Henderson and I fought through buses and shifting formations of tourists to get there. "Two laps to go," he said when we were done, meaning of the island. Chubby, middle-aged lei girls lassoed us with wreaths of plumeria. Henderson looked up at a phalanx of white-haired, thickset women applauding us from the hotel *lanai*, and said, very loudly, "The irony of that is that if their husbands had run and not died early, those biddies wouldn't have been able to use the insurance money to come over and cheer us on."

Surely we were tired. But it was here in Waikiki that our surroundings seemed most of a trial. We wished to sleep at nine; the singing from the parking lot didn't cease until two. We craved fresh sea air; the elevators were full of smokers. The next day we ran rapidly out of town to the coast, past Diamond Head, out Kalanianaole Highway, the route of the December Honolulu Marathon. We finished the seventeen miles over two large lava hills at Makapu Point.

John McCormack won the leg, giving us five winners in our first five days. Henderson and I finished a minute and a half back, a few seconds of which was spent cowering in a ditch where we had gone to escape an enormous earth mover being carried on a still more gargantuan truck.

We let turquoise waves batter us silly at Makapu Beach, the best body surfing area on Oahu. When we staggered out, we collapsed on the hot sand.

"My Lord, I can't even lift the can to my lips," said Jeff Jones.

"You know," said John McCormack, lying spread-eagled, staring into the expanding blue sky, "There's nobody better than us. I don't mean we're better than everybody, but there's *nobody* better than us." Our ready assent, besides expressing the feeling that such tiredness ought to be worth something, seemed a reaction against the indolence and excesses of Waikiki, a wish for recognition of an equally legitimate way to go. Reduced to basics, we were becoming a mobile tribe.

Perhaps reduced to fewer than basics. Ed Shaffer suddenly appeared like a stork over us, saying, "I don't know what's the matter with you guys. There are five Colorado coeds over there who don't know a soul on the island and here you sit. . . ."

Camp was down the road at Waimanalo Beach Park upon thick turf. Through feathery ironwood trees we watched the green and fluted cliffs of the Koolau Range. Warm water lapped a soft sand beach. The sun would rise through our tent flaps. "You can see why Lindbergh was so affected by this place," said Doug Middleton, a Denver investment counselor who often ran with a "Money Runner" T-shirt. Round and incandescently pale at first, Middleton had turned patchy red, then tan, his beard coming out thick salt and pepper. Fat melted away daily. Only the calmly professional modulations of his voice stayed. Later, he would engage math professor

Norm Locksley of Washington, D.C., in abstract conversations about interest rates and inflation and what could possibly be on Jimmy Carter's mind. Middleton had been running a year and a half. "I decided one day, taking stock, that I'd invest some time in myself." So he had begun, but in a modest way, walking and jogging. Never had he covered the distance we were doing. "I've developed a craving for onions," he said, "but I'm holding up."

We all were, except for Harvey Shultz, who was back in Waikiki with a case of diarrhea. The first results of the enzyme and hormone monitoring showed that despite the unaccustomed stress, everyone was responding well.

We had picked up a few new people. Bert and Earlene Smith of Odessa, Texas, he a red-faced trial lawyer, she a tiny blonde woman given to outfits of shocking pink, had signed on for a week. They reminded Henderson of Chester and Jessica Tate on "Soap." Bert did tend toward resonance in his speech, and Earlene did show a wondrous solicitude for Bert's welfare. As they neared the finish of each day's run, Bert would put his head down and outkick Earlene. Then as he stood panting she would kneel and untie his shoes for him.

Day six presented us with our hilliest section, 19.7 miles above the cities of Kailua and Kaneohe and along the shore of Kaneohe Bay to Kualoa Point, near the tiny island known as Chinaman's Hat. Ed Shaffer led the first five miles before stopping abruptly on top of a hill and waving Henderson and me past. "What am I doing?" he said in answer to Leon's question. "I'm resting."

By now we knew how to keep track of mileage by reference to mileposts and markers put down by Roberto Deuriarte, the chief recorder. In these we invested a childish faith, such that when this day's run went on a mile farther than advertised, Henderson ended saying, "They flat out *lied* to us."

The finish was beside an arboretum of some kind. Walking through rows of quite large decorative trees, I met a manager, who explained that this was where all the trees were grown for the City and County of Honolulu. "They have to be at least four inches in diameter when they're planted in the parks or they'll be broken off or torn out by the locals." Later, Jack Scaff nodded. "It's the same reason there are no mirrors or toilet seats in the Beach Park rest rooms.

Cashew trees spread over our camp. Scaff this afternoon was animated, reporting behind-the-scenes events. "The caterer thinks we're sandbagging him. He keeps saying, 'Are you *sure* you only have thirty-six people out there?'" Reassuringly, he spoke of our taxed cardiopulmonary systems as fail-safe. "The lungs can absorb more oxygen than the blood can hold; the blood can carry more oxygen than the muscles can accept. It'd be stupid to have it the other way. You'd twitch a finger and pass out."

Dr. Ben Kuchar normally blew his bugle for reveille at 5:30 A.M. Now he did it at 5 P.M., heralding the return of Harvey Shultz, who was wan and confused after a day spent on buses trying it find us.

Over a dinner of noodles he strengthened, describing a lifelong train of ordeals: his diabetes, his being in the wrong place at the wrong time at the wrong speed. "I had a motorcycle wreck nine years ago. Broke my back, hip, ribs, everything. My right leg is still an inch thinner than my left. But the running—ah, it's been a godsend, although I still don't know what I'm doing out there. This was observable. Harvey ran as he lived, with such force of footstrike that his shoes tended to explode under him. The resulting soreness and blisters he tried to put out of mind, in much the same fashion that he requested no novocaine when he had a tooth drilled. "I have developed a fairly high threshold of pain," he said. "But think about it. The really bad pain of a dentist only adds up to fifteen seconds or so but that horrible flabby numbness of novocaine lasts half a day." It was such a rational assessment of trade-offs that had led Harvey here. "I'd only been on my machinist's job a week when I left to try this thing," he said. "It's not worth worrying whether it will be there when I get back."

Our seventh day, another twenty-three-miler, would more than complete our first circuit of the island. It was a strangely paced run, Jeff Jones starting us off at his unchanging speed, then John McCormack passing crisply at eleven miles. Henderson and I said to each other, "Now let's not go with him," and after a mile, we went with him. Through the Kahuku sugar area McCormack increased the pace on every downhill. Despite the hot sun I felt good but Henderson, heavier, needing more fluid, was in trouble by twenty miles. He dropped back, the first time that we had not kept company through an entire leg. Cut adrift from his sensible counsel that to last out the race required caution in the early stages, and that no matter if it felt like we had been born on these roads it was still early, I tossed my hat to the film crew and took off. For a couple of miles at 5:30-mile pace the lift of new muscles was exhilarating. Then, as heat dizziness began to creep in, I was sustained by the thought that the end was near. Indeed, there was the blue van two hundred yards ahead. But as I watched, it started up and drove away—another misjudged end. For a mile I struggled on, furious, developing a bile-filled speech, which I finally delivered to Deuriarte, he nodding, abject, as I raged that *that* was never going to happen again. After two minutes of jogging recovery, I was back, abject myself, apologizing for my derangement. We ended up hugging, escorted into these wild I swings of emotion by the chemistry of slight changes of pace. Henderson walked in fifteen minutes later and put ice on his head. "Will it ever feel good," he whispered, "to get back to my true sport, off these roads."

We were on Ehukai Beach, site of the Banzai Pipeline. We sat on the sand and watched the surfers and shared bits of our day. A little poodlelike dog had come yapping out of a yard after Dave Benson's ankles, but before it reached him a car hit it. "A lady ran out," said Benson, "and said, 'That dumb boy. I told him tie that dog. Now I make him dig one hole!'"

A kid on a skateboard had asked Jack Scaff what he was doing. Scaff shouted, "Give me your food!" grabbed the kid's Fritos, and ran on.

Kathy Emerick and Suzanne Bella of the film crew declared that Hawaiian drivers were the rudest they'd ever seen. I disagreed, arguing for South Americans, but dwelling on the seemingly fundamental principle of all driver/runner relationships, that the harder it is for the driver to understand the runner, the more vicious he will be. Thus one who has devoted a life to the accumulation of status bestowing goods such as overpowered cars will find the reception of same by runners an incomprehensible affront, and so insist with all two tons of his authority that the road remain under the automobile's sway. The runner, if he is to survive, knows that justice must be tempered with cowardice. As Sancho Panza remarks in *The*

Man of La Mancha, it matters not whether the pitcher hits the stone or the stone hits the pitcher, it's bad for the pitcher. You stay alert, and when a bus or Cadillac drives you onto the broken coral shoulder or into the hedge of oleander, you shake it off and stride on. Of course, the arithmetic of stress being inexorable, miles of this take their toll. Coming into camp always seemed a marvel. We stopped, crossed a lawn or dune, and sat down among ourselves, sanctuary regained, and often I felt like shedding tears of thanksgiving.

Here at Ehukai we feasted on *mahi mahi* Florentine and pineapple-lichee-cherry salad. The Shiatsu massage school, half a dozen Japanese women arrived and fell to work on us. Now the race leader on elapsed time, I was escorted to the Sensei, the professor, for his particular treatment, which, since he had to catch a plane to Maui in an hour, consisted of hurried stretches, twists, and snaps of delicate regions, including the horrifying act of rubbing my kneecaps around in circles as though they were scouring pads. In five minutes the professor was on the way to the airport. Bruised, I reflected that his school seemed to permit individuality in technique. I watched Henderson slide into blissful unconsciousness under the tender and careful touch of a masseuse named Kathy, who soothed him for an hour and a half without going near his kneecaps. "Wait'll I tell the guys they threw in a *massage*," said Ralph Mittman.

The next morning the vans took us to the cool, fragrant glades and soggy parrots of Waimea Falls Park. Peacocks wailed as we breakfasted in misty rain on papaya slices from silver platters. We departed on our run just as an old-time revival got going in a big park tent. Harvey Shultz missed the start. He was singing hymns in the service.

It was only a thirteen-mile day, and now we were retracing our steps. Certain fields and vistas were familiar to the point of nostalgia. Henderson, rejuvenated by his rubdown, tied with John McCormack and Doug Peck for the leg, two minutes ahead of Dave Erb and me and the Race Bunny.

I was stiff, either from the hard burst at the end of the previous run or from the ruinous massage. "Get your mind off it," said the Race Bunny. So we went soaring. Dillingham Field is across the road from where we camped at Mokuleia, and there a young woman named Wendy Hunt will take you two at a time into the updrafts that climb the cliffs. Soon the world was divided beneath us, the blue hemisphere of the sea and the green of the land; the latter further divided into lumps of green mountains and soft folds of green cane. As we rose Hunt said that she was twenty and had been a glider pilot for six years. "This is all I want to do," she said, a signal cry of satisfaction, as we entered a dive, dropping in a tight, double helix descent with a sister ship.

Stomach tense, I said, "This is like a dog fight."

Her tone was remonstrative. "It is a dance."

Later, when Jack and Donna Scaff were up with the same pilot, Jack grew so exhilarated that he began to sing, "I can fly, I can fly, I can fly," from *Peter Pan*.

"That's why my parents named me Wendy," said Hunt, happily.

In the golden light before sunset, Donna Scaff and her three sisters, all raised on Molokai, passed around lengths of splashy red cloth and taught us how to wear them as Polynesian *lavalavas*, requisite dinner dress. Soon they had us all taking hula lessons. Afterward, Scaff and I walked in the sea, a more salubrious massage than the manipulations of the Shiatsu.

We remarked on the good cheer of all our adventurers. These are special people because they're self-chosen, doing this for the only good reason—that they want to.

"And the stress is just enough to bring our personalities into sharp relief, but not so much that we're at each other's throats."

"Yeah, and it can never be the same, should we do it again. Because word will get out, from these brave people, that it was easy, so easy anyone can do it."

I smiled, because in the competitive division the rigor was mounting. Our midrace rest was two days away, but first we had to again cross roadless Kaena Point, then run through the cane fields to Pearl Harbor. Since I could be expected to put my track runner's speed to the test on that last day, Henderson's strategy concentrated on Kaena Point, where his cross-country gifts might either get back a lot of my thirteen-minute lead or make me run so hard my effectiveness was cut for the morrow.

Thus after Jeff Jones led the three miles to rough going, Henderson for the first time showed us the kind of running he loves. With a low, balanced stride that calls on the power of his hips and thighs, he went away over the rocks and hollows and ledges. For a couple of miles I kept within 40 yards, benefitting from his pathfinding, but then my arms ached from the arrhythmic struggle, my breath came in uncontrollable gasps. He had me by 200 yards when we reached the road. A mile later, he had me by 400. Try as I did past the condominiums of Makaha Beach, at the end he beat me by a minute, and I was so full of ache that my mind rebelled from the idea of racing hard again the next morning. We had run the seventeen-mile leg twenty minutes faster than a week earlier.

We camped at Nanakuli Beach Park, beside an inviting gem of bay. Snorkling in the clear shallows we saw the *Humuhumunukunukuapuaa* of song and then, farther out, black fins a foot high, moving at speed. There is a churning mixture of fear and delight at the appearance of large creatures in the ocean, a sensation that is memorable later but paralyzing at the time. As the shapes came on, watchers on the beach shouted that they were dolphins.

Steve Marts, of the accompanying film crew, and I swam out. The group of what seemed four or five mammals turned away, our spirits falling. Then they turned again and swept past us, their language of high-pitched tones and clicks filling the sea, and as the underwater shadows resolved into dolphins we saw with wonder that there were at least fifty of them, each larger than the imagination was ready for, elegant and aloof embodiments of the freedom of perfect self reliance.

When they had passed, we were euphoric, dazed, it seemed, with honor. I sat on the beach for an hour, scanning the sea, wondering if there were any service a man could do them to encourage their return, able to think of none.

But in the night—perhaps in answer to my question on the beach—I dreamed I was again swimming near the dolphins. They were all around me, agitated, nudging. A female was in trouble. She was trying to give birth, a tiny tail protruding from her sleekness. I reached in—such warmth in the cold sea—and got my hands around the infant dolphin, folding its fins down and sliding it free, supporting on the surface until its new breath began. It shot away, and the group formed around it. At once

I was alone, suspended over the cobalt abyss.

The next day I raced Henderson over the hills of the Farmington Highway, through the eternally burning cane. The last six miles were upon a traffic-clogged road into Eva Beach. Down a hill I heard his footsteps fall away. I ran on past sugar towns and dilapidated stores, past working Hawaii with its trucks and smoke and dust. I took the pace down another notch. Near the finish I remember thinking that to the drivers of the trucks and vans this straining man was as foreign, as incomprehensible as any dolphin. I wanted it that way.

Harvey Shultz had turned collector. He brought in a pair of mismatched gloves, a can opener, a bowling pin, a hat, a dipstick, and a round of live ammunition. "I'm going to throw it in the bonfire tonight," he said, an angry mood having overtaken him on the road.

"Promise me, promise me you won't," said Scaff, having forgotten that we never had a bonfire.

It was May First, Lei Day in Hawaii, and Donna Scaff had some experts in Hawaiiana arrive with bales of flowers to teach us the sticky craft of garlands. After dinner we walked the beach, bedecked, watching the lights of Honolulu across the water.

"It looks pretty from here," I said.

"So does New York," said Henderson, "from outer space."

We got to the city the next day, following a circuitous route. By means of the Scaffs' prodigious pull, we were cleared to drive through the West Loch of Pearl Harbor, a secure naval area where strange buildings crouch behind hedges of barbed wire. Photography was forbidden, for here are entombed the nuclear weapons for the military in the Pacific. We were to be picked up by a catamaran for a tour of the harbor. While we waited, Henderson made the guards edgy, saying sweetly, "Vladivostok, Irkutsk, and Smolensk, my friends. Dostoyevsky, Pushkin, and Tolstoy, Brumel, Yashchenko, and Baryshnikov.

The catamaran ride was an odd juxtaposition, a sobering inspection of the rusted remains of the *Utah*, the *Nevada*, the *Arizona*, the *West Virginia*, the *Tennessee*, these tombs of Pearl Harbor still holding thousands of men, and, minutes later, a loud party beneath our own decks, a company musician conducting a limbo contest in which Harvey Shultz practically hung himself on the broomstick. In a serious moment, Bert and Earlene Smith received gold medals for the completion of their week's run. Touched, Bert said "You can't know what these few days have meant. Sometimes you have to go a little crazy to keep your sanity."

We passed a scattered day and a half in Waikiki. When we gathered for a dinner, the talk was all of the road, of each other. "I've benefitted from knowing Tippy Dias," said Doug Middleton. "She exudes such a sense of gentleness and patience. And when Gil goes to set the nets or bring them in she goes too, and her relationship with the sea is something you feel embarrassed to intrude upon."

Our relationship with our own run was becoming something like that, ever more personal. A movement was growing to move the finish, now only a lap away, from the grating surround of Waikiki to somewhere more private. "Maybe we shouldn't finish at all," said Henderson. "Maybe we should just go our separate ways and rejoin on other islands. Ireland, say, or New Caledonia."

We began again with 20.5 miles around Makapu Point, stopping at Bellows Beach Park, an Air Force facility which had a sign on the rest room saying "Dry Paint." On a beach of powdered sugar sand, John McCormack said, "I wish this thing were starting over. A few sore muscles, some hard uphill pulls, no price at all for such an experience."

With only a week to go we were consciously savoring, casting about with devouring eyes, finding we still didn't really know half our fellows. Here were Pat Garland and Doris Muse who ran a newspaper delivery service in Chattanooga, Tennessee, who jogged walked every day at a modest pace, and who by now could recommend the best roadside inns for omelettes or steak and eggs. It had been early rumored that they kept a revolver in their tent, but if so, it was out of character with their sweet-tempered calm. Pat, especially, tall and with every appearance of an athlete, trotted contentedly along at nine or ten minutes a mile when it seemed she could go much faster. "But I'd miss so much, she said, irrefutably, because we front runners often came to arresting landscapes we'd somehow been blind to twice before. Jeff Jones was the master of this, claiming not to have noticed the ocean for two weeks.

Behind us, duels were fought, the fiercest between George Conlan, forty-eight, an executive in a juice dispenser firm, and Bill Zappas, fifty-eight, for the over-forty title. Conlan, from Belvedere, California, on San Francisco Bay, had arrived admirably lean and fit from training a hundred miles per week. Zappas, who runs a real estate company in Los Angeles, had begun less strongly, but now was gaining, having passed his twenty-eight-year-old son, Mike. His secret, he said, was the Shiatsu massage and an unbending competitiveness. He goaded himself with Conlan's lead, calling him "Sneaky George," saying, "I'm going to hang on to him, I'm going to drive him crazy."

"But Bill, that's cruel. Can you sustain that cruelty for another hundred and twenty-five miles?"

"Sure. That's what it's all about.'

Also a hard man was Pat Gorey, thirty-eight, who tends bar at The Red Blazer on Second Avenue and Eighty-first in Manhattan. A strong starter and ashen, wobbly finisher who had a disturbing tendency to lie down with his head in the road, Gorey had smoked two packs a day for twenty-five years. After two weeks of our remarks he quit—for a day—and looked so grave the more humane among us urged him to keep on with his disgusting practice. If we were protective of anyone, it was Carlene Lucas, thirty-eight, of Novato, California, who combined boundless energy with a faint air of hesitancy. In 1970 she was a housewife with three children. Then she contracted Guillain-Barre syndrome, a disease that destroys the myelin sheath covering the nerves, and for four months was paralyzed. She recovered slowly, taking up running both as therapy and as an affirmation of her return to a full life. She had seen a circular for the footrace at a friend's, and had decided to run in it "as my first truly selfish act."

We had a windfall when our fourteenth day's run, from Bellows to Lainani Beach Park, ended three miles shorter than expected, at only fifteen miles, and right beside a little fruit stand, whose proprietor sold forty pounds of Chinese bananas in half an hour. Lieutenant Dave Benson, now down to 227 from his original 245, finished in two hours and eighteen minutes, triumphant that he'd run off and left Jack Scaff. Twenty minutes later Scaff trotted in and announced that he'd only stopped his watch when he had paused to commune with our walkers, the Kuchars. "My elapsed time," he read, "is two hours exactly."

Benson was incredulous. "He'd have had to walk with them for five miles to come in with that time."

Henderson said, "The story here is how we all were created by Jack Scaff and then turned against our maker."

The next two days, sixteen miles to Hukilau Beach Park near the Mormon Temple at Laie, and nineteen miles to Alii Beach Park in Haleiwa, seemed to fray our nerves more than any earlier passage. A garbage truck passed with its driver and hauler screaming invective at us. A truck went for John McCormack, a bus veered off after Henderson and Peck, its driver bearing the serene face of the angel of death. The feeling of always being hunted grew, moving us to an ascending hatred of the automobile, the monstrous power and opportunity for evil it places in the fingertips of those who don't deserve it. Thus the Indians must have seethed over the white intruder's rifles.

Later, calmed by a cool beach, beautiful colors, spray floating over black rocks, we examined our deteriorating feet in the soft glow of survival.

"Well, your lead is up to half an hour," said Henderson as the Race Bunny rubbed our sore calves.

"So I can give you ten minutes a day."

"But you might cramp up and fall down in the rocks of Kaena Point tomorrow."

"And lie there kicking in random jerks," said the Race Bunny, "like a cockroach when you spray him with Raid."

She regarded Henderson's feet. "Looks like this one got caught in a meat grinder. Turn over quick now. I have to service twenty-five other guys before dinner."

As he did, he saw Ed Shaffer approaching. "This Haleiwa town has more lovely women than anywhere in Hawaii," he said. "C'mon, Leon, come with me as bait."

Harvey Shultz had run with a vengeance, having been passed by Pat Corey, the Red Blazer, with six miles to go. "No self-destructive smoker was going to pull that," he said. "I ran behind him for a while, then when he hit the wall I passed him and beat him by six minutes." Harvey rubbed it in by continuing for a half-mile past the finish. Corey had a Primo and walked into town for some cigarettes.

Haleiwa offered many diversions besides its beauties. Soon we were strewn across the beach or sailing canoes or taking lessons in windsurfing. We had begun to consider ourselves a raffish collection, scraggly, bony and—like Ed or Harvey— unconstrained by a strict sense of propriety. We were now to see what real incivility was.

When Gorey returned from town he passed a knot of local young men in the parking lot. One called out to him that he'd heard that.

"Heard what?"

"What you called me."

Gorey hadn't said anything. An able bartender, he recognized the man was drunk and kept walking. The fractious local stumbled after him and took a wild swing.

Gorey easily ducked and kept moving. The drunk followed, trailed in turn by half a dozen of his friends. This procession came into our camp and once there, the intruders went wild, attacking firemen Dave Gutierrez and George Collins, apparently because they were Chicano and black respectively, and tentmates, and this had aroused some racist ire in the observing locals. They couldn't have picked a worse man to fight than Gutierrez, who stunned first one man with a single punch and took two more to the ground. Gil Dias ran to help, as did Mike Zappas. Donna Scaff called the police, while Jack went about the camp picking up axes and hammers, tossing them into tents to keep them from being used as weapons.

At length the attackers, shouting that they would return, retreated across the park. Gutierrez had a scraped collar bone, and his left big toenail had been torn away, apparently by a tent peg. Mike Zappas had a bloody nose.

The police, in the form of two large patrolmen, arrived and talked the locals, who made no move to leave, and us.

"We classify this as third degree assault, a misdemeanor, said one of the police, an Officer Donnelly, after assessing our stories. "We have to actually witness the offense before we can make an arrest. . . .'"

This was met with cries of disbelief. "Arrest them for being drunk and disorderly," said someone.

"If we arrest them for drinking in public, we have to arrest half of you, said Donnelly. "I'll stay around as long as I can, but I'm afraid I can't guarantee you a quiet night."

As these negotiations went on, the park seemed to fill with twelve- and fourteen-year-old kids, many doing exaggerated little dances of combat feinting, darting.

"Jackals," said Henderson. We shared a sense of a society gathering against us. Finally our protector, Lieutenant Dave Benson, arrived from duty in Honolulu. "I can't leave you guys alone for a minute," he said, grinning. He had brought a superior, a major. Soon five patrol cars ringed our camp. One officer put on a lavalava and helped Gil Dias get in the nets.

Officer Donnelly and I had a talk, in which he expressed some sympathy for the frustrations of many local people, priced out of owning a home (as is Donnelly himself) by the influx of mainland *haoles* with money. "We Hawaiian boys, we don't get encouraged to stay on in school," he said. "With one exception, the guys who came after you are not bad. I know them. They just some feel there's nothing to do but hit somebody."

They apparently felt that way fairly regularly because they came back twice in the night. Encountering 280-pound policemen with dogs, they crept away again and we slept undisturbed.

The next morning we escaped around Kaena Point, beginning apprehensively, finishing relieved at Keaau Beach Park to discover that we had been followed, not by assailants but by a gangly white poi dog, probably with dalmatian in his ancestry. He collapsed with blistered paws, and was thereafter fed and petted so much that Keaau Park surpassed his every notion of the kingdom of heaven. By acclamation we named him Primo. "I'm taking that dog back to South Carolina," said Ed Shaffer, who relented when one of our police escorts said he'd give him a good home.

The next day Leon and I were bone-weary. He had sore Achilles' tendons; I favored a calf. "We've come too far to blow up now," we said. Doug Peck and John McCormack romped ahead of us past industrial parks to Barber's Point, where the lawn was filled with "sleeping grass," little fronds that curled up at a touch.

With time and distance, it had begun to seem that the fight at Haleiwa had been a rude but necessary awakening, first to the real dangers of some regions—"Nowhere is paradise," said Gil Dias. "Every place got its thugs."—then to the subtle unreality that had been claiming us. It was one thing to reduce our wants to those of animal subsistence, to reject for a time the coveting of property or power, and treasure instead a soft stride, a good tan, a fine heat tolerance, a vivid character to run with. But to fancy that, like the dolphins, we might fashion a lean and mobile society on these values was folly in a world where there was no escape from the vengeful and dispossessed. "We all have to live together," said Henderson. "It's a shame, but there it is."

Our penultimate day took us twenty-one miles to Keehi Lagoon Park near the Honolulu airport. From there it would be only a 10,000-meter sprint to the finish we had voted in Ala Moana Park—out and away from the towers of Waikiki. Again Peck and McCormack won the leg. "We're million-meter racers," they said. We had run past the Primo brewery. Two days later it was shut down by its corporate master—Schlitz.

This day was the hardest. "Those cane and earth trucks," said Dave Gutierrez, back running after one day of caring for his foot "make my ass pucker every time they pass." George Conlan had had diarrhea for four days, losing twelve pounds, but hung with Bill Zappas anyway, and there was no more talk of anyone driving anyone else crazy.

Carlene Lucas finished in ecstasy, delivered into a new life, and hugged everybody in sight.

Jack Scaff and Harvey Shultz were long in finishing. When they arrived they were walking, both completely spent. Jack had pleaded for a ride from Donna.

"No, poor dear," she had said, driving on.

They came in with arms linked. "We took a tour of a taffy factory," said Scaff, shaking his head. "Harvey was yanking it out of the machine and eating it by the greasy fistfuls."

Harvey sat down and dropped his day's findings, a land snail shell, a tube of Lip Lustre, twenty feet of nylon cord, a red flag from the back of a lumber truck, and a bolt that must have weighed four pounds. "Three hours, thirty-one minutes," he said, stopping his watch. We all looked at Scaff.

"3:18:05," he said.

Harvey stiffened. "We were together the whole way!"

"I can't help it if you don't know how to time."

After that the celebrations seemed to bleed into each other. We made the final six miles the next morning, escorted by police on motorcycles. The early finishers turned to embrace the followers. We ended up in our *lavalavas* at a sentimental award ceremony at the Scaff home. It turned out that I had run the 312 miles in 35 hours, 11 minutes, and 54 seconds, an average of 6:45 per mile. I gained one pound. Henderson did 36:01:00, McCormack, 36:38:53, Jeff Jones, 37:21:48, Doug

Peck, 38:02:54, Dave Erb, 41:16:37, and Pat Gorey, 41:59:06. George Conlan was ninth in 42:09:45, Ed Shaffer tenth in 43:01:02. Harvey Shultz was fourteenth in 44:20:57, and Jack Scaff sixteenth in 48:58:28, a time lustily booed.

Formalities over, we found we couldn't leave. (Indeed, Breon, Mittman, and Hargis, the high school kids, were still camped on Scaff's *lanai* three days later.) We talked of doing one grand lap of the much larger Island of Hawaii. We kept casting back, describing everything to hold the memory clear. I thought of the last time around Kaena Point.

Again Henderson had swept away, knowing eight and ten steps ahead where to put his feet. He talked later of "catching my rhythm," but to me, the runner of smooth roads, that sounded like nonsense. A rough country man's rhythm must be dictated by the rocks, the holes. "There was one stretch there,"' he said, "where we had to cross the tops of all those jutting sharp rocks and I hit each one perfectly. It was like a dance." I remembered it as a terrifing ordeal. Doug Peck, trained on Tahoe trails, gave the best chase.

As I stumbled behind, I had a sudden conviction. I would win the race, but only because there was little more ground like this. The larger conclusion was that all racing, all competition, was arbitrary, the chance elements of distance, of terrain, of temperature combining to choose a winner. What was left, what was important was how the long struggle moved us, how it toughened and stretched and then mingled all these disparate souls.

As I reached the paved road, I saw Henderson inexplicably standing there, turned to me, white teeth shining out of a polished walnut face. "As far as I'm concerned," he had said, transported, "it's all over."

—October 1979

How often do you hear about someone borrowing a friend's book, then later buying his own copy because he liked it so much? Or a book so treasured that it gets passed from friend to friend until it simply falls apart from so many readings? *Once a Runner* is such a book.

It has become a cult classic and remains our all-time best seller. It has been acclaimed over the years by Frank Shorter, Bill Rodgers, Alberto Salazar and many other top runners as the best running novel ever. The story of college runner Quenton Cassidy's battle to the top is widely regarded as the most accurate portrayal yet written of the little known world of world class runners.

Many readers say they learned more about running from this novel than from all the training books they have read.

It won *Running* magazine's award as the best book of the year, and has been highly acclaimed by *Running Times, Racing South, and Track & Field News,* as well as by writers like Joe Henderson, Don Kardong and Kenny Moore.

"I've read *Once a Runner* six times and still enjoy it immensely. It continues to renew my heart to 'go after the fire, not the smoke.'"
—**J.A. Sandoz,** Olympia, WA

"Please send me two more copies of *Once a Runner*. It makes an excellent gift to my running friends. It might interest Mr. Parker to know that one [copy] is presently circulating among the members of the München Ost (East Munich) Track Club in West Germany. I had two of their members stay with me as exchange students last year and gave them a copy upon departure. One of them, a 1500-meter man and miler, wrote that his pulse went to 130 during the description of the last race. 'That's *exactly* how it is,' he said. In return I received a t-shirt from the Greek marathon from Marathon to Athens—an equitable trade. My thanks to Mr. Parker for a great book."
—**Dave Slaughter,** Florence, KY

"I have read *Once a Runner* at least 20 times, even going as far as playing *Once a Runner* trivia when I travel to races. It has been very influential in my running."
—**Andy Palmer,** Saco, ME

"I have just finished reading *Once a Runner* and would like to tell you how much I enjoyed it. I am an assistant cross country coach in Jacksonville at Bishop Kenny High School. Our runners are preparing for the state cross country meet in two weeks. As part of this preparation a lot of them are reading *Once a Runner*."
—**James Bryan,** Jacksonville, FL

"The passage describing the aggressive feelings Quenton has in 'Night Run' is (without intention of gushing) one of the best I've ever read. 'There Are No Secrets' is probably the best advice I've come across yet, and that includes a voracious reader's gleanings of both running magazines as well as every book on running I can get my hooks on."
—**David Grant**, Albuquerque, NM

"Perhaps the best novel ever written about running. There are parts of *Once a Runner* that are pure poetry. I enjoyed it thoroughly and have never read descriptions of what it is to run and race as accurate and compelling as Parker's. . ."
—**Tom Jordan,** *Track & Field News*

"I hate to use a cliche, but I couldn't put it down." —**Joe Henderson,** *Runner's World*

"I'm jealous. This is very close to the kind of book I've wanted to write for years. . . [Parker] has shown an ability to find that vein that runners have within them, and write about it better than anyone ever has."
—**Don Kardong**, of *Runner's World*

"By far the most accurate fictional portrayal of the world of the serious runner. . . a marvelous description of the way it really is." —**Kenny Moore,** of *Sports Illustrated*

What really made Jim Ryun tick? Why did Jim Fixx really die? What is the Cinnamon Bun Theory and what does it have to do with Pat Porter, high altitude sickness, and four national cross country championships?

Parker's writing is as powerful as ever and his many readers will find the answers to such questions and a great deal more in his latest work.

This one is destined to become a cult classic like *Once a Runner* and *Runners and Other Ghosts on the Trail.* In fact, this latest collection of Parker's non-fiction pieces contains everything that originally appeared in *Ghosts on the Trail* (now sold out) plus much, much more. Profiles on Jim Ryun, Pat Porter, Barry Brown, Frank Shorter and others. Incisive essays on Courage, Coming Back, The Aging Athlete, and Missing the Poetry, all from his highly regarded *Ultrasport* columns. Lighter moments like "The Great Dragon Run," "The TeeVee Olympics," "Training in Greece," and "Getting Beat by a Woman."

RUNNERS
& Other Dreamers

by John L. Parker, Jr.

". . .Parker excites and tantalizes the reader. . . Every runner should read this jewel." **–Ruben Flores**, *San Antonio Light*

". . .a collection of true stories about runners, for runners, by a runner. John Parker knows running from the inside out and knows how to tell a story." *–California Track and Running News*

An Excerpt

A high desert, like a war, is a very good place to find out some things about yourself that you may not have wanted to know.

How you handle it is your business.

It has always been a favorite of Saints and Madmen and Lost Tribes. A lot of people just leave. The Light gets to them. Or the Space. Or something quite a bit less ethereal, such as the way rattlesnakes like to crawl into your sleeping bag to stay warm. The letters back, though, are always wistful:

. . .I was born and raised in Alamosa. I love every inch of the valley and all the happy memories it holds, and yes, even the sad ones. . .

And:

. . .My grandfather settled in the valley not awfully long after the Indians left! Talk about "soul" —

Mine lies deep in that river land surrounded by the Rockies.
. .

Those from a literary magazine called *Alma,* Spanish for "soul," published out of Alamosa, Colorado, a small town on the floor of the San Luis Valley. "Floor" here is deceptive usage. Alamosa is one and one-half miles above sea level. And anywhere you go from here is up. To live in such a place is to break yourself of your oxygen habit.

And there is something else about the high desert, something you think you already know, but which if you haven't been there you can't really *feel.* It is this: the desert doesn't care what kind of hurry you're in or how fast you're going, it's not going to let you get anywhere. You can sit in your rent-a-car going just under a hundred in a perfectly straight line toward the airport at Denver and after a couple of hours you will still be, relatively speaking, in the same place.

You cannot breathe here and you cannot make any progress against the backdrop. It is the long distance runner's most perfectly articulated nightmare.

Pat Porter, a 26-year-old Olympian, a four-time national cross-country champion, voluntarily lives in Alamosa. He *likes* it. Are you beginning to get the idea?

—From "Rare Atmosphere, Astringent Light"

Runners & Other Dreamers
By John L. Parker
©1989, paper, 178 pgs. **$9.95**
Code: RDR

For the others, it may have been a race, but for Brad Townes it was a quest for salvation. He had run all the way from death's door and he had lost everything along the way. In the final mile, he had nothing left to lose except the race. You'll find your heart racing right along with the protagonist in this compelling story, beautifully told by a veteran runner.

The grand daddy of all marathons is the backdrop for this exciting story, with the chapters taking you right through the Great Race itself: Brookline to Hopkinton, Hayden Rowe Street, Hopkinton to Ashland to Framingham, Framingham to Natick, Natick to Wellesley, Wellesley to Newton Falls, The Newton Hills, Brookline, and finally Boston. When you finish, you'll feel as if you'd just run the race alongside Bradley Townes!

The scene shifts back and forth from the heat of the race to Bradley's secret past and the reasons for his impossible quest. Tuckman's narrative keeps you right on the edge of your seat during the entire story. We've heard from some readers who said this book kept them reading all night, others who reported themselves in tears at the end.

Reading this book is a great way to prepare mentally and spritually to run Boston.

"This book will appeal to a lot of runners, particularly those who, over the years, have felt the urge to 'do Boston.'"**–Bill Rodgers**

"I admit it. I couldn't put the book down. I needed to know–did Bradley Townes win? Did he beat Rodgers and Seko in the premier non-Olympic 26-miler–Boston?. . .Tuckman draws you quickly into the Townes' story and his quest for victory over 26 miles and death." **–Chuck Morris,** *Maine Running*

". . . enough true details and a fast enough pace to please even an envious writer who looked hard for ways to be critical. I read the book in one sitting, which has only happened two other times in the past ten years. . ."**–Joe Henderson,** *Running Commentary*

An excerpt

Brad could still make out snatches of the radio coverage over the crowd noise. So they still don't know who I am, he thought. They can just call me Mighty Joe from Hannibal, Mo, he chuckled to himself, despite the fire now spreading through his lungs and back muscles.

Twenty yard ahead he could see Seko and beyond him in the distance, Rodgers. In front of Rodgers was only the motorcycle policeman. Now if I can just tie myself to Seko with an invisible cord, and slowly start to pull the son of a bitch in, he thought, just like Bannister did to Landy. He focused on the rhythmically moving shoulders of the Japanese champion, established contact in his mind, and then grimly set about his task.

Rodgers has just passed the 23 mile point, folks, and still looks as loose and easy as he did when he took the lead back on the hills. Seko is behind him but looks tired. And then there's that mystery man. We still don't have. . . . Oh, excuse me. . . . They're trying. . . . Uh, here it is, I have it. I now have the information! Number 2022 is. . . Bradley Townes. . . whose name is not familiar to me. Nor. . . I'm just checking now. . .No? Nor to anyone else on the press truck.

Repeating: Bradley Townes is in third place. He is from Boston. He is 28 years old, and his best previous time is 2:22:35. He is not affiliated with any club and he lists no sponsoring company or product. I hardly need emphasize that he was not included in any of the pre-race publicity information handed out by the Boston Athletic Association. Again, I apologize, but that is all the information that has been released. We are trying to find out more and we'll let you know as soon as we do.

Brad reached the bottom of the hill and now was just three miles out. Twenty-three down and three to go, he thought. Good God! Just give me the strength. He gave Seko a little tug on the cord. . .

Long Road to Boston
By Bruce W. Tuckman
©1988, paper, 169 pgs. $9.95

A wonderful novel about a mysterious, reclusive runner haunting London's Hampstead Heath. And would you believe, A long-running hit.

This enchanting novel was written by Boulderite Paul Christman, editor of the *Running Stats* newsletter. This is one of those hard-to-find books that you will treasure for years.

THE PURPLE RUNNER

a novel by
PAUL CHRISTMAN

"Anyone who considers himself (or herself) a hopeless running nut is going to get a serious kick out of it."—*Running Times*

"Great fun to read and the climactic conclusion boldly rewrites running history, and predicts the future as well."
—*Women's Sports & Fitness*

"There are parts of the narrative that are so familiar you'll feel as if you've been caught thinking aloud."
—*Rocky Mountain Running News*

"This book is like a good race: it starts out easy, picks up in the middle, and finishes with a dazzling sprint. Runners everywhere will enjoy it."—**Lorraine Moller**, Olympian

"An exciting yarn that holds the reader to the tape. . ."—**Dick Quax**, Olympian

An excerpt

God dammit! she thought to herself as Christa and a pack of men began to ease by her like a formation of drenched egrets. *You're not slipping by that easily!* Solian tried picking up her knees, but her mind was making a promise her legs couldn't keep. Christa and company evenly receded from her grasp.

Oh, no, not you too! Solian mentally lashed herself as Mary struggled by her 90 seconds later. *I'm going to drop out. . .no, got to keep going. . .third woman. . . you can still break 2:50. . .*

Minutes later she stumbled to a stop at a feed station just beyond the 38-kilometer mark, gulped a cup of water, then grabbed a sponge and squeezed it over her head. Her first few steps made her feel nauseous. She probably needed some salt, but in the last few miles of a marathon replacement drinks upset her stomach worse than water. Solian could feel the water sloshing around in her stomach and she was getting very dizzy. The sun seemed to be penetrating right through her AUCKLAND UNIVERSITY singlet and navy-blue nylon shorts. *Don't do it! Don't!* Her mind and body were engaged in a contest: the former urging her to keep running, the latter telling her to walk. *Just make it to the 39-kilometer mark. . . you might start feeling better. . .* But 100 meters later she found herself walking. God, she hated those pitying looks from the spectators when she wasn't doing well.

"C'mon, Solian, only three kilometers to go!" a man supporting himself on two metal arm-braced crutches shouted from the side of the road. Solian felt tears well up in her eyes. Here was a man who would give anything to walk properly, and she was walking when she could still be running. *But, there's no disgrace in saving yourself for another day. Why kill yourself? Walk off the course and admit you just didn't have the miles.* But it was no go: she knew she would have to finish; the man on crutches merely a reminder of what a gift it was to be able to use her legs. Painfully she began to run again. . .

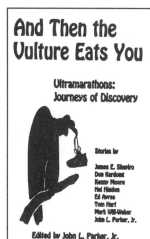

And Then the Vulture Eats You

Ultramarathons: Journeys of Discovery

Stories by
James E. Shapiro
Don Kardong
Kenny Moore
Hal Higdon
Ed Ayres
Tom Hart
Mark Will-Weber
John L. Parker, Jr.

Edited by John L. Parker, Jr.

The best writers in the sport of running take up a fascinating subject, the last frontier of long-distance events: races longer than a marathon.

Who runs these 50-milers, 100-milers, multi-day events, multi-event events? And *why* do they do it? And (okay, admit you're a little curious) what's it like to do one?

James Shapiro, a long time ultra-runner, whose *Meditations from the Breakdown Lane* is a classic piece of running literature, begins by relating with heart-rending detail his experiences in a 6-Day Race in "Swifts on the Wing."

In "To the Limit and Beyond," Kenny Moore takes you through a gut-wrenching experience in his first-person account of the Great Hawaiian Footrace, a horrendous 6-day ordeal that seemingly changes his life.

Don Kardong, one of the wittiest and most personable writers in the sport, in "Le Grizz" goes the 50-mile distance at the infamous race that gives this piece its name. Along the way this former Olympic marathoner, like so many participants in these events, makes startling discoveries about himself.

Ed Ayres, editor of *Running Times*, takes on the Western States 100 in "Wings of Icarus," and the event turns out to be a kind of catharsis in his life.

In "Road Warriors," Hal Higdon's report on his group's informal attempt to run across the state of Indiana is another kind of ultra tale: a light-hearted, self-imposed challenge that turns, like most ultra events, into a revealing spiritual odyssey.

Tom Hart's self-imposed challenge, to run a solo 37-miler on his 37th birthday, is the basis for his ultra story. He finds out, as do the others, that an effort on the magnitude of an ultra is more than a feat of endurance, it is a journey into self.

John Parker ends with "And Then the Vulture Eats You," an uproarious analysis of today's ultra runners ("Mystic Ultras"). Your sides will ache from reading his account of

the war between the "Track Men" and the "Mystic Ultras" in the Jackson, Michigan Ultimate Runner contest, in which the entrants race a 10K, a 440, a mile, a 100-yd dash, a mile, and a marathon, all in the same day.

If you are an ultra runner, have ever been even *mildly* curious about such events, or if you are just a lover of great writing, you will greatly enjoy this book.

An Excerpt

From Shapiro's "Swifts on the Wing"

Most of us would be on the track 16 to 18 hours a day. Some would sleep in a trackside tent that swarmed with activity; others like myself would dash off to nearby hotels for a few hours of troubled sleep, tormented by burning feet, sore joints and overtired bodies. Some runners would say much later, when we emerged on the other side of this trial, that they didn't dream about the race while it was actually on but that they did during the first free night.

Certainly there was no way to escape the feverish intoxication of the race. Only once during those six days and nights did the number of competitors sink to just one. At every moment somebody or some bodies moved round the track, ceaselessly at work, so that no matter when you slept, the relentless advance of your competitors seeped through the chill night air, made you awaken with that sobering sense that not another instant could be wasted. It was like war.

And Then the Vulture Eats You
Edited by John L. Parker, Jr. ©1990,
paper, 166 pgs. **$9.95**
Code: VUL

This critically acclaimed novel, first published in 1969, has for years been regarded as one of the true classics not only in the literature of footracing, but in general interest literature as well.

Glanville's beautifully portrayed relationship between runner Ike Low and the eccentric and charismatic coach Sam Dee has become a set piece in the tales of athletes: *Rocky, Chariots of Fire,* even *Long Road to Boston* owe a debt to this work.

There are echoes of *Loneliness of the Long Distance Runner* as well. You will be captivated by the story of the working-class stiff, Ike Low, as Sam Dee "discovers" him thrashing through inconsequential races, a mediocre sprinter at a local running club.

"The first time I met him, I thought he was a nut case," said Ike of his coach.

"You are built to run the *mile,*" Dee told him. "You are the perfect combination of ectomorph-mesomorph; long calves, lean, muscular thighs and arms, chest between thirty-seven and thirty-eight, and broad, slim shoulders. A miler is the aristocrat of running. A miler is the nearest to a thoroughbred racehorse that exists on two legs."

And thus begins the relationship that will transform Ike into one of the great distance runners in the world.

". . . brilliantly told, rushing to a wildly exciting climax. . . as serious an effort as anyone has made to explore the tortures and indecisions of the totally dedicated athlete."
—*Newsweek*

"Until *Once A Runner*, this was my favorite running novel." —**Bill Rodgers**

"When I was a miler in college, this book was my *Once a Runner*." —**John L. Parker**

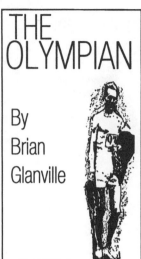

THE OLYMPIAN
By Brian Glanville

Cedarwinds Publishing Company

An Excerpt

This thing, this pain thing, in a way I saw what he meant, but in another way, I didn't understand it. Why run at all if it was going to hurt you? Sport, to me, was something you enjoyed, and if you didn't enjoy it, you packed it in. On the other hand, I could see he was right, that this sort of attitude wasn't going to get you nowhere, not with everybody else so dead serious and more or less dedicating their lives to it. Either you did it properly, or you might as well let it alone.

And mind you, it wasn't like there was no enjoyment in it at all, that it was all slog. The training was hard, of course, and all the things you had to give up, but the races, they could really be great, if things were going well; so exciting that everything else in the world seemed dead; that moment when it was time to go and you felt this power thrumming away in you like a great, big engine and you knew you were going to do it, beat the lot of them. In a way it was better than actually doing it, like a meal or making love to a bird; I mean, it usually looks better beforehand. Though winning was great, too, breaking that old tape, the little, light touch against your chest, and the first feeling you always had, didn't matter how tired you were, was always this flutter in the guts, like to say, I've done it.

The other way I could see Sam was right was obviously if you want something, you ain't going to get it for nothing, not unless you inherit it, and you can't inherit running, and there was a hell of a lot to want in athletics—breaking records, running for Britain, traveling abroad, and maybe one day, please God, an Olympic medal. Because records, they were here today and gone tomorrow, but an Olympic gold medal they could never take away from you.

The Olympian
By Brian Glanville
©1969, paperback, 253 pgs., **$9.95**

This is the wonderful autobiography of Clarence DeMar, seven-time winner of the Boston Marathon. In an age that had not yet conceived of masters running, his last Boston victory came in 1930 when he was nearly 42!

Originally published in 1937, this little gem was nearly forgotten for many years. It was discovered and reprinted in 1981, then forgotten again. Charmingly written in DeMar's own heartfelt words, it provides a fascinating glimpse into an America of a simpler time.

Perhaps the best-known distance runner of his era, DeMar never profited monetarily from his prowess. He prided himself on his simple New England values: his work as a typesetter, his leadership of a Boy Scout troop, his church work. Much of his training was accomplished during his runs to and from work each day.

He discusses a great many of the unsolicited suggestions about diet, training, and lifestyle he received over the years, a few of which he dutifully tried on himself by way of experimentation. He was a shrewd analyst, open to new ideas, yet with enough skepticism to give weight to his findings. Amazingly enough, *nearly all* the conclusions he reached over 50 years ago about these complex issues have been validated by subsequent research.

In so many ways, DeMar was way ahead of his time. You'll be fascinated by his story.

"Clarence DeMar may have run through—and to the top of—another era, but his story will ring true to all modern marathoners. Today's runners will not only enjoy reading about the way it was; they may even learn a little about the way it should be."
—Amby Burfoot, *Runner's World*

"Long after many of the current running books are forgotten—and deservedly so for some of them—*Marathon* will continue to be in the front of the pack. That's where Clarence DeMar always was himself."**—Colman McCarthy,** *The Washington Post*

MARATHON
The Clarence DeMar Story

By Clarence DeMar

Cedarwinds Publishing Company

"His record as a runner is fantastic. His story deserves to be read by anyone interested in running." **—Johnny Kelley,** marathoner.

DeMar dominated the marathon in a fashion that would be the envy of a Rodgers or a Shorter. His story, which precedes the running boom, endorsements, and television coverage of the major events, should warm the heart of any jogger."**—George A. Hirsch,** *The Runner*

An Excerpt

During the summer of this year I received a letter from Dr. Kellogg of Battle Creek, Michigan. (This is not the Kellogg of cornflake fame.) The doctor had some ideas on diet which he said should improve my endurance.

He invited me to spend a few weeks at his sanitarium and find out for myself. Since I couldn't afford to lose my wages for the sake of the doctor's experiment I declined, but expressed my interest in the matter and my willingness to eat as he would suggest for a year or so. So Dr. Kellogg wrote me a lot about calories, proteins, carbohydrates and fats and the advantages of abstaining from meat. With the cooperation of my mother I conscientiously followed the program of eating no meat (except Thanksgiving) and tried to count the proper number of calories for a year.

When I went away from home or anyone visited us, it was embarrassing to have to explain about my eating habits. Many people thought me "persnickety" but I felt that my running would be more justified if I contributed something to the noble experiment in science! After eating this way for a couple of months I saw no change for better or worse.

MARATHON by Clarence DeMar
©1937, paper, 156 p. **$9.95**
Code: CDM

A collection of John Parker's humorous writing about sports. The lead piece is a quiz the status-seeking runner can take to determine just how "with it" he or she is. (Hint: If you think a Rosa Mota is a new four-cylinder Japanese roadster, you lose 50 points.) Here's a rundown of the other chapters: "Harry Winkler and the Awesome Attack of the Toothless Shark" is about a phony shark attack pulled by some of Parker's skin-diving buddies. "Won't you come home, Irv Taylor?" is the story of an old-timey runner who retires in disgust because of all the newcomers in their fancy running togs. "Big Stakes at Twin Lakes" is about Parker and a friend running a mile relay against four other guys. "My Latest Marathon" is a survivor's account of his first 26-miler. "Mountain Climbing in Florida" tells of Parker's quest to reach the highest point in his not-so-mountainous home state of Florida. "The Blister Derby" recounts his first and last attempt at race-walking. "Stalking the Wild Pelota" is Parker's side-splitting account of playing Jai Lai for the first and last time.

Needless to say, this is a great gift or back-of-the-john book.

"I laughed till I thought I would have to send out for a truss..." —**Ron Wiggins**, *Palm Beach Post*

ISBN 0-915297-03-5

$2.95

AEROBIC CHIC
& other delusions

By John L. Parker, Jr.

Confessions of a Sportsman of the '80s

An Excerpt

I remember it as if it were yesterday.

Sure I had had challenging assignments as a budding writer before, but this one threatened to end a promising career before the dew of youth had dried from my cheek.

"Parker," said the editor of the St. Petersburg Times Sunday magazine, "we want you to climb the highest mountain in Florida and write about it for us."

"You've got to be kidding!" I practically screamed into the phone. "I'm nowhere near an experienced technical climber. Why I've been known to go into oxygen debt just getting up to change the channel. The weather could complicate an expedition horribly, the trails might be slick with the spring run-off, and I wouldn't have time to train properly. It's absurd! It's impossible!"

"We'll pay $50."

"Sold American!"

Well, sir, mountain climbing in Florida is no sport for the faint of heart. The slopes are treacherous, the trails hard to maneuver, and the mountains themselves are often difficult to locate...

Aerobic Chic & Other Delusions
By John L. Parker, Jr.
©1983, paper, 50 pgs. **$3.95**
Code: ACO

This is simply the most comprehensive book on endurance training ever compiled. Somewhere in its 832 pages is a discussion of nearly every conceivable topic of interest to the serious athlete. Noakes is a medical doctor and exercise physiologist as well as a long-time runner, with more than 70 marathon and ultramarathon events in his log.

He explores the physiology of running with entire chapters on muscle structure and function, oxygen transport, energy metabolism, and control of body temperature.

You'll discover important new ideas in research, such as recent doubt about the VO2 max concept and its implications for predicting running performance, and the newly realized importance of drinking patterns during exercise in determining fluid and energy replacement.

Noakes considers all aspects of training, offering practical guidelines on shoes and apparel, tips for beginners, and advice on finding the right races for your skill level. He includes fascinating insights from pioneer training theorist Arthur Newton, chapters on training the mind, the problems of overtraining, and the approaches taken by 34 of the world's greatest runners.

Noakes also deals with the down side: injuries and other health considerations. He demonstrates convincingly that injuries don't "just happen," and tells you how to recognize, diagnose, avoid, and treat them. He includes chapters on nutrition and weight control, as well separate chapters dealing with issues relating to both women and children.

Finally, he examines both the benefits and hazards of endurance training as it relates to the body's major systems, including the respiratory, gastrointestinal, genitourinary, endocrine, immune, and central nervous system. He devotes considerable space to environmental hazards, coronary heart disease, longevity issues, and instances of sudden death in athletes.

Dr. Noakes is the Liberty Life Professor of Exercise and Sports Science, and director of the Bioenergetics of Exercise Research Unit of the Medical Research Council of the University of Cape Town. He is an editorial board member for many international sport science journals and the 1991 president of the South African Sports Medicine Association as well as a Fellow of the American College of Sports Medicine.

"Noakes has a training, an intelligence, a sensitivity, and experience that few writers on the athletic life can equal. On every page we see the work of the scientist. . . Noakes is a runner who has gone through the varied experiences of running: The contemplation, the conversation, the competition. He is familiar with both the joy and the boredom of running. Its peaks and valleys, its elation and depression. If we are to study man we must study man in all aspects: body, mind, and spirit."

—George Sheehan, MD

The Lore of Running
By Tim Noakes, MD
paper, 832 pgs. ©1991 **$19.95**
Code: LOR

Other books from Cedarwinds...

The world's leading distance experts set out to write a book aimed primarily at coaches, but to their surprise, runners as well began to discover this remarkably complete and up-to-date text.

Sebastian Coe's rise to the top of world-class middle-distance running was no accident. It was the direct result of an approach to training that combines practical principles with scientific knowledge—the approach described in this book by Coe's coach/father Peter and by Dr. David Martin, one of the sports leading physiologists.

The book's 82 photos, 72 figures, and 40 tables make the extensive technical information easy to understand. You'll find practical examples of how this training approach transformed Coe, Keith Brantly, Wendy Sly, Pat Porter, Tom Byers, Janis Klecker, and others from fast runners into world-class winners.

This book bridges the gaps between scientific information and the day-to-day realities of training.

You'll learn about the biomechanics and biochemistry of running; goal-setting for competitive runners; developing a plan for total body fitness; the importance of multi-tier and multi-pace training; strategies for successful racing from the 800-meter through the marathon; integrating psychological and physiological aspects of athlete development; techniques for scientific assessment of fitness; stress management to avoid burnout; and the dangers of overtraining.

The chapters include:

1. The Coupling of Movement and Metabolism

2. Heart, Lung, and Blood Dynamics During Exercise

3. A Unified Strategy for Training Distance Runners

4. Comprehensive Conditioning for Runners

5. Successful Racing: Preparation and Achievement

6. Stress Management in Training

"A Rolls Royce of running manuals. . .This is certainly the most complete work I have encountered that tackles the multi-disciplinary demands of training runners." —*Athletics Today*

"I can honestly say that this book is, without a doubt, the best presentation on the subject of distance preparation and training I have ever read." —Joe Newton *Head Track and Cross Country Coach, York High School, Elmhurst, IL*

Training Distance Runners
By David E. Martin and Peter N. Coe
hardcover, 312 pgs. ©1991 **$27.95**
Code: TDR

A hard-to-find little gem about a 40-year-old Fairfax, VA mother who decides to accompany her 14-year-old daughter to a track meet, and is so inspired by the masters competition she sees that she decides to join her daughter's track team. After some early painful training, she begins to set her sights on what seems at first a nearly-impossible goal: the 6-minute mile barrier. Inspirational, with good training insights.

The Six-Minute Mile
by Jinny Beyer
©1984, paper, 207 pgs. **$8.95**
Code: SMM

There has never been another Pre.

Steve Prefontaine, a true American original, captured the imagination of running fans in the 70's like no one before or since. An American record-holder many times over, the charismatic, fearless, outspoken Pre attracted hordes of fans to the University of Oregon's Hayward Field to watch him take on the best in the world. They were called *Pre's People.* Thousands of others around the world were avid followers of this magnetic personality. They still grieve his tragic death in a 1975 car wreck, just hours after winning his latest 5000-meter race at Hayward.

Jordan covers Pre's meteoric career from his early high school races in Coos Bay, Oregon (where he set a national two-mile record of 8:41.5 in 1969), through his college days racing the likes of Frank Shorter, Kenny Moore, Greg Fredericks, Harold Norpoth, Don Kardong, Lasse Viren, and Rod Dixon. He covers Pre's agonizing

fourth in the '72 Olympic final (13:28.3 to Viren's winning 13:26.4), his great '73 and '74 seasons (six American records), and the start of what should have been the greatest racing year of his career.

Jordan, a former associate publisher for *Track and Field News,* interviewed hundreds of Pre's friends, family, teammates, and competitors to put together a compelling, insightful portrait of one of America's greatest runners.

PRE! by Tom Jordan
©1977, paper, 129 pgs., **$9.95**
Code: PRE

Dr. David Costill's *Inside Running* is the ultimate scientific resource for the serious runner. This is simply THE book on the science of long distance training, by the premiere physiologist in the U.S.

Contains many charts and graphs, and outlines the latest research in the field of exercise physiology. But Costill, an athlete himself, is ultimately after the same thing you are: the practical application of this knowledge. He spends much of the book translating the scientific findings into principles the runner can understand and use.

"What he offers is practical. It works. We can take it out the next day and use it."—**George Sheehan, M.D.**

"...a gold mine of information for the runner who is genuinely curious about the nature of endurance. He has a way of clarifying things we knew to be true but never understood."—*Running Times Magazine*

"...an expertly written, scientifically sound, up-to-date, primer on the latest medical and technical data on running."
—**Dr. Alfred F. Morris**

Perhaps the best all around novice/intermediate training guide on the market, Galloway's guide has become the best-selling training book in the country.

Galloway's low-strain marathon program has been used successfully by tens of thousands of aspiring marathoners. He makes his points simply and gracefully, with no preaching, lecturing, or jargonizing.

A widely known lecturer and training adviser, Galloway was a 1972 Olympian and member of the early Florida Track Club in the Shorter/Bacheler glory days. He is now an excellent masters runner with 10K times in the low 30's. He was the founder of the Phiddipides running store chain.

Covers everything from getting started, to nutrition, to shopping for shoes, to his famous plan for running a marathon on as little as 3 miles a day.

"Jeff Galloway is perhaps the one individual in the American running community who can combine a superior knowledge of our

sport with the highest level of achievement—the U.S. Olympic team."—**Bill Rodgers**

"His marathon plan, a masterpiece of simplicity and practicality, mixes a few very long runs with lots of short ones."—**Joe Henderson**

"Galloway doesn't gossip, philosophize or speculate. He just gives you the facts."
—**George Sheehan, M.D.**

"Galloway articulately dispels the macho tenet that you must hurt and strain to be fit. . ." —**Jim Pettigrew**, *Sky Magazine*

"Jeff Galloway's experience as a nationally ranked distance runner and years of promoting running at all levels makes him the best possible source for the wealth of information contained in this book." —**Dr. David Costill**, author of *Inside Running*

This is an enthralling true story of the little-known, reclusive tribe in the mountains of Mexico whose members think nothing of running hundreds of miles at a time. One Tarahumara is known to have run nearly 600 miles in five days to deliver a message. One of the tribe's favorite hunting methods is to chase a deer until it simply drops from exhaustion.

Lutz explores the Tarahumara culture in some detail, including the game of *rarajipari*, in which teams compete by kicking a small wooden ball to a distant goal, sometimes several days away.

This very interesting little book is a quick read and contains sections of interest to children. With its beautifully colored cover and color photographs, it would make an ideal and hard-to-find gift for a running

friend. Forward by Joe Henderson.

"Have the Tarahumara received a special dispensation from some of the human limitations known to us? If they have, I suspect it is because these limitations are artificial. They have been based on our imperfect knowledge of what man can and cannot do."

—Dr. George Sheehan

"The Tarahumara may be the finest natural distance runners in the world." **—Michael Jenkinson**

For ultrarunners as well as us mere 10kers and marathoners. This is the fascinating, true story of the legendary Ted Corbitt, a pioneer ultra-distance runner of the 1950's. More than a compelling personal story of a black athlete in a little known sport, this book is also filled with Corbitt's hard-earned wisdom from thousands of miles of training and racing in the "pre-boom" days. Corbitt's courage and determination will enthrall and inspire you. This hard-to-find book makes a great gift.

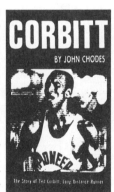

An Excerpt

The gun barked and they were off. They had to circle the track 3 1/2 times before heading out of the stadium and onto the road.

After two laps Ted noticed a familiar figure cruising alongside him.

The famous facial contortions were missing, but his powerful stride was unmistakable. The "Prague Express" [Emil Zatopek]

glided by without effort, gradually moving up on the leaders. At the head of the long procession, England's Jim Peters cut himself loose from the pack with a devastating burst. Ted's dream of glory ended almost before it began. Leaving the stadium at the fastest pace of his life, he felt an agonizing pain in his right side. It was the worst stitch he had ever known.

Maybe it was the exceptional pace or the terrible tension he had suffered all these weeks. Immediately the pain slowed him and he started losing ground. Yet, despite the stitch he remained with men who would eventually finish in the top ten. Then Jones and Dyrgall swept past. Dyrgall called out, "Watch the pace, it's awful fast." At that moment the pain was at its worst, but even when it eased there was a binding sensation which persisted throughout the remaining distance...

Shipping Rates
(please add to your order form)

Type of Service	FIRST BOOK	EACH ADDITIONAL
Standard Book Rate U.S. Mail	$3	$.50
Priority Mail in U.S. (delivery in 3-4 days)	$5	$1
UPS 2nd Day	$7	$1
Canada & Mexico Surface	$4	$1
Air Mail	$5	$2
Other Western Hemisphere Countries Surface	$4	$2
Air Mail	$6	$3
Europe Surface	$4	$2
Air Mail	$8	$6
Asia, Africa, Pacific Rim, etc. Surface	$4	$2
Air Mail	$10	$8

Cedarwinds Publishing Company
P.O. Box 351, Medway, OH 45341
Credit Card Orders only:
800-548-2388
Hours: 9 am to 6 pm EST
(or use recording after hours)
Information: 513-849-1689
FAX Orders: 513-849-1624

Editorial Offices:
Box 13618, Tallahassee, FL 32317
904-224-9261

ORDER FORM

Quantity	Title	Amount

(Note: Shipping is already added in price of non-book products)	Sub-total	
Florida and Ohio residents please add 6% sales tax		
Standard Shipping: Add $3 for first book, $.50 for each additional		
Special Shipping: See box at left for foreign or special shipping charges		
	TOTAL ENCLOSED $	

NAME_____

ADDRESS_____

CITY_____STATE_____ZIP_____

Important: please furnish telephone numbers below in case we need to contact you.

Day phone: _____

Night phone: _____

❏ Check or money order enclosed (do not send cash)
❏ Visa/MC

Card No._____

Expiration _____
Signature _____

To order by mail, send check, money order, or credit
card authorization above—payable in U.S. funds—to:
Cedarwinds Publishing Company
P.O. Box 351— 1305 Park Dr.
Medway, OH 45341

FAX: 513-849-1624
Phone Orders: 800-548-2388